The Ultimate Handbook of Motivational Quotes for Coaches and Leaders

Cindy — Stay Fired Up!
Pat Williams 2011

Pat Williams
with Ken Hussar

COACHES CHOICE™

ISBN: 978-1-60679-128-8
Library of Congress Control Number: 2010935555
Cover design: Brenden Murphy
Book layout: Studio J Art & Design
Front cover photos: (top, from left to right)—©John Kavouris/Icon SMI/ZUMA Press, ©Jeff Moreland/Cal Sport Media/ZUMA Press, ©AJ Mast/Icon SMI/ZUMA Press; (bottom) Hemera/Thinkstock

Coaches Choice
P.O. Box 1828
Monterey, CA 93942
www.coacheschoice.com

Dedication

This book is dedicated to Andrew Herdliska and Latria Leak, my outstanding associates in our Orlando Magic office, who keep things running smoothly. I could not run the daily race without them.

Acknowledgments

With deep appreciation, I acknowledge the support and guidance of the following people who helped make this book possible.

Special thanks to Bob Vander Weide, Alex Martins, and Rich DeVos of the Orlando Magic.

I'm grateful to my associates Andrew Herdliska and Latria Leak, to whom I have dedicated this book, and to my ace typist, Fran Thomas, who typed thousands of quotes found in this book.

Thanks also to my writing partner, Ken Hussar, for his superb contributions in shaping this manuscript.

Hearty thanks also go to my friend and publisher of Coaches Choice books, Jim Peterson, and to editorial manager Kristi Huelsing for believing that we had something important to share and for providing the support and forum to say it. Kudos to the entire staff of Coaches Choice/Healthy Learning books for their skill and dedication.

Finally, special thanks and appreciation go to my wife, Ruth, and to my wonderful and supportive family. They are truly the backbone of my life.

Contents

Preface

It's confession time. At the outset of our "run" together, I admit to you that I am an incurable multi-tasker. As a young adult, I glommed onto these "timely" truths: "Time is ours but once. Waste it, and it is gone forever. Invest it, and it has not passed in vain," and, "The man who makes the most of every minute becomes the man of the hour."

As senior executive vice-president of the National Basketball Association's Orlando Magic, I know the importance of being well-informed on issues present and past. On a typical day, I read at least one entire book, seven newspapers, and an assortment of magazines and newsletters. I make marginal notations and then deliver the material to my ace typist, Fran Thomas, who types the marked items on 4x6 index cards.

I have been a jogger and fitness/nutrition buff since my days as a minor league catcher in the Philadelphia Phillies' farm system. It wasn't until 1996, however, that I challenged myself to run a marathon. My objective was not to set a new "land speed" record, but rather to prove to my 19 children (14 of whom were adopted from four foreign countries) and to myself that with goal-setting, hard work, determination, and training, what was once thought *impossible* can become a reality.

But I digress. Let's return to those index cards. Prior to running a marathon (and I have run 55 of them as of the publication of this book), I would laminate my favorite index cards. Then, during the 26.2-mile journey, I'd whip out the selected cards and read them over and over to commit them to memory for use in my speeches and for my own personal motivation. Believe me, at my running pace, there is, shall we say, *plenty* of time to maximize and to meditate on and admire these wonderful gems!

I soon found that I had thousands of index cards that begged to be shared with others. I contacted my friend in Lancaster, Pennsylvania, Ken Hussar, who has worked with me either writing or editing more than 50 of my books. I sent the cards to Ken, and he developed a MARATHON acronym:

Making commitments
Acting on your plans
Rigorously pursuing
Achieving goals and attitude
Truth or consequences (character)
Helping others
Occupying your mind
Noting what is important

Profit from my gleaning. You will quickly note that this is not a book about running, nor is it a self-help study. It is my hope, however, that many of the thoughts in the following eight chapters will propel you to a more productive journey, future achievement, and greatness until you reach the finish line.

1

Making Commitments

iStockphoto/Thinkstock

"Let's start at the very beginning—a very good place to start," lyricist Oscar Hammerstein wrote in the opening line of "Do, Re, Mi" from *The Sound of Music*. This simple, yet profound, reminder states what many might consider to be obvious: to achieve success, it is necessary to "start at the beginning" with commitment.

My late friend and outstanding basketball coach, Chuck Daly, used to give a speech: "You're Either in the Box or Out of the Box." The essence of Chuck's thesis was an individual is either committed or is not. A person must be 100-percent, joined-at-the-hip, key-in-the-lock, and throw-the-key-away committed.

Whether it be a business, marriage, or sports venture, without commitment you have nothing. Commitment is a vital anchor of society. The following thoughts reflect this philosophy.

"The bottom line is this: You can discover your authentic leadership, right now.
You do not have to be born with the characteristics or traits of a leader;
You do not have to wait for a tap on the shoulder;
You do not have to be at the top of your organization;
You can step up and lead at any point in your life."

—Bill George

✦

"The authentic leaders bring people together around a shared purpose and empower them to step up and lead authentically in order to create value for all stakeholders."

—Unknown

✦

"He had to hold the reigns to do the driving alone. It was the only kind of leadership he knew."

—A biographer of Woodrow Wilson

✦

"Leadership is not a role, privilege, title, or money. It is responsibility."

—Peter Drucker

✦

"The leader sees leadership as responsibility rather than rank and privilege."

—Peter Drucker

✦

"Taking full responsibility is an area of leadership called management of self, which, when done correctly, can build incredible loyalty for the leader."

—Michael Lombardi

✦

"Leadership usually gravitates to the man who can get up and say what he thinks."

—Dale Carnegie

✦

"A strong leader must be willing to listen aggressively."

—D. Michael Abrashoff

"My main job was developing talent. I was a gardener, providing water and other nourishment to our top 750 people. Of course, I had to pull out some weeds, too.

—Jack Welch

✦

"Whatever you put in that pie, that's what you're going to get out of it. If you put minimal ingredients in, like one ham hock, don't expect three when you open that pot and it's done."

—Sam Mitchell

✦

"Once, two privates were fighting and needed to be disciplined. Instead of confining them to their quarters, General Dwight D. Eisenhower ordered the pair to wash every window in the barracks. While one private cleaned the inside, his rival washed the outside of the same window. Initially the two grimaced at the other and exchanged evil looks, but soon enough the grimaces turned into comical faces, then laughter. By day's end, the privates had forgotten their disputes, harmony had been restored to the battalion, and the men began to realize that, in Eisenhower, they had a unique officer."

—John Wukovits

✦

"The ultimate test of any presidential decision is not whether it's popular at the time, but whether it's right. If it's right, make it, and let the popular part take care of itself."

—Harry S. Truman

✦

"I think the basic thing is to take as much time as possible before acting, to talk to as many people as you can before you formulate a decision."

—Pete Rozelle

✦

"Visions are born in the soul of a man or a woman who is consumed with the tension between what is and what could be. Anyone who is emotionally involved, frustrated, brokenhearted, maybe even angry ... about the way things are in light of the way they believe things could be, is a candidate for a vision. Visions form in the hearts of those who are dissatisfied with the status quo."

—Andy Stanley

Former President Ronald Reagan enjoyed telling the following story about himself. He claimed it was how he learned early in life to make firm and resolute decisions. According to the story, a kindly aunt once took him to a cobbler to have a pair of shoes custom made for him. The shoemaker asked, "Do you want a square toe or a round one?" The young Reagan hemmed and hawed, so the cobbler said, "Come back in a day or two and tell me what you want."

A few days later, the cobbler saw Reagan on the street and asked what he had decided about the shoes. "I haven't made up my mind," said Reagan.

"Very well," the cobbler said. Then he announced to his customer, "Your shoes will be ready tomorrow."

When Reagan got the shoes, one had a round toe and the other a square toe. Reagan concluded, "Looking at those shoes every day taught me a lesson: If you don't make your own decisions, somebody else will make them for you." Always remember that no decision is a decision.

✦

"Leadership is getting players to believe in you."

—Larry Bird

✦

"As a manager you are responsible for everybody. You are the final decision maker."

—Joe Torre

✦

"I pledge you, I pledge myself, to a New Deal for the American people."

—Franklin D. Roosevelt

✦

"Abraham Lincoln had the ability to look forward. He had the ability that a leader has—a leader like George W. Bush, a leader like Ronald Reagan—to look into the future."

—Rudy Giuliani

✦

"The world must be made safe for democracy."

—Woodrow Wilson

✦

"I make my decision, and I don't look back."

—Sandra Day O'Connor

"There stands the decision and there stands the President."

—John F. Kennedy

✦

"When the time comes that a leader feels he must make a decision, he must make it in a clean-cut fashion on his own responsibility, and take full blame for anything that goes wrong."

—Dwight D. Eisenhower

✦

On February 19, 1903, Milton S. Hershey revealed plans that he was building a town where his chocolate factory would be. His wife, Kitty, said, "Milton, you ought to go have your head examined."

✦

"You get all the facts and you make up your mind."

—Harry S. Truman

✦

"The capacity for decision is God's rarest gift of mind to man.

—Dean Acheson

✦

"Make your decision and never show doubt."

—Albert Benjamin "Happy" Chandler

✦

"Billie Jean King is a visionary and knows what she wants tomorrow to look like, and how to get there."

—Donna Lopiano

✦

"The future doesn't just happen. It's shaped by decision."

—Paul Tagliabue

✦

"You'll never have all the information you need to make a decision. If you did it would be a foregone conclusion, not a decision."

—David Mahoney

"Ultimately in the Presidency greatness is measured by decision making."
—Tom Wicker

✦

"There is no such thing as a born leader. Leaders are made by the way they respond to circumstances. You can take two people in exact opposite situations and one of them will end up being a leader; the other washes out because of the choices he makes."
—Rick Warren

✦

"Four questions to ask yourself if you want to live your dreams (If you don't answer them your dreams won't come true. You'll continue to live in a fantasy world.):

1. Why do I want to do this? This reason must be connected to some value you have—family, financial, health. If not, you won't have enough drive and motivation to complete it.
2. What do you want to do specifically? It must be so clear it can be measured. If not, how do you know when you get there?
3. When do you want to achieve it? A dream without a deadline remains a someday forever and it never happens.
4. How am I going to do this step-by-step? Start with baby steps to achieve quick success, then keep moving forward."

—Ruth Williams

✦

"Marvin, what do we do now?"
—Robert Redford in *The Candidate* as a newly elected senator speaking to his campaign manager

✦

"An executive is a person who always decides; sometimes he decides incorrectly, but he always decides."
—John H. Patterson

✦

"Some snicker and say I'm ridiculous because I'm meticulous with details, but what do you see near those who succeed? Perfected details are ubiquitous."
—Michael James Cronen

"Pleasant memories must be arranged in advance."
—Unknown

✦

"Leaders are those who can see the invisible."
—Theresa Grentz

✦

"Who's going to lead today?"
—Vince Lombardi at the beginning of every Thursday practice

✦

"Leaders don't force people to follow; they invite them on a journey."
—Charles S. Lauer

✦

"The crux of leadership is that you must constantly stop to consider how your decision will influence people."
—Michigan State Police maxim

✦

"As Administrator-in-Chief, George Washington insisted on accountability, diligence, and speed—and attention to details, details, details. If the details were mastered, everything else—the big plans and ambitious projects—would follow. Only 'systematic and solid arrangements,' he wrote, could protect the nation from the hazards of chance."
—James MacGregor Burns

✦

"This Administration, today, here and now, declares unconditional war on poverty."
—Lyndon B. Johnson

✦

"Small plans do not inflame the minds of men."
—Bill Bright

✦

"Leadership is the ability to decide what is to be done, then to get others to want to do it."
—Dwight D. Eisenhower

"For of all sad words of tongue and pen, the saddest are these: 'It might have been.'"
—John Greenleaf Whittier

✦

"Our Federal Union. It must be preserved."
—Andrew Jackson

✦

"Liberty and union, now and forever, one and inseparable!"
—Daniel Webster

✦

"As a leader, you have to be a big-picture person."
—J.P. Pawliw-Fry

✦

"A vision keeps you focused, fueled, fresh, fruitful, faithful."
—Jay Strack

✦

In *The Adventures of Alice in Wonderland,* Alice came up to the caterpillar and asked him which road she should take. He asked where she was going. She replied that she didn't know. He said, "Then it doesn't matter what road you take."

✦

"When a man does not know what harbor he is making for, no wind is the right wind."
—Seneca

✦

"To grasp and hold a vision that is the very essence of successful leadership—not only on the movie set where I learned it—but everywhere."
—Ronald Reagan

✦

"We don't take applications. Only commitments."
—United States Marine Corp advertisement

"If your vision is for a year, plant wheat. If your vision is for ten years, plant trees. If your vision is for a lifetime, plant people."

—Chinese proverb

✦

"Nothing happens unless first a dream."

—Carl Sandburg

✦

"I believe this nation should commit itself to achieving the goal, before this decade is out, of landing a man on the moon and returning him safely to Earth. If we are to go only halfway or reduce our sights in the face of difficulty, in my judgment, it would be better not to go at all."

—John F. Kennedy

✦

"Martin Luther King, Jr. was endowed with the gift to see beyond his years. You might call it a dream, but I think it was a vision of what America could become. Dr. King was the greatest communicator in the history of America, and could get others to see his vision as he shared with them what he visualized. As a result, he had the ability to get people to follow him."

—John Lewis

✦

"Paint a picture of your vision for the team and each player. Players need to see what the end results are before they get it. They need a picture for the end of the day."

—Mike Thibault

✦

Sam Houston served as President of the Republic of Texas from 1836–38 and 1841–44, before guiding the independent Republic into the Union in 1845. In 2003, his great-great-granddaughter, Margaret Rost, told the *Houston Chronicle*: "A lot of people had sight, but few had Houston's vision."

✦

"George Bush could have beaten me, but he always talked about what he had done, not what he was going to do. I kept waiting for him to talk about the future. He never did."

—Bill Clinton

"The best leaders are talent magnets. They are the coach people want to play for because they build their careers and send them onto bigger and better things."

—Liz Wiseman

✦

"When newly elected Prime Minister Winston Churchill addressed Britain over BBC radio in 1941, he communicated his vision to the beleaguered Nation: 'Upon this battle depends the survival of Christian civilization. Upon it depends our own British life and the long continuity of our institutions and our Empire. Hitler knows that he will have to break us on this island or lose the war. If we can stand up to him, all Europe will be free, and the life of the world may move forward into broad sunlit uplands. Let us therefore brace ourselves to our duties and so bear ourselves that if the British Empire and Commonwealth last for a thousand years, men will say, "This was their finest hour."' Churchill's vision became Britain's vision that would carry them through the strenuous war years."

—Greg Morris

✦

"To do all which may achieve and cherish a just and lasting peace among ourselves and with all nations."

—Abraham Lincoln

✦

"Leadership can't wait."

—A billboard along highway I-4 in Orlando, Florida

✦

"Having a vision and being able to sell it is an essential task of leadership."

—Warren Bennis and Robert Thomas

✦

"You lead by voice."

—Frances Hesselbein

✦

"I shall not seek, and I will not accept, the nomination of my party for another term as your president."

—Lyndon B. Johnson

"I solemnly swear that I will faithfully execute the office of the President of the United States and will, to the best of my ability, preserve, protect, and defend the Constitution of the United States, so help me God."

—George Washington

✦

"Let us dedicate ourselves to what the Greeks wrote so many years ago: 'To tame the savageness of man and make gentle the life of the world.'"

—Robert F. Kennedy

✦

"I'm in!"

—Banner outside Oakland Raiders' practice facility

✦

"With malice toward none, with charity for all, with firmness in the right as God gives us to see the right, let us strive on to finish the work we are in, to bind up the nation's wounds, to care for him who shall have borne the battle and for his widow and his orphan, to do all we may to achieve and cherish a just and lasting peace among ourselves and with all great nations."

—Abraham Lincoln

✦

"There are only two options regarding commitment: you're either in, or you're out. There's no such thing as life in-between."

—Pat Riley

✦

When the Declaration of Independence was adopted, the chances that the Revolution would actually succeed were slim. At the signing ceremony, John Hancock remarked, "We must be unanimous; we must all hang together," Benjamin Franklin agreed, "or most assuredly, we shall all hang separately."

✦

"I wanted a kinder, gentler nation."

—George H.W. Bush

"Tonight, we are a country awakened to danger and called to defend freedom. Our grief has turned to anger and anger to resolution. We will not tire, we will not falter, and we will not fail."

—George W. Bush

✦

"All free men, wherever they may live, are citizens of Berlin; therefore, as a free man, I take pride in the words: *'Ich bin ein Berliner.'*"

—John F. Kennedy

✦

"With confidence in our armed forces ... with the unbounding determination of our people ... we will gain the inevitable triumph ... so help us, God."

—Franklin D. Roosevelt

✦

"Senator Barkley and I will win this election and make those Republicans like it, don't you forget that!"

—Harry S. Truman

✦

"I would say to the House, as I said to those who have joined this government: 'I have nothing to offer but blood, toil, tears, and sweat.'"

—Winston Churchill

✦

"Commitment is what transforms a promise into a reality."

—Abraham Lincoln

✦

"It's not that I want to paint or I want to sing. I have to."

—Tony Bennett

✦

"We stand at Armageddon and we battle for the Lord!"

—Theodore Roosevelt

In November 1978, Ronald Reagan stood in front of the Berlin Wall and told his aides: "We have got to find a way to knock this thing down." In June 1987, he predicted in a speech at the Berlin Wall, "Yes, across Europe this wall will fall, for it cannot withstand faith, it cannot withstand truth. The wall cannot withstand freedom." Then, on November 9, 1989, the Iron Curtain that had separated East from West fell. Ronald Reagan had been stubborn, tough, and right. He had won the Cold War. "I never dreamed that in less than three years, the wall would come down, and a 6,000-pound section of it would be sent to me for my Presidential library," said Reagan, but, even if he hadn't dreamed that the wall would come down as fast as it did, he had dreamed that it would come down.

✦

"I will prepare and some day my chance will come."
—Abraham Lincoln

✦

"If you can't motivate yourself, you'll never be able to motivate others."
—Jay Strack

✦

"Everyone wants to win. The special person has the will to prepare to win."
—Marv Levy

✦

"You know, what you did last night is history. You're only as good as your performance today."
—Tony La Russa

✦

"As I looked out a moment ago, from the Reichstag, that embodiment of German unity, I noticed words crudely spray-painted upon the wall, perhaps by a young Berliner: 'This wall will fall.' Beliefs become reality."
—Wynton Hall

✦

"Discipline is the key to success—financial discipline, nutritional discipline, workout discipline—and only five percent of the country has it, but if you have it, you will dominate."
—Colin Cowherd

"Mother always said that was what set him off."

—Curtis LeMay's younger sister on the first time her brother saw an airplane

✦

"Your dream is not big enough if it doesn't scare you."

—Matthias Schmelz

✦

"People with goals succeed because they know where they are going."

—Earl Nightingale

✦

"You may fire when you are ready, Gridley."

—George Dewey

✦

"Every problem has a gift for you in its hands."

—Richard Bach

✦

"If you want to go fast, go alone. If you want to go far, go together."

—African proverb

✦

"Commissioner Roger Goodell has a vision of where he wants his league to go, and he wants people around him who can help him get there."

—Donald Watkins

✦

"Great leadership has to be sustainable and not a one-shot deal. It's a matter of redefining the possible and creates the attitude of, 'Hey, we can do this. We can go places and do things we previously did not think possible.' The leader helps people understand this."

—John Ashcroft

"Great leaders are not 'poll vaulters.' They don't wait to see where everyone is headed and then get out in front of them. True leaders believe that consensus is the enemy of leadership."

—John Ashcroft

✦

"Millions of words have been written about leadership, but no one has been able to define it. The closest I can come is that you must have a great personal desire to lead. People become leaders because they decided to become leaders."

—Joe Drach

✦

"Glad to hear you have someone pushing you for the catching job. That helps you and the ball club. Hustle a little more every day."

—Note from Bob "Peanuts" Riley to Pat Williams when he was a catcher at Wake Forest University (1961)

✦

"Don't ever lose your confidence and remember the other fellows put their uniforms on the same way you do. Never stop swinging and you will be rough on all of them."

—Bob "Peanuts" Riley to Pat Williams

2

Acting on Your Plans

Jupiterimages

Now that you are committed to a goal, you need a plan. The Wizard of Westwood, John Wooden, is considered by many to be the greatest basketball coach in the history of the game. He preaches: "Failing to prepare is preparing to fail," and his UCLA Bruins championship teams were personifications of preparedness.

We need road maps to guide us to our destinations. The "maps" are of no use, however, without action. Many individuals have great inspirations in the shower, but when they dry off, the visions evaporate and nothing of substance is achieved.

The much-traveled itinerant evangelist, Vance Havner, put it this way: "You can't just stare up the steps; you have to step up the stairs." Thomas Edison observed: "Even your best plans won't work unless you do."

Read over the following quotes to get your action act together.

"Be bold."

—The advice Theo Epstein received from his father when he became the general manager of the Red Sox at age 28

✦

"Don't cuss, don't argue with the officials, and don't lose the game."

—John Heisman on coaching football

✦

"Throughout history, the most common debilitating human ailment has been cold feet."

—Robert Venditto

✦

"A man really determines himself by what he does. I wonder how a man feels when he isn't defined?"

—Vin Scully

✦

"You don't become a leader because you say you are. It's much more what you do than what you say."

—George Lee "Sparky" Anderson

✦

"If leaders don't have someone to whom they can hand off the baton, we're nothing but foam on the beach. Success, without successors, is not success."

—Jay Strack

✦

"People of the Philippines, I have returned. By the grace of Almighty God, our forces stand again on Philippine soil ... The hour of your redemption is here ... Rally to me ... Rise and strike. Strike at every available opportunity: for your homes and hearths, strike. For future generations of your sons and daughters."

—Douglas MacArthur

✦

"Coaching is making players do what they don't want to do so they can become what they want to become."

—Tom Coughlin

"Be the boss. It's not a dictatorship, but it's not a democracy either."

—Jim Mora, Sr.

✦

"I sit here all day trying to persuade people to do the things they ought to have the sense to do without my persuading them. That's all the powers of the president amount to."

—Harry S. Truman

✦

"You cannot lead from the crowd."

—Margaret Thatcher

✦

"It's better to put ten men to work than to do the work of ten men."

—D.L. Moody

✦

"There is an epidemic of EFWIC disease going around: Excuses For Why I Can't."

—Hal Urban

✦

"She was extremely focused—big time. All she ever saw was the ball, the court, and being number one."

—Rosie Casals on Steffi Graf

✦

"Never look back, unless you are planning to go that way."

—Henry David Thoreau

✦

"Work, work, work is the main thing."

—Abraham Lincoln

✦

"Hire people who already have the motivation and the drive to be eagles, and then just let them soar."

—Jim Rohn

"Do what you don't want to do to get what you want."

—Dawn Staley

✦

"The only quality that can be developed by studious reflection and practice is the leadership of men. The art of leadership is deciding what to do and then getting the men to want to do it."

—Dwight D. Eisenhower

✦

"A president has got to be the calcium in the backbone. If he weakens, the whole team weakens."

—George W. Bush

✦

"I don't believe in looking back. If you make a decision that you think is the proper one at the time, that's the correct decision."

—John Wooden

✦

"A rock pile ceases to be a rock pile the moment a single man contemplates it bearing within him the image of a cathedral."

—Antoine de Saint-Exupéry

✦

"Vision is built on reality; it's not mystical. It's not what is, but what can be. After the vision, a bridge must be built to turn it into reality."

—John Maxwell

✦

"Once I determine to move, I seldom, if ever, fret."

—Gerald R. Ford

✦

"Every child is born blessed with a vivid imagination, but just as a muscle grows flabby with disuse, so the bright imagination of a child pales in later years if he ceases to exercise it."

—Walt Disney

"I read a great book years ago about the Supreme Court that said the Court's challenge was 'to remember the future and imagine the past.' That's a great phrase because it says so much. You imagine the past in order to make it relevant to the future that you are creating. The future doesn't just happen; it's shaped by decisions."

—Paul Tagliabue

✦

"What great cause would have been fought and won under the banner: 'I stand for consensus'?"

—Margaret Thatcher

✦

"If your horse is dead, for goodness sake, dismount."

—Eddy Ketchursid

✦

"The Queen had only one way of settling all difficulties, great or small. 'Off with his head!' she said, without even looking around."

—*Alice's Adventures in Wonderland*

✦

"The ideal leader is one who invariably acts kindly and with consideration and is still decisive and bold. The greatest blunder in war is indecisiveness, slowness, and hesitation."

—Dwight D. Eisenhower

✦

"When I've heard all I need to make a decision, I don't take a vote, I make a decision."

—Ronald Reagan

✦

"The most difficult thing is the decision to act; the rest is merely tenacity."

—Amelia Earhart

✦

"I act with decision."

—Nathanael Greene

"Every man must rake his own leaves."
—Dusty Baker

✦

"If you can't explain it to your mother or grandmother, don't do it."
—Glen Salow

✦

"Be right or wrong, but be decisive in your actions."
—Brian Billick

✦

Lynda Johnson Robb asked Harry Truman how he had felt about dropping the first atomic bomb. "He said he was sure it was the right thing to do, and he got a good night's sleep."

✦

"Standing in the middle of the road is very dangerous; you get knocked down by the traffic from both sides."
—Margaret Thatcher

✦

"When a decision has been made and the die is cast, then murder the alternatives."
—Unknown

✦

"In any moment of decision the best thing you can do is the right thing. The next best this is the wrong thing. The worst thing you can do is nothing."
—Theodore Roosevelt

✦

"Indecision kills."
—Richard Cheney

✦

"Talk is cheap. Let's go play."
—Johnny Unitas

"The papers may circulate around the government for a while, but they finally reach this desk. Then, there's no place else for them to go. The president—whoever he is—has to decide. He can't pass the buck to anybody. No one else can do the deciding for him. That's his job."

—Harry S. Truman

✦

"When Bear Bryant was asked about a play call or a substitution he made, he had a standard answer to the media: 'I was just trying to win the game.'"

—Wimp Sanderson

✦

"An indecisive mind is one of the greatest misfortunes that can befall an army."

—Joseph Reed

✦

"My word is out to these people and I can't take it back."

—Abraham Lincoln

✦

"An unwillingness to accept risk has swamped more leaders than anything I can think of."

—Max DePree

✦

"A great deal of talent is lost to the world for want of a little courage. Every day sends to their graves obscure men whose timidity prevented them from making a first effort."

—Sydney Smith

✦

"I am here to make decisions, and whether they prove right or wrong, I am going to make them."

—Harry S. Truman

✦

"If you don't live it, you don't believe it."

—Marion Wade

"If you have a dream, you need the courage to make it come true."

—Walt Disney

✦

"Many years later, E.D. Nixon, the black Montgomery lawyer who represented Rosa Parks, met a woman on an airplane who told him she couldn't imagine what would have happened to black people if Martin Luther King had not come to Montgomery. He said, 'If Mrs. Parks had gotten up and given that white man her seat, you'd never have heard of Reverend King.'"

—Gail Collins

✦

John Gunther, author, once asked Eleanor Roosevelt, "Just how does the President think?" She responded, "My dear, Mr. Gunther, the President never thinks. He decides."

✦

For many years, George Morris worked at the Truman Library in Independence, Missouri, and knew Harry S. Truman personally. Mr. Truman kept an office at the library, and one day he noticed 12 Japanese students who were on tour. Truman invited them into his private office, sat on the edge of his desk, and removed his glasses. He spoke with them briefly and said, "I'm very sorry for the heartache I caused your nation. I'm sorry you had to suffer, along with your families and your friends, but I'd do it again if I had to."

✦

"I saw something on a bumper sticker a long time ago that said, 'It's not *what if*; it's *what now*.' If you allow yourself to play those 'what if' games, especially [with] the repetitiveness and day-in, day-out grind of the game of baseball, you will absolutely start driving yourself crazy. You make your decision and say, *'What now? What's next?'* not *'What happened?'*"

—Bob Brenly

✦

"Disneyland will never be completed. It will continue to grow as long as there is imagination left in the world."

—Walt Disney

✦

"It's kind of fun to do the impossible."

—Walt Disney

"Let us have faith that right makes might, and in that faith, let us, to the end, dare to do our duty as we understand it."

—Abraham Lincoln

✦

"General Secretary Gorbachev, if you seek peace, if you seek prosperity for the Soviet Union and Eastern Europe, if you seek liberalization: come here to this gate! Mr. Gorbachev, open this gate! Mr. Gorbachev, tear down this wall."

—Ronald Reagan

✦

"The future belongs to those who are prepared."

—Jay Strack

✦

"If you want to accomplish something, go do it."

—Rudyard Kipling

✦

"Between saying and doing, many pairs of shoes are worn out."

—Italian proverb

✦

The Nine Ps: "Previous preparation and planning prevent pretty poor performance and problems down the pike."

—Unknown

✦

"His only motivation was to win football games."

—Dick Hoak on Chuck Noll

✦

"If you are willing to give up credit, you can get anything done."

—Benjamin Franklin

✦

"There are no movements moving ahead without someone at the head moving them."

—Ravi Zacharias

"There's an old saying that victory has a hundred fathers and defeat is an orphan. What matters is that I am the responsible officer of the government."

—John F. Kennedy

✦

"A mature leader has the confidence to wait until the last moment to make major decisions. Like a game of chess, your move is predicated on what the other side does."

—John C. Maxwell

✦

"Real leadership is about creating a consensus where none exists."

—Arianna Huffington

✦

"Leadership is action, not position."

—Donald McGannon

✦

"He consulted much, pondered much, resolved slowly, resolved surely."

—Alexander Hamilton on George Washington as President, and how he faced complicated issues

✦

"To be a top-notch leader, you have to have an edge. Good leaders see reality and then go make tough decisions."

—J.P. Pawliw-Fry

✦

"You can't lead the charge unless you know how to sit in the saddle."

—George Steinbrenner

✦

"The first rule of leadership is to lead."

—Donald F. Kettl

✦

"To lead is to make decisions."

—Jack Uldrich

"I don't do committees, I am direct. Sometimes someone has to draw a line between informing, consulting, and deciding."

—Condoleezza Rice

✦

"Dave was a decider, not a ducker."

—George Shultz, former Secretary of Defense, at the funeral of David Packard

✦

"The characteristics that make some people better leaders than others are setting the right goals, reaching them the right way, and doing both in the right amount of time. This is what leadership is when you get right down to it."

—Jack Welch

✦

"Leadership is not something you live but something you behave. Leadership has to be fleshed out by action. Powerful leadership emerges when your life matches the message."

—John Maxwell

✦

"A leader is a person with a magnet in his heart and a compass in his head."

—Vance Havner

✦

Once, the young Franklin D. Roosevelt was scolded by his mother for being too bossy with the other children. Franklin replied, "Mummie, if I didn't give the orders, nothing would happen."

✦

"When the country is in chaos, everybody has a plan to fix it, but it takes a leader of real understanding to straighten things out."

—Proverbs 28:2 (The Message)

✦

"We've got to take out the boss element. We're going to win on our ideas, not by whips and chains."

—Jack Welch

"The leader who makes no mistakes is the leader who makes no decisions, takes no risks, and achieves nothing for us."

—Bill O'Neil

✦

"The job of a leader is to define reality and give hope."

—Kenneth Chenault

✦

"The most important leadership principle I learned was simple: Do the right thing."

—Norman Schwarzkopf

✦

"I'm intense and I'm a driver. I'm a firm believer in the old adage that if you're going to lead, lead."

—George Steinbrenner

✦

"Ninety percent of leadership is learned by doing."

—Bill Hybels

✦

"As a politician, Abraham Lincoln had an intuitive sense of when to hold fast, when to wait, and when to lead."

—Doris Kearns Goodwin

✦

"The best lead by example."

—Woody Hayes on players at Ohio State who were his best leaders

✦

"You're driving the train. Your job is to keep the train rolling every day."

—Bill Parcells

✦

"I've always found that the speed of the boss is the speed of the team."

—Lee Iacocca

"A leader's message must be communicated so that every listener understands and knows what to do. The vision must be memorable (words inventive); the visions must be measurable (words insightful); and the vision must be motivational (words give incentive)."

—John Maxwell

✦

"How do you define leadership? In order to demystify it for people, we have come up with The Four Es of Leadership:

1. Energy. Leaders provide their own energy. They wake up in the morning and get going because they are self-starters.
2. Edge. They make tough decisions because they believe 'the buck stops here.'
3. Execution. Great leaders get things done because they know how to turn strategy into reality.
4. Energize. It's not about you. It's getting a team of people to do it together."

—Jack Welch

✦

"You can have brilliant ideas, but if you can't get them across, your ideas won't get you anywhere."

—Lee Iacocca

✦

"He followed the dictum of Douglas MacArthur. MacArthur said that in order to establish authority, precipitate action immediately. In other words, do something bold. We all know the boldness of MacArthur's Inchon landing and his actions in the South Pacific. Gillman, above all else, was a bold—in some cases—audacious coach."

—Jack Kemp on coach Sid Gillman

✦

"*Now* is the operative word. Everything you put in your way is just a method of putting off the hour when you could actually be building your dream. You don't need endless time and perfect conditions. Do it now. Do it today. Do it for 20 minutes and watch your heart start beating."

—Barbara Sher

✦

"Management is nothing more than motivating people."

—Lee Iacocca

"Surround yourself with the best people you can find, delegate authority, and don't interfere."

—Ronald Reagan

✦

"In a Democracy the President Is Also Salesman in Chief."

—A headline in the Sunday *New York Times* (September 28, 2003)

✦

"Opportunities multiply as they are seized."

—Sun Tzu

✦

"He was a great teacher who had the ability to make hard things simple. Chuck was a remarkable collector of knowledge."

—John Fox, NFL coach, on Chuck Noll

✦

"I never hire anyone unless he knows something about the game I don't."

—Bear Bryant

✦

"The world hates change, yet it is the only thing that has brought progress."

—Charles Kettering

✦

"A leader offers a clear vision on the way to go. It's all about seeing beyond the fuzziness. A leader has to make a plan and stay with it. You can't overreact to a few rough days. It's important to be consistent and stick with your plan for the long haul."

—Joe Torre

✦

"I've never left the field saying, 'I could've done more to get ready.'"

—Peyton Manning

✦

"At the end of the day a great team will beat a great individual."

—Magic Johnson

"I have only done what any red-blooded American would do. We gonna do our part, and we'll win because we're on God's side. Thank you."

—Joe Louis

✦

"On Christmas night 1776, the most daring exploit of the Revolutionary War took place. George Washington's password that night was 'victory or death.' A snowstorm with near zero visibility shielded Washington's movements as he launched a two-pronged surprise attack on Trenton, New Jersey. During the battle, Washington rode up on horseback to a major and his troops and called out, 'March on, my brave fellows, after me!' while he spun his horse toward the enemy. His victory at Trenton, and a few days later at Princeton where he whipped the British, turned the tide of the Revolutionary War."

—Herbert Warden III

✦

"The quicker they are whipped the quicker we can go home. The shortest way home is through Berlin and Tokyo and when we get to Berlin I am personally going to shoot that paper-hanging Hitler, just like I'd shoot a snake."

—George S. Patton

✦

"And you know, my friends, there comes a time when people get tired of being trampled on by the iron feet of oppression."

—Martin Luther King, Jr. to a huge overflow crowd at Holt Street Church, his first national appearance, December 1955

✦

"You want your company to run well? Here's an ironclad rule: Get everyone on the same team. Get everyone working together for the same goal; get them to win or lose together."

—Gordon Bethune

✦

"Sometimes the window of opportunity is only open briefly. Waiting is not a decision, although many people think it is. Be willing to make decisions. That's the most important quality in a good leader. Don't fall victim to what I call the ready-aim-aim-aim-aim syndrome. You must be willing to fire."

—T. Boone Pickens

"Don't be afraid to coach the team."

—Jerry Buss, Lakers' owner, to Pat Riley after he became the head coach

✦

"The greatest danger for most of us lies not in setting our aim too high and falling short, but in setting our aim too low and achieving our mark."

—Michelangelo

✦

"Some people think that a lot of things I do are unbalanced and probably do seem so if one thinks only in terms of the present, but I'm thinking of 25 years from now."

—Franklin D. Roosevelt

✦

"A good plan today is better than a perfect plan tomorrow."

—George S. Patton

✦

"I work off a model. When I talk to kids I say the first thing you have to do is dream. When you get it on paper it becomes a goal. Once on paper you can study it to find out the best way to achieve your goal."

—Arte Moreno

✦

"A vision's just a vision if it's only in your head.
If no one gets to hear it, it's as good as dead.
It has to come to life.
Bit by bit, putting it together
Piece by piece, the only way to make a work of art.
Every moment makes a contribution.
Every little detail plays a part.
Having just the vision's no solution.
Everything depends on execution.
Putting it together, that's what counts."

—Stephen Sondheim's lyrics from *Sunday in the Park With George*

"The vision must be followed by the venture. It is not enough to stare up the steps; we must step up the stairs."

—Vance Havner

✦

"Leadership is the capacity to translate vision into reality."

—Warren Bennis

✦

"Vision without action is a daydream. Action without vision is a nightmare."

—Japanese proverb

✦

"Once I made up my mind, I acted and I did not worry about the action I took."

—Harry S. Truman

✦

"Saddle up, Pilgrim, and get to work."

—John Wayne

✦

"Nothing is more important than what you are doing, when you're doing it."

—Pete Carril

✦

"With leaders, the future calls to them in a voice they can't drown out. The future is more real than the present. It compels them to act."

—Marcus Buckingham

✦

"A wealthy person plans for three generations; a poor person plans for Saturday night."

—Gloria Vanderbilt

✦

"Think beyond your lifetime if you want to accomplish something truly worthwhile."

—Walt Disney

"He that has no plan becomes the victim of everyone else's plan."

—Bill Gaither

✦

"Orville Wright's vision was so intense that it served as a sort of 'cosmic magnet' pulling him toward destiny."

—Mark Eppler

✦

"Leadership is the ability to articulate a vision and the ability to get others to act on that vision."

—Jack Welch

✦

"A distant reference point makes the path straight."

—Wayne Hastings and Ron Potter

✦

"A vision becomes a goal when you put a date on it."

—James Davis

✦

"I saw the angel in the marble and carved until I set him free."

— Michelangelo

✦

"My wife, Ruth, is pursuing her doctorate in organizational leadership. It will take three years of hard work. She has a sign posted next to her desk that says, 'The office of Dr. Ruth Williams, 2010.'"

—Pat Williams

✦

"You need to live with a clock and a compass. The clock helps you deal with the routine issues of life. The compass sets the direction for your life and gives you a vision. It drives you to your goals."

—Stephen Covey

"It does not matter how slowly you go, so long as you don't stop."
—Confucius

✦

"Let's get where we're going."
—General John Pershing

✦

"*Mr. Meant To* has a comrade
And his name is *Didn't Do.*
Have you ever chanced to meet them?
Did they ever call on you?
These two fellows lived together
In the *House of Never Win*
And I'm told that it is haunted by
The *Ghost of Might Have Been.*"
—John Wooden

✦

"Winning is the science of being totally prepared."
—George Allen

✦

"You start with having to win and you work back."
—Don Shula

✦

"Defensive strategy never has produced ultimate victory."
—Douglas MacArthur

✦

"I thought I was going to win it."
—Pat Robertson on why he entered the 1988 Republican presidential primaries

✦

"I don't want to win every game, just the next one."
—Lou Holtz

"People with goals succeed because they know where they're going."

—Earl Nightingale

✦

"A leader must walk a tightrope between the consent he must win and the control he must exert."

—Vince Lombardi

✦

"The art of leadership is not saying 'yes'. It's saying 'no'."

—Tony Blair

✦

"I have a perfect horror of words that are not backed up by deeds."

—Theodore Roosevelt

✦

"We must behave as if we have a volunteer workforce because that, in fact, is what we have."

—Scott Cook

✦

"She's a chameleon when it comes to motivation. Whatever she needs to do to get her team motivated is what she does."

—Marsha Frese on her sister Brenda Frese

✦

"Leadership is not about money, fame, and power. Leadership is responsibility."

—Peter Drucker

✦

"The fierce urgency of *now*."

—Martin Luther King, Jr.

✦

"The task of a leader is to get his people from where they are to where they have not been."

—Henry Kissinger

"Leadership is character in motion."

—Les Csorba

✦

"You get all the facts and you make up your mind ... Presidents have to make decisions if they're going to get anywhere, and those presidents who couldn't make decisions are the ones who caused all the trouble."

—Harry S. Truman

✦

"'The time had come.' Those four words are the essence of any great decision. Great decision-makers possess a fine sense of the ripeness of things. They know when the time has come, and it is this knowledge that drives the decisions they make."

—Alan Axelrod

✦

"Empowerment starts with four small, yet unbelievably powerful words: What do you think? Then utter four more powerful words: You make the call."

—Steve Ventura

✦

"When you run GE, there are seven to 12 times a year when you have to say, 'You're doing it my way.' If you do it 18 times, the good people will leave. If you do it three times, the company falls apart."

—Jeff Immelt

✦

"If my people understand me, I'll get their attention, but if my people trust me, I'll get their action."

—Cavett Roberts

✦

"All this will not be finished in the first 100 days, nor will it be finished in the first 1,000 days, nor in the life of this administration, nor even in our lifetime on this planet, but let us begin."

—John F. Kennedy

"I think my management style is direct. I want very fast decisions. I think the worst decision is usually no decision."

—Roger Ailes

✦

"I never did. I only prepared for the next play."

—Karch Kiraly on how he prepares to win Olympic gold

✦

"When I need to make a decision, I don't take a vote. I make a decision."

—Ronald Reagan

✦

"If you would not be forgotten as soon as you're dead and rotten, either write things worth reading or do things worth the writing."

—Benjamin Franklin

✦

"Some problems can't be solved, but they can be managed."

—Mario Cuomo

✦

"A crisis is a terrible thing to waste."

—Dick Clark, former CEO of Merck

✦

"Life isn't about waiting for the storm to pass. It's about learning to dance in the rain."

—Unknown

✦

"My father didn't think people were the problem, but the solution."

—Jack Kemp's son Jimmy

✦

"I see the big picture first, then I go backwards to execute it."

—Billie Jean King

"If you don't like bad news, you should get out of the leadership business. Your job is to hear as much bad news as there is out there, and to figure out ways of dealing with it."

—Kim Campbell

✦

Sandra Day O'Connor has a needlepoint pillow on her couch that reads: "Maybe in error, but never in doubt."

✦

"The one word that makes a good manager: decisiveness."

—Lee Iacocca

✦

"George Washington's mother is supposed to have greeted news of one of her son's victories in the Revolutionary War by saying, 'George generally carries through anything he undertakes.'"

—Richard Brookhiser

✦

"I once asked Coach Wooden what it was that made him so successful. He spent 15 minutes arguing with me that he was not successful. Finally, he told me two qualities:

1. Organization, preparation, and efficiency in practice
2. Caring

   He truly cared about us as human beings."

—Jamaal Wilkes

✦

"The greatest leaders of history seem to have two universal qualities:

1. They have an audacity, but also a caution born of careful study. They know when and how long to plan, but when the point of action is reached, they cast aside their doubts and act aggressively and with total confidence. The secret is knowing when that point is reached.
2. These leaders imagine and envision a successful outcome to whatever venture they are leading. They don't spend time imagining failure, but instead imagine a reality to their dream and go about creating it."

—Alan Axelrod

"The chief gem of my character is the ability to keep resolves when they are made."
—Abraham Lincoln

✦

"You call the game. Go out and be a catcher."
—Jamie Moyer, Phillies' pitcher, to rookie catcher Carlos Ruiz

✦

"Lyndon B. Johnson insisted that Jackie Kennedy be present when he took the oath of office aboard Air Force One on November 22, 1963, 98 minutes after her husband was declared dead. Continuity mattered now, and legitimacy. When everyone was gathered in the steamy, gold-carpeted Presidential cabin, she had still not arrived. 'We'll wait for her,' Johnson said. 'I want her here.'

"He urged Lady Bird to take notes on everything that happened, found a Dictaphone to record the ceremony, and made sure the photographer got it, too. When Jackie came, she stood by him and his wife as he raised his hand. When he had finished, he turned and hugged them both; then, he gave his first order as Commander-in-Chief: 'OK, let's get this plane back to Washington.'

"On the flight, he imagined what it would be like if something happened to the pilot and someone else had to bring the plane in, 'with no plans showing how long the runways were, with no maps and no notes.'"
—Nancy Gibbs and Michael Duffy

✦

"Don't fire until you see the whites of their eyes; then fire low."
—General Israel Putnam at Breed's Hill

✦

"Live it up. The meter is running!"
—Harry Caray

✦

"Doing nothing is almost the worst thing a president can do."
—Michael Beschloss

✦

"I like 'Decisive One.'"
—Jim Irsay, NFL team owner, on what nickname NFL commissioner Roger Goodell should have

"I made my final decision and that final decision was mine alone to make."

—Harry S. Truman on dropping the atomic bomb on Japan

✦

"I would rather lose making a move than do nothing."

—Earl Weaver

✦

"I'm not a big vision guy. I think it was Einstein who said that vision without execution is an hallucination."

—Mike Hurd

✦

Todd Beamer on United Flight #93 on September 11, 2001, to Verizon Airfone supervisor Lisa Jefferson as they prayed together: "Our Father, Who art in heaven, hallowed be thy Name"; then Todd spoke the famous words, "Let's roll."

✦

"The highways of life are full of flat squirrels who couldn't make up their minds."

—Unknown

✦

"The ancestor to every action is a thought."

—Ralph Waldo Emerson

✦

"There comes a time when a man has to take a stand, and history will record that he has to meet these tough situations and ultimately make a decision."

—John F. Kennedy

✦

"What must be done eventually should be done immediately."

—Jeremy Foley

✦

"Read my lips: No new taxes."

—George H.W. Bush

"General Douglas MacArthur said that every military defeat can be explained by two words: too late. 'Too late in anticipating danger; too late in preparing for it; too late in taking action.'"

—George Will

✦

"The president is managing this war, the draft, foreign relations, and planning a reconstruction of the Union all at once. I never knew with what tyrannous authority he rules the Cabinet until now. The most important things he decides, and there is no cavil."

—John Hay's diary, August 1863, on his boss, Abraham Lincoln

✦

"Not to decide is to decide."

—Harvey Cox

✦

"I'm the decider and I decide what is best."

—George W. Bush

✦

"I don't second-guess myself. I'm in the decision-making position and I make the call."

—Ernie Accorsi

✦

"Doug, councils of war bring timidity and confusion."

—Advice to Douglas MacArthur from his father

✦

"I did not run for president to pass these problems to the next generation. I ran for president to solve these problems for the next generation."

—Barack Obama

✦

"Problems don't go away on their own. Handle them quickly and find solutions right away. Waiting to address problems is a deadly trap."

—Paul J. Meyer

"Move the ball; make shots."

—Phil Jackson in a huddle with the Los Angeles Lakers during a timeout

✦

"A problem is something you have hopes of changing. Anything else is a fact of life."

—C.R. Smith

✦

"You must envision the future deeply and in detail—creatively—so that the unforeseeable becomes foreseeable. Then you write your script for the foreseeable."

—Bill Walsh

✦

"He was my hero even before I was born. One day, many years later, I telephoned my father to tell him I was leaving Harvard Law School and that I wanted to be a football coach. Thirty seconds of painful silence followed, and then the old marine said simply, 'Be a good one!' I hope I haven't disappointed him."

—Marv Levy on his father

✦

"You guys stop jabbering. I call the plays. You guys just do your job. Is that clear?"

—Bart Starr, former Green Bay Packers quarterback, in the first huddle of his first game, when he was a high school junior

✦

"Knock it down."

—Dean Smith, former University of North Carolina coach, to Michael Jordan before the last shot of the 1982 NCAA title game

✦

"The enemy is there, and I'm going to strike him ... I am going to take them where they are on Cemetery Hill."

—Robert E. Lee

✦

"My old Duke coach would say, 'Next play.' Coach K says it all the time. Learn from it and get better."

—Greg Paulus

"The question is: Is it right to surrender to this army? If it is right, I will take all the responsibility."

—Robert E. Lee

✦

"Dad always used to say, 'Hit it hard, hit it hard. Don't worry about it; just hit it, go find it, and hit it again.'"

—Arnold Palmer

✦

"To the fans and everybody in Gator Nation: You will never see any player in the entire country play as hard as I will play the rest of the season. You will never see someone push the rest of the team as hard as I will push everybody the rest of the season, and you'll never see a team play harder than we will the rest of the season." (The University of Florida won the rest of their games and beat Oklahoma for the national title.)

—Tim Tebow

✦

"On the day I'm performing, I don't hear anything anyone says to me."

—Luciano Pavarotti

✦

"Damn the torpedoes. Full speed ahead."

—David Farragut

✦

Forrest Clare "Phog" Allen, longtime basketball coach of the University of Kansas, was once asked to pick his best team. His answer was, "Ask me in 25 years and let me see what they have done in their lives."

✦

"You can't have a good football team unless you get a team committed to get a little bit better every day in practice. You've got to prepare yourself to practice well."

—Joe Paterno

✦

"It is said that leadership is that unique quality which enables special people to stand up and pull the rest over the horizon."

—Bill Polian

"His was a case of brain-hunger. It remained so until the end of his life."

—Father Cavenaugh at Notre Dame on Knute Rockne as a learner

✦

"I give the same halftime speech over and over. It works best when my players are better than the other coach's players."

—Chuck Mills

✦

"America loves a winner. America will not tolerate a loser. ... Americans play to win."

—George S. Patton

✦

"Your mission remains fixed, determined, inviolable ... it is to win our wars. In war, there is no substitute for victory."

—Douglas MacArthur

✦

"Admiral Kimmel, we are under attack."

—Admiral Husband Kimmel, commanding officer in charge of American Naval forces at Pearl Harbor, Hawaii, December 7, 1941

✦

"Teams only win titles when their best players forget about their statistics, sublimate their own games for the greater good, and put their egos on hold."

—Isiah Thomas

✦

"I have studied all the greatest American business leaders for years, and I have noticed one thing: they understand their company and have a vision of where to go, but more important, they are great cheerleaders and know how to inspire the troops and move them along."

—Jack Trout

✦

"The reason I saw things was that I was so intense. I was intent on seeing them."

—Ted Williams

"Focus on the finish line, not on all the pain you feel."
—A sign at mile 18 of the 2010 Disney Marathon

✦

"I didn't make a living acting until I was 35. Tenacity is critical."
—Harrison Ford

✦

"I was once dining with Horace Greeley and he asked me if it was not necessary to swear at your men and 'whoop them up,' as the saying goes. I replied that I thought not. There is nothing like quiet assurances and confidences. A general need never be noisy, and I think quiet troops are the best fighters."
—General James Longstreet

✦

"We have met the enemy and they are ours."
—Oliver Hazard Perry

✦

"There is no backdown in old Abe."
—Stephen Douglas, senator, on Abraham Lincoln

✦

When three-star general Hal Moore (played by Mel Gibson in *We Were Soldiers*) was asked if there was a tip-off sign of extraordinary leaders, he replied, "Unplanned acts of kindness."

✦

"I am a warrior and part of a team."
—American soldiers' pledge

✦

"I was always worried about my next win—always—because if you didn't have enough of them you were going to get fired, and I didn't want to get fired—not after five years, not after 10, not after 15 years. So, I was proud of the fact that that never happened to me."
—Earl Weaver

"War is waged only with vigor, decision, and unshaken will. One must never grope or hesitate."

—Napoleon

✦

"Do you want to matter in life? You have to have a passion for something ... when you have a passion you rise above your peers."

—Colin Cowherd

✦

"To critics of his decision to drop nuclear bombs on Japan, Harry Truman responded in effect: 'You don't understand. We had to win.'"

—Lance Morrow

✦

"For we must consider that we shall be as a city upon a hill. The eyes of all people are upon us."

—John Winthrop, first governor of the Massachusetts Bay Colony

✦

"There is no use saying, 'We are doing our best.' You have to succeed in doing what is necessary."

—Winston Churchill

✦

"Great leaders leave their people exhausted but exhilarated."

—Liz Wiseman

✦

"You're the leader; you're the boss, and you can't blame others. You must give direction."

—George Steinbrenner

✦

"Leaders are either multipliers or diminishers. Multipliers give people space and freedom to make mistakes. They remove fear from an organization. Diminishers may get short-term gains, but they don't get people's best thinking when they are working out of fear."

—Liz Wiseman

"The greatest leaders are ferocious listeners and question-askers. They have a high level of intellectual curiosity."

—Liz Wiseman

✦

"Self-discipline is the ability to do what you should do, when you should do it, whether you feel like it or not. There are 999 other success principles that I have found in my reading and experience, but without self-discipline, none of them work. With self-discipline, they all work."

—Elbert Hubbard

✦

"If you have a different colored shirt on, I want to whip you."

—Bear Bryant to a writer at Texas A&M on why he competed so intensely

✦

"One morning in the middle of the summer I came to work and took a look in the weight room. Over in the corner I saw someone working out and as I looked closer I saw that it was Kobe Bryant. I talked to him and asked, "What brings you here at this time of year?" He told me he'd brought his family on vacation to spend a week at Disney World. I asked him about his workout schedule and here's what I discovered. He was in our facility at 6 a.m. and worked out hard until 9 a.m. Then he showered, drove the 30 miles back to the hotel, picked up his family, and got to the park by 11 a.m. That meant he had to be up by 4:30 or 5 a.m. to get to our place by 6 a.m. This went on from Monday through Friday of his vacation week. Any questions why Kobe is the best player in the game and one of the greatest of all time?"

—Tom Smith, former Orlando Magic athletic trainer

✦

"Bear Bryant was a great leader because he was a great psychologist and motivator. Before the start of my senior season in 1953, he called me into his office and said, 'Steve, you know what? You can't make this team. I don't know where I can play you.' Boy, that got me really pumped up and made me want to do better. I only went out and made All-SEC and All-American that year."

—Steve Meilinger

3

Rigorously Pursuing

Jupiterimages

Study great and successful people and you will soon discover a common thread that runs among them: intense desire. These champions possess laser-like focus and an uncommon work ethic.

Whether it be Tiger Woods, Michael Jordan, Bill Gates, or Warren Buffet, each of these achievers is relentless in his desire to achieve at the highest level.

Read on to learn what it takes to achieve excellence.

"Anyone can hustle."
—Chris Hatcher

✦

"Motivation comes from within. The best coaches or managers help their teams to find that motivation within themselves rather than just cramming it down their throats."
—Larry Bird

✦

"Get up early in the morning in a three-point stance, and love what you do."
—David Baliff

✦

"If my doctor told me I had only six minutes to live, I wouldn't brood. I would type a little faster."
—Isaac Asimov

✦

"Anything's possible if you've got enough nerve."
—J.K. Rowling

✦

"He is no fool who gives what he cannot keep to gain what he cannot lose."
—Jim Elliott

✦

"When I played in the NFL, I never tried to hit anyone hard to really try to hurt them, unless it was a league game or something."
—Dick Butkus

✦

"Good leaders grab opportunities as they come…'they take the cookies when they're passed' as Mount Vernon's chairman of the board, Gay Hart Gaines, likes to say. They don't let their lack of funds, education, or standing in society prevent them from achieving a high level of success. Good leaders use their existing connections, and perhaps more important, they aggressively seek new connections. They don't wait around for lightning to strike."
—James C. Rees

"I'm not a football coach. I'm a salesman."
—Tommy Tuberville

✦

"Red was a straight-shooter with his guys, and he was the greatest salesperson ever. He came to Boston, a hockey town, in the 1950s and sold basketball because he believed in the product."
—M.L. Carr on Arnold Jacob "Red" Auerbach

✦

"The greatest compliment I ever got in my whole career came from Walter Alston, my former manager with the Dodgers. When he was retiring, he gave me a copy of his book and wrote inside the cover: 'To Don. When it's on the line, I want you to have the ball.' That's all a pitcher can hope for. That's it. Say no more. That's the height of a compliment you can give a professional athlete: when it's on the line, they want you to have the ball. I still get goose bumps when I think of having read that the first time when he wrote it for me."
—Don Sutton

✦

"Very, very, very few leaders have the temperament or the stomach for it. You have to perform every day or you will get slit to pieces."
—Ron Peltier

✦

John Kiernan, *New York Times* columnist, wrote the inscription for the trophy presented to Lou Gehrig by his teammates on July 4, 1939:

"We've been to the wars together,
We took our foes as they came,
And always you were the leader
And ever you played the game."

✦

"She'd never ask me to do a job she wouldn't do herself. No job was too big or too small for her to do. It never wavered with Pat, and that approach cultivated tremendous loyalty."
—Mickie DeMoss on Pat Summitt as a leader

"If anyone gives you a hard time because of the bomb, you tell them that if they have anything to say, they should call me. I'm the one who sent you."

—Harry S. Truman to pilot Paul Tibbets in the White House after World War II (Tibbets flew the Enola Gay B-29 that dropped the bomb on Hiroshima.)

✦

"I was like a pilot in a storm, and my job was to get the plane through the storm and land it safely."

—Chuck Daly

✦

"The origin of the word 'motivation' comes from 'motive,' which Webster's defines as 'that within the individual rather than without, which causes him or her to act.' In other words, all of our actions have motives or reasons. They come from needs felt deeply inside, and no one else can fill them for us. It isn't real motivation unless it comes from us."

—Hal Urban

✦

"Red Auerbach's genius was mostly in his skills as a motivator."

—Bill Russell

✦

"You motivate your players on an individual basis, not a group basis. Don't believe players are self-motivated. You have to motivate and inspire them every day."

—Paul Mainieri

✦

"The essence of coaching to me is pushing and pulling, encouraging and counseling each young guy to yearn for greatness. In today's world it has become easy to make excuses and to accept falling short. No parent, teacher, or coach should allow this attitude. Greatness is an honorable goal."

—Phil Martelli

✦

"When you do something, you should burn yourself up completely, like a good bonfire, leaving no trace of yourself."

—Shunryu Suzuki

"No matter how good a picture we turn out, I can always see ways to improve it when I see the finished product."

—Walt Disney

✦

"Walt Disney was a man who always wanted to be enthusiastic about something, to have a project that consumed his interest."

—Michael Barrier

✦

"I once asked Floyd Patterson if he knew he had been knocked down more times than any other boxer in history. He mildly answered, 'Yes, but I got up more times than anyone.'"

—Bert Sugar

✦

"Whatever happens, the flame of the French Resistance must not be extinguished and will not be extinguished."

—Charles de Gaulle

✦

"If you have a job without aggravation, you don't have a job."

—Malcolm Forbes

✦

"You've got to be 100 percent there. If you're only slightly not there on a big mountain, it can cause you to fall or to get in trouble."

—Ed Viesturs on climbing mountains

✦

"The key to being successful in life and with your business is focus, knowing how and where to focus your time and efforts. If you want to be successful, the key is finding something you're good at and focusing your efforts to help people."

—Brian Tracy

✦

"Focus, focus, focus—then get it done. That's the Jordan way."

—Tim Russert on Michael Jordan

"People ask me what I did last night. I can't remember. They think I'm joking. Every second you think about the past is a second when you can't think about the future."

—Randy Shannon

✦

"Concentration is sequential action to detail."

—Donna Lopiano

✦

"Some people just cut the grass, and they're like, 'Phew. That's it. I ain't going to plant the flowers, chop the wood, cut the grass, hit the hedges, and rake the leaves. Then I've got to rake the little scraps up from when I cut the grass! I ain't going to do all that stuff.' But that's why Ben Wallace works in this league. He uses the broom. He uses the rake. He doesn't take the blower and blow it. If you're a country boy, you understand that."

—Kevin Garnett on Ben Wallace

✦

"I had no natural gift to be anything; not an athlete, not an actor, not a writer, not a director, a painter of garden porches, not anything. So, I've worked really hard because nothing came easily to me."

—Paul Newman

✦

"I was born for the storm, and a calm does not suit me."

—Andrew Jackson

✦

"We have wished to avoid shooting, but the shooting has started and history has recorded who fired the first shot. In the long run, however, all that will matter is who fired the last shot."

—Franklin D. Roosevelt

✦

"He had great discipline on the Steelers. He got after all the stars—Bradshaw, Joe Greene, Greenwood. As a result, all the other guys fell into line. Most coaches get after the easy guys and leave the stars alone."

—George Perles on Chuck Noll of the Steelers

"Self-discipline is getting yourself to do something even though you don't feel like it, because the reward for getting it done far exceeds the temporary unpleasantness of the task itself."

—Hal Urban

✦

"Passion is putting everything you've got into everything you do."

—John Maxwell

✦

"The day that I don't have passion, I would quit and just get out."

—Richard Daley

✦

"Will and I could hardly wait for the morning to come to get at something that interested us. That's happiness."

—Orville Wright

✦

"For me, knowing that I've done all the work is a magical feeling. When I'm on the starting line knowing that I've worked harder than anyone else, that is a great source of strength and inspiration for me."

—Lance Armstrong

✦

"I can't guarantee that if you work hard you will be successful, but I can guarantee that if you don't work hard you will not be successful. For years, I thought that if you work hard you succeed. That's wrong. Everyone is working hard. The truth is: if you don't work hard, you won't be successful. If you do, you just improve your chances."

—Jim Valvano

✦

"Problem-solving is the primary job of CEOs."

—Carl Bass

✦

"Boldness has genius, power, and magic in it."

—Goethe

"The problem is not that there are problems. The problem is expecting otherwise, and thinking that having problems is a problem."

—Theodore Rubin

✦

"Anyone who sells anything that we do is a competitor."

—David Glass

✦

"You don't manage for the money or the publicity. It's about the competition."

—Tony La Russa

✦

"If the other guy's getting better, then you'd better be getting better faster than that other guy's getting better, or you're getting worse."

—Tom Peters

✦

"If Pepsi-Cola didn't exist, I would try to invent it. It keeps us and them on our toes and keeps us lean."

—Roberto Goizueta, Coca-Cola CEO, 1981–1997

✦

"The late Edwin Bennett Williams used to say that as a trial lawyer and a sports team owner, his entire life was built on 'contest living.' Everything he did each day was built around competition and trying to beat the other guy."

—Ernie Accorsi

✦

Jackie Robinson: "Do you want a player who's afraid to fight back?"

Branch Rickey: "I want a player with guts enough not to fight back. You've got to do this job with base hits and stolen bases and fielding ground balls, Jackie. Nothing else."

Jackie Robinson: "I promise you there will be no incident."

✦

"All successful people who have had great success are lacking in one thing: fear. Most people stop themselves before they start because they're afraid. They quit before trying to do something."

—Mitch Albom

What is discipline?

1. Burning the midnight oil when you would rather sleep.
2. Taking the extra step when you would rather sit.
3. Going the extra mile when you would rather stop.
4. Lifting up your pride when you would rather quit.

✦

"Fortune favors the bold."
—Machiavelli

✦

Dan Rather closed newscasts with: "Courage."

✦

"These are the boys of Pointe du Hoc. These are the men who took the cliffs. These are the champions who helped free a continent. These are the heroes who helped end a war."
—Ronald Reagan

✦

"The first and great commandment is: Don't let them scare you."
—Elmer Davis

✦

"Courage is the power to let go of the familiar."
—Raymond Lindquist

✦

"Men don't follow titles; they follow courage."
—Mel Gibson in *Braveheart*

✦

"Courage is the main quality of leadership. Courage to initiate something and to keep it going."
—Walt Disney

✦

"The real hero is the man who fights even though he is scared."
—George S. Patton

"Courage is doing what you're afraid to do. There can be no courage unless you're scared."

—Eddie Rickenbacker

✦

"Cancer can take away all my physical ability. It cannot touch my mind; it cannot touch my heart; and it cannot touch my soul. Those three things are going to carry on forever."

—Jim Valvano's farewell speech, March 4, 1993

✦

"The time to be nervous is before you place the bet, not after the wheel is spinning. Scared money never wins."

—Bill Parcells

✦

"The true meaning of courage is to be afraid, and then with your knees knocking and your heart racing, to step out anyway."

—Oprah Winfrey

✦

"I have ploughed and planted and gathered into the barns, and no man could hear me! And ain't I a woman? Obligated to you for hearing me, and now old Sojourner ain't got nothing more to say."

—Sojourner Truth at the Women's Convention in Akron, Ohio (December 1851)

✦

"You can learn from failure, but don't dwell on it."

—Joe Montana

✦

"The ability to learn faster than your competition may be the only sustainable competitive advantage."

—Arie DeGeus

✦

"You're three weeks from being fired. Do not lose three in a row."

—Joe Gibbs on the perils of coaching in the NFL

"The only skill that will be important in the 21st century is the skill of learning new skills. Everything else will become obsolete over time. It has been said that, 'Whatever got you to where you are today is not enough to keep you there.'"

—Peter Drucker

✦

"Whatever you are doing well today, you will have to be doing it vastly better one year from today if you want to keep your position."

—Tom Peters

✦

"Pro sports is 90 percent adversity and 10 percent success. You've got to be aware going in that it's going to be rough. It's all about survival, and you've got to be ready for the battle every day. When you get to experience that ten percent, enjoy it."

—Phil Simms

✦

In a *Peanuts* comic strip, Lucy missed yet another fly ball. As she apologetically approached Charlie Brown on the mound, she said, "I thought I had it, but suddenly I remembered all the others I've missed—the past got in my eyes!" When we let failures of the past get in our eyes, we are inviting further frustration.

✦

"Yesterday, December 7, 1941, is a date which will live in infamy ... the United States of America was suddenly and deliberately attacked by Naval and Air Forces of the Empire of Japan ... No matter how long it may take us to overcome this premeditated invasion, the American people in their righteous might will win through to absolute victory."

—Franklin D. Roosevelt

✦

"Franklin Roosevelt was a rare mix. He somehow combined instinct with calculation, exasperating improvisations with what some of his contemporaries called 'longheadedness.' He had a way of peering forward, fixing a point far away on the horizon, then tacking toward it without much worry about the day-to-day choppiness en route. This long-range thinking was not the same as long-term planning. He didn't waste a lot of time detailing it, but his focus on the bigger picture would serve him well."

—Jonathan Alter

"The Lord of the gentle breeze is Lord of the rough and tumble."

—Steven Curtis Chapman, songwriter (from "King of the Jungle")

✦

"That we here highly resolve that these dead shall not have died in vain, that this nation under God shall have a new birth of freedom ... and that government of the people, by the people, and for the people, shall not perish from the Earth."

—Abraham Lincoln

✦

"Let every nation know whether it wishes us well or ill, that we shall pay any price, bear any burden, meet any hardship, support any friend, oppose any foe to assure the survival and the success of liberty."

—John F. Kennedy

✦

Amid the appalling cascade of bad news that ushered out of 1941, Winston Churchill could joke about the moment when he realized France was not only defeated but turning hostile: "When I warned them that Britain would fight on alone whatever they did, their generals told their Prime Minister and his divided Cabinet, 'In three weeks, England will have her neck wrung like a chicken.' Some chicken! Some neck!"

✦

"The man who can drive himself further once the pain starts is the man who will win."

—Roger Bannister

✦

"I was standing in the tunnel before our game with the Colts on September 10, 2006. The players from both teams were waiting to go out on the field. You could cut the pressure with a knife as the players were dancing and jumping around. Peyton Manning of the Colts just stood there with this look on his face that just overwhelmed me. In all my years in sports I've never seen such a look of focus on an athlete's face. That look almost took my breath away."

—Ernie Accorsi, recalling the first time two brothers (Peyton and Eli Manning) played at quarterback against each other in the NFL

"You've got to get obsessed and stay focused."
—John Irving

✦

Al McGuire inscribed a photo to Tom Crean: "Tom, 'Only once—enjoy the run.' Al"

✦

"If the power to do hard work is not talent, it is the best possible substitute for it."
—James Garfield

✦

"There's no one who's dropped on top of the mountain. You've got to work your way to the top."
—Al McGuire

✦

"The heights by great men reached and kept were not attained by sudden flight, but they while their companions slept were toiling upward in the night."
—Henry Wadsworth Longfellow

✦

"Every hour misspent is lost forever."
—George Washington

✦

"I do not know anyone who has got to the top without hard work. That is the recipe. It will not always get you to the top, but it should get you pretty near."
—Margaret Thatcher

✦

"One of my great days in baseball was the night in 1985 that Pete Rose broke Ty Cobb's hit record. The 30 days leading up to that were unbelievable. One night, he went 0-4 and said, 'Kitty, tell the writers I'll be there in a little while.' He took Billy DeMars, one of the coaches, and he went to the batting cage under the stands and took batting practice at 11:00 at night."
—Jim Kaat

"I try as hard as I can. I never dog it."
—Tiger Woods

✦

"When the storms of life hit, you have to be prepared for them and put your rain coat on."
—Dorothy Gabriel

✦

Once in a while Franklin D. Roosevelt would end a letter to Winston Churchill: "Keep up the good work."

✦

"I think my greatest asset is that I practice more than anyone to develop my talent."
—Tiger Woods

✦

"Every time you do something, go a little bit farther than you did before. Pretty soon you'll have gone twice as far as you originally thought you could."
—Bill O'Neil

✦

"Unless you are willing to drench yourself in your work beyond the capacity of the average man, you are not cut out for a position at the top."
—James Cash Penney

✦

"Whether you like him or not, he's tenacious."
—Barbara Bush on her son, George

✦

"When Marty Schottenheimer coached the Browns for me in Cleveland, he used an expression, 'Row your boat backward.' In other words, you can't always see the finish line, and you don't know the outcome in advance; therefore, just keep using your oars every day and keep stroking the boat. If you do, the outcome will take care of itself. That's really all you can do anyway."
—Ernie Accorsi

"Leaders are not born. Leaders are made, and they are made by effort and hard work."
—Vince Lombardi

✦

"When it came to work, he never spared himself."
—Ken Blackburn, aide, on Branch Rickey

✦

Former Phillies' manager Larry Bowa had a needlepoint that sat on a filing cabinet in the corner of his office at Veteran's Stadium: "Last year? History. Last night? In the books. Tonight? 110 percent."

✦

"No one works harder than Michael. He just wants to get better."
—Doug Collins on Michael Jordan

✦

"Quit competing, and you dry up like a peach seed."
—Sam Snead

✦

"You either work hard or Michael has no use for you."
—Phil Jackson on Michael Jordan

✦

"I once asked Ted Williams if he could do it all over again, what would he do differently? Ted answered, 'Practice twice as long.'"
—Tommy Holmes

✦

"There has never yet been a man who led a life of ease whose name is worth remembering."
—Theodore Roosevelt

✦

"She believed more than ever that work—the harder the better—was the essence of life."
—A. Scott Berg on Katharine Hepburn

"I'm convinced that children come out of the womb looking for shortcuts."

—Bill Gaither

✦

"The best advice I ever got when I was a kid, I remember meeting Bob Hope and I said to Bob, 'Have you got any advice?' He said to me, 'Remember, kid, nobody ever got discovered laying off. You've got to work. You don't get better laying off."

—Alan King

✦

"True champions are made when no one is looking."

—Sign in the weight room at the Cincinnati Reds' spring training site, Sarasota, Florida

✦

"The difference between a job and a career is the difference between 40 and 60 hours a week."

—Robert Frost

✦

"Difficulty is the excuse history never accepts."

—Edward R. Murrow

✦

"The tougher you are on yourself, the easier life will be on you."

—Zig Ziglar

✦

"Just plain working at it. Work, that's the real secret."

—Ted Williams on the key to hitting

✦

"It's not an easy life. Nothing worthwhile is ever easy. If David had slain a dwarf instead of a giant, who would have cared? Who would remember?"

—Victor Kiam

✦

"Hard work wins it."

—Lance Armstrong

"Most of the other kids would play in the pool or be off shooting pool, playing around. Tiger was always practicing or in his room with his father. He took the road less traveled while we took the road most traveled."

—Brad Zwetschke on Tiger Woods

✦

"The harder you work, the harder it is to surrender."

—Vince Lombardi

✦

"If you push the human body, it will respond."

—Bobby Clarke

✦

"In the NBA, 75 percent of the players don't want to work. When you get a guy like Ben, who goes overtime, he's going to stand out."

—Charles Oakley on Ben Wallace

✦

"I was made to work. If you are equally industrious, you will be equally successful."

—Johann Sebastian Bach

✦

"Any stupid donkey can die. Dying is easy. Living's a pain in the backside. You've got to work at it."

—Jack LaLanne at age 89

✦

"My theory has always been, you put your head down and work hard, and good things happen."

—Donald Rumsfeld

✦

"You wonder how they do it, and you look to see the knack; You watch the foot in action, or the shoulder, or the back; But when you spot the answer where the high glamour's lurk; You'll find in moving higher up the laurel covered spire; That the most of it is practice, and the rest of it is work."

—Grantland Rice

"If you want to become the best at what you do, it's hard—really hard."

—Jack Welch

✦

"You're either getting better or you're getting worse, so if you're not working hard enough to get better, you're getting worse."

—Woody Hayes

✦

"If players work hard, they usually improve. Hard work will give them the chance to get better."

—Jerry Sloan

✦

"I used to do four shows a day in vaudeville, then drop into a nightclub. I might do 30 or 40 minutes off the cuff. I thought nothing of working from noon to one o'clock the next morning."

—Bob Hope

✦

"I've got a theory that if you give 100 percent all of the time, somehow things will work out in the end."

—Larry Bird

✦

"A man is never satisfied. You go up there and get four hits, and you want five; you can taste it."

—Joe DiMaggio

✦

"Success is exhausting. In fact, the more success you achieve, the harder you'll have to work. Not only is more expected of you when you gain some fame, but more people will be rooting for your collapse. Sometimes staying on top is harder than getting there."

—Gene Perret

✦

"Good timber does not grow with ease. The stronger the wind, the stronger the trees."

—J. Willard Marriott

"Being successful carries an obligation to continue to work hard to be successful. There are very few plateaus where you can stop and rest, because those who don't stop will go right past you."

—Unknown

✦

"Success doesn't have an auto-pilot. You need to work every day."

—Gordon Bethune

✦

"We have become a shortcut culture."

—Michael Jordan

✦

Gary Player was one of the world's great golfers for years and years. Over that time, many fans told him, "I'd give anything to hit a golf ball as well as you." After one tough day on the course, he responded to that comment with complete honesty. "You would love to hit the golf ball like me if it was easy. Do you know what I have to go through to hit a golf ball the way I do? You've got to get up every morning at five o'clock, go out to the range and hit 1,000 balls. Your hands start bleeding, then you walk back to the clubhouse, wash the blood off, slap on some bandages, and go out and hit another 1,000 balls. That's what it takes to hit a golf ball the way I do."

✦

"It is really funny when you watch young players. They work so hard to get from the low minor leagues into the high minor leagues. They work hard to finally get to the big leagues, and then they work hard to become an established player. Suddenly, they think, 'Oh boy! I can finally take it easy. I am a star and don't have to work anymore.' The better you are in this game, the more you have to work."

—Roberto Clemente

✦

"If anybody swung more than he did, they had to be staying up all night."

—Dell Oliver, boyhood friend of Ted Williams in San Diego

✦

"You must do the thing you think you cannot do."

—Eleanor Roosevelt

"You can get through any circumstance, but the question is: who will you be on the other side?"

—Ryan Dobson

✦

"Delay in war is fatal."

—Napoleon

✦

"There never were such men in an army before. They will go anywhere and do anything if properly led."

—Robert E. Lee

✦

"Sometimes the best leader is a teammate. Cal Ripken always took infield, did his pre-game work, never missed anything (as we all know). That kind of example is a kind of leadership that a lesser player cannot ignore. If a guy like Cal Ripken goes about his business that way, I had better do the same. Similarly, a manager who is willing to do the work is looked up to the same way."

—Terry Kennedy

✦

"In 1967, as I shipped out to Vietnam, I asked my dad, 'What do I do now?'
He told me 'Be *FEISTY*.'

F: Have *focus* in your life.
E: Put some *energy* behind your focus.
I: Once you lose your *integrity*, you can never get it back.
S: *Solve* the problem.
T: *Take* the blame.
Y: *Yes*, I do windows.

Do what it takes to be successful."

—Tommy B. Franks

✦

Carlos Tosca once asked Atlanta Manager Bobby Cox what was the most important piece of advice Cox could give him should he ever be given the responsibility of leading a Major League team. Cox told Tosca: "Don't ever sweep unpleasant things under the rug. Confront them."

"No man loved being president more than T.R. or missed being president as much."
—Karl Rove on Theodore Roosevelt

✦

"Lyndon would always have to be the leader."
—A cousin of Lyndon B. Johnson on the young LBJ

✦

"Leaders see:

1. Beyond others: They look past their own future to the generations that follow.
2. Before others: They see what must happen long before others are ready.
3. Bigger than others: They have a larger and unusual vision of what can happen."

—John Maxwell

✦

Michael Jordon's brother, Sgt. Major James R. Jordon, 47, asked to stay in the Army a year beyond his mandatory 30-year retirement date to go to Iraq: "We are doing things, and it requires leaders to do certain things. That's what I am, a leader."

✦

"Dr. King would be 75 now had he lived. I think he'd be very pleased with the amount of progress we've made. He always saw the possibility of the future and viewed life with a positive approach even when things were tough."
—Andrew Young on Martin Luther King Jr.'s leadership skills

✦

"In calm water, every ship has a good captain."
—Grover Cleveland

✦

"George Washington really was the Father of our Country. He was out in the field all eight years of the war with his troops. Despite the fact that they had no salary at times, no vacation, no food, he kept them together until the war was won."
—Donald T. Phillips

✦

"You don't lead from a distance. You lead up close."
—David Uth

"Coaching's a dictatorship. Nobody else gets to step in and tell you how to run your team."

—Al McGuire

✦

"I'll tell you what leadership is. It's persuasion and conciliation and patience. It's long, slow, tough work. That's the only sort of leadership I know or believe in—or will practice."

—Dwight D. Eisenhower

✦

"If you step out and people follow, you are a leader. If you are able to do it over a period of time, you have the gift of leadership. Lots of people can lead for a while, but the key is to get people to follow you over time when they don't have to do that."

—Ed Young

✦

"All the NFL coaches have a common trait—they are teachers. Most of the great ones were teachers before they became coaches. Also, all the great ones are never satisfied. They are always striving for perfection."

—Ernie Accorsi

✦

"The best song ever written says: 'Life is not tried. It is merely survived if you are standing outside the fire.' (Garth Brooks). Nothing more true was ever written. Leadership puts you inside the fire. You must act, react, make decisions, and be alive. That is what life is all about in my opinion."

—Rick Hartzel

✦

"Leadership is not rank, privilege, titles, or money. It's responsibility."

—Colin Powell

✦

"Why, do you know that, not withstanding our discouragements, we are now fast recovering and could make a big fight today if we have someone to inspire us with confidence."

—A captain in the Union Army, 1863

"The three most important characteristics of a good leader are these that I borrowed from Dr. Bruce Ogilvie, a pioneer in psychological testing of athletes:

1. An intense desire for success
2. Learning about the task and working hard to master it
3. Be who you are, and don't try to adopt another's personality."

—Jack Ramsay

✦

"He knew talent, and he knew how to motivate it. A lot of his approach came from Psychology 101 and the rest was fear and intimidation."

—Bob Cousy on Red Auerbach

✦

"He made you feel that there was no way we'd win unless you played well. That was his greatest strength as a leader. He could really motivate you."

—Jerry Stovall on his LSU Coach Paul Dietzel

✦

"Bear Bryant was the best marketing man I ever saw. He sold Alabama football non-stop. He never stopped selling. He sold, sold, sold to everybody. He sold to the media, fans, alumni, his players, and especially to Mama while he was recruiting her son. If Bear got to Mama in the kitchen, it was generally all over."

—Keith Jackson

✦

"I lived in a place where restaurants wouldn't serve me a hamburger, but my parents were telling me I could be president."

—Condoleezza Rice

✦

"They shall still bear fruit in old age; they shall be fresh and flourishing."

—Psalm 92:14 (NKJV)

✦

"I believe that the moment I tell myself I've had a full and satisfying life, that will be the end. No matter how old I get, I intend to always embrace the future."

—Eiji Toyoda at age 92

"Old age is not a time to coast but to climb."
—Unknown

✦

"I'm not friendly with my competitors until I beat them."
—Roger Bannister

✦

"I was yelling at Father Time, 'Take that, you old man!'"
—George H.W. Bush on why he was skydiving on his 80th birthday

✦

"Old age ain't no place for sissies."
—Bette Davis

✦

"Two-things seemed pretty apparent to me. One was, in order to be a Mississippi River pilot, a man had got to learn more than any one man ought to be allowed to know, and the other was that he must learn it all over again in a different way every 24 hours."
—Mark Twain, *Life on the Mississippi*

✦

Oliver Wendell Holmes, Jr. was and still is generally regarded as one of the most outstanding justices in the history of the U.S. Supreme Court. He was known as "the Great Dissenter" because he disagreed with the other judges so much. Holmes sat on the Supreme Court until he was 91. Two years later, President Franklin Roosevelt visited him and found him reading Plato.

"Why?" FDR asked.

"To improve my mind," Holmes replied.

✦

"I have often been asked, 'What is the best age for producing?' I know only one answer: the age you are now."
—Milton S. Hershey at age 85

✦

"However long I have left, I want to live to the fullest."
—Milton Berle at age 93

"Retirement at 65 is ridiculous. When I was 65, I still had pimples."

—George Burns

✦

"I spoke in Peoria, Illinois, September 2004. We visited the home of Pete Hanssen, a South African, and around a cookout he told us about the problems with the rhinos in South Africa. In trying to drive them from one area to another, they will break through any barrier, no matter how strong. Finally, Gary Player's brother had an idea. Spread sheets of black visqueen along the barriers. It worked. The rhinos wouldn't even attempt to break through. They couldn't see through the material, so they didn't even try."

—Pat Williams

✦

"I have a burning incandescence in my gut."

—Vince Lombardi

✦

"I do wear a watch, but I don't need one. That's how much I love what I'm doing. Do whatever you have to do to be excited about what you're doing every day."

—Jim Calhoun

✦

"His enthusiasm would soar, his sights would focus, and his passion would stir."

—Dick Wirthlin, pollster, on Ronald Reagan during the last days of a close election

✦

"Basketball is my life. When 28 other head coaches are sleeping, I can probably guarantee you that I'll be up."

—Eric Musselman

✦

"Passion is contagious, so is a lack of it."

—D.A. Benton

✦

"Let me tell you the secret that has led me to my goal. My strength lies solely in my tenacity."

—Louis Pasteur

"We shall fight for the things we have always carried nearest to our hearts. The world must be made safe for democracy."

—Woodrow Wilson when he asked Congress to declare war on Germany and its allies (April 2, 1917)

✦

"The world belongs to the energetic."

—Ralph Waldo Emerson

✦

"Countless times in youth soccer, college soccer, and the pros, teams that weren't nearly as talented as their opponents won the match because they contested every ball as if it were their last."

—Mia Hamm

✦

When Condoleezza Rice was eight years old, her parents took her to see the White House in Washington, DC. She told her dad, "One day, I'll be in that house."

✦

"I like the color red because it's a fire, and I see myself as always being on fire."

—Arnold Schwarzenegger on his favorite color

✦

"A leader is someone who selects a noble cause and pursues it with such passion and intensity that he brings others along with him."

—Unknown

✦

"All people are in one of three categories:

1. They are just coming out of a storm.
2. They are right in the middle of a storm.
3. They are heading for a storm."

—David Uth

✦

"He bristled with energy."

—Jerry Kramer on Vince Lombardi

"Your heart is about to jump out of your chest."

—Joe Gibbs on game day in the NFL

✦

"I am so ill-rounded that the 10 things I love to do are: write, write, write, write, write, write, write, write, write, and write. Oh, I do other things. I even like to do other things, but when asked for 10 things I love, that's it."

—Isaac Asimov

✦

"A bold heart is half the battle."

—Dwight D. Eisenhower

✦

"One person with passion is better than 40 people merely interested."

—E.M. Forster

✦

"The point is not to arrive at the grave safely in a well-preserved body, but rather to skid in sideways, totally worn out, shouting, 'Holy cow! What a ride!'"

—Zig Ziglar on the end of his life

✦

"He was the most intense man I've ever met. If he was cooking a steak he was intense about it."

—Paul Dietzel on Vince Lombardi

✦

When Mickey Mantle died, *Sports Illustrated* wrote a tribute to him, which included this line: "The world will always belong to those who swing from the heels."

✦

"He was the only person I ever knew who was never afraid."

—Lyndon B. Johnson on FDR

✦

"Victory belongs to the most persevering."

—Napoleon

The Financial Times of London (1982) labeled Jack Welch "Neutron Jack," writing "He takes out the people and leaves the buildings standing." *Fortune* wrote: "He's the toughest boss in America and conducts meetings so aggressively that people tremble."

✦

"He knew that triumph was transient and that defeat was neither fatal nor final. There would be another game tomorrow."

—David Cough on manager Burt Shotton

✦

"In an article titled "What Makes Olympic Champions?" seven common characteristics are identified:

1. They all have a dream—often a vision from childhood.
2. They are passionate about always giving the very best performance.
3. They bounce back—all of these athletes have known defeat and have used those losses as motivation.
4. They aim high—they all compete to win the gold medal.
5. They plan for trouble—setbacks and adjustments are inevitable, so they prepare for them.
6. They never quit.
7. They make their own luck by seizing every opportunity and break.

These characteristics will not only be evident while the Olympic flame is burning, but they will be evident in the life of every champion—athlete or not."

—Ronnie Floyd, *The Meaning of a Man*

✦

Cyrus McCormick gave the first public demonstration of his new reaper in 1831. He did not sell one reaper for 10 years. In 1842, he sold seven of them.

✦

"Here's what I've noticed about champions. They are all so determined to succeed. It doesn't come easy to them, but they hang in there and don't give up."

—Frank Deford

✦

"It is the dogged pertinacity of Grant that wins."

—Abraham Lincoln on Ulysses S. Grant

"He was constantly reminding me that you can get better, an inch at a time. Come in every day and get better. One day you'll look back and be surprised at how much progress you've made."

—Ed Wade on Paul Owens

✦

"When Grant once gets possession of a place, he holds on to it as if he had inherited it."

—Abraham Lincoln on Ulysses S. Grant

✦

"Most guys somewhere along the line will meet an obstacle they aren't willing to clear, whether it's shooting or dribbling or something off the court, like girls or partying. They will not keep on going. I kept on going."

—Steve Nash

✦

"My thing is no matter who's guarding me, I believe that you're going to crack before I will. I'm just going to keep on pushing at you until you give in."

—Kobe Bryant

✦

"Success grows out of the problems you go through, not the problems you go around."

—C. Mason Weaver

✦

"Never give in, never give in, never, never, never, never—in nothing, great or small, larger or pretty—never give in, except to convictions of honor and good sense."

—Winston Churchill

✦

"My son Bobby and I ran the Philadelphia Marathon on November 20, 2005. I saw an advertising sign that read: 'Success goes to those who are driven. Ride the Philadelphia Transit System.' A play on words, but a very accurate statement."

—Pat Williams

"The most common trait I have found in all successful people is that they have conquered the temptation to give up. It's true—people who win never quit."

—Peter Lowe

✦

"The cleaning fluid, Formula 409, got its name because there were 408 failures before the manufacturer found a successful combination. You learn from your mistakes. If we take something away each time, you get something from experience."

—Ben Carson

✦

"Many of life's failures are people who did not realize how close they were to success when they gave up."

—Thomas Edison

✦

"In 1968, Hubert Humphrey lost a very tough Presidential election to Richard M. Nixon. The next morning, Humphrey spoke to his staff, even though he had to be exhausted. Dressed in his best blue suit, he said, 'We lost. Now let's go make government work.'"

—Jim Oberstar

✦

Elvis Presley failed his audition for *Arthur Godfrey's Talent Scouts*.

✦

"This great nation will endure as it has endured, will revive and will prosper ... The only thing we have to fear is fear itself."

—Franklin Roosevelt on Inauguration Day after the 1932 election

✦

"I know of no way but to persist."

—Vince Lombardi

✦

After the capture of the Western Wall by Israeli soldiers during the June 1967 Six-Day War, Prime Minister Yitzhak Rabin addressed the Israeli soldiers: "It's with affection and pride that the whole nation salutes you today for the decisive victory you have brought us ... it was not handed to us on a silver platter. The fighting was savage and hard. Many of our comrades in arms have fallen in action. Their sacrifices shall not have been in vain."

"The great theme of Winston Churchill's life was: never surrender."

—Gretchen Rubin

✦

When Donovan McNabb finally got to play football as an 11-year-old for St. Jude Flying Jays in the south suburbs of Chicago, his dad reminded him of the family's house rule: Once you start something, you finish it. "The first day of practice, they only passed out the equipment," Sam McNabb said. "The second day they had some contact. He came back and said to me, 'You know football is kind of a serious sport. You can get hurt at it.'

I said, 'Yeah.'

He said, 'They hit pretty hard in football.'

I said, 'Yeah, they do. Where are you going with this?'

He said, 'Well, you're probably not going to let me quit are you?'

I said, 'You're right.'"

✦

"Sweat, pain, and exhaustion are all temporary. Finishing Boston is forever. It is now safe to add 'Boston Finisher' to your vocabulary."

—A sign in the Boston Marriott at the 2004 Boston Marathon

✦

"We must all suffer from one of two pains: the pain of discipline or the pain of regret. The difference is that discipline weighs ounces, while regret weighs tons."

—Jim Rohn

✦

"Legendary hill seeks runners with nose-to-the-grindstone stick-to-itiveness. Legs of steel a plus."

—A sign in the 2004 Boston Marathon as the runners headed up to "Heartbreak Hill"

✦

"Adversity causes some to break and others to break records."

—A slogan on the back of a runner's T-shirt

✦

"Quitting is the only way you'll ensure that you won't succeed."

—Craig Breedlove

"Age wrinkles the body. Quitting wrinkles the soul."
—Douglas MacArthur

✦

"Self-discipline is the ability to make yourself do what you should do, when you should do it, whether you feel like it or not."
—Brian Tracy

✦

"These guys have been planning what they want from their lives since they were young kids. They're single-minded in their pursuit of being the best players in their games."
—Jason Giambi on Alex Rodriguez and Tiger Woods

✦

"The difference between winning and losing is frequently not quitting."
—Walt Disney

✦

"You are either a salmon or a jellyfish. A salmon swims upstream and faces the risk and danger to get there. A jellyfish just sits in the water and floats along wherever the tide is going."
—David Uth

✦

"I like taking gambles. I walk into each situation knowing it could flop. I won't like it, but I'm not going to roll over and die."
—Reba McEntire

✦

"Nothing in the world can take the place of persistence. Talent will not; nothing is more common than unsuccessful men with talent; genius is almost a proverb. Education will not; the world is full of educated derelicts. Persistence and determination alone are omnipotent."
—Calvin Coolidge

✦

"Never give up and never give in."
—Frank Crosetti to Jerry Coleman

"I think and think for months and years. Ninety-nine times the conclusion is false. The hundredth time I am right."

—Albert Einstein

✦

"You never get it right. Never once was it the way I imagined it lying awake at four o'clock in the morning, thinking about it the next day. My goal always remained to get it right, one time."

—Charlton Heston on his relentless drive

✦

"I saw not a despairing look nor did I hear a despairing word. We had our solacing words always ready for each other. 'Come, boys, we shall do better, another time,' sounded throughout our little army."

—Captain Enoch Anderson on September 11, 1777, after the Battle of Brandywine

✦

"What is the easiest thing in the world to do? To quit! Quitting takes no effort, no time, no thought, and quitting is cheap. It won't cost you a dime. All you have to do is simply stop what you're doing."

—Michael Youssef

✦

"In the movie *A League of Their Own*, when the star catcher, played by Geena Davis, declares she wants to quit the team to return home to be with her husband, the team manager, played by Tom Hanks, tells her she cannot give up. 'It's supposed to be hard,' Hanks tells her. 'If it wasn't hard, everyone would do it ... the hard is what makes it great.'"

—Jeff Gerth and Don Van Natta, Jr.

✦

Vincent Van Gogh only sold one painting during his lifetime, and that was to his brother, Theodore.

✦

"Everyone is dealt a problem in life and mine is missing four fingers."

—Jim Abbott

"Difficulty is the excuse history never accepts."
—Edward R. Murrow

✦

"The nose of the bulldog has been turned upwards so he can breathe without letting go."
—Winston Churchill

✦

"A champion is simply one who didn't give up when he wanted to."
—Tom Landry

✦

In Baltimore, Maryland, in May of 1982, a lanky shortstop by the name of Cal Ripken, Jr. played the first game of what has become known in baseball circles as The Streak. He just kept plugging away and on September 6, 1995, 2,131 games later, "Iron Man" Ripken set the all-time record for consecutive games played by a Major League Baseball player, shattering a record that had stood for 56 years. He wasn't finished, however. Ripken continued to play, not missing a game until he reached a new milestone of 2,632 consecutive games spanning 15 years.

✦

In 1940, five days of frenzied efforts to evacuate British and French soldiers from Dunkirk in France prompted Churchill's famous war-time speech: "We go on to the end ... We shall defend our island, whatever the cost may be. We shall fight on the beaches, we shall fight on the landing grounds, and we shall fight in the hills. We shall never surrender."

✦

Asked to describe his stepson, Jeff Gordon, in one word, John Bickford said slowly and clearly, "Relentless."

✦

"He who has never failed cannot be great. Failure is the true test of greatness."
—Herman Melville

✦

"If you fail a test in life, you'll face it time and time again until you pass it. The stakes keep getting higher if you don't learn how to pass."
—Dawn Staley

"Walt Disney had such tenacity. He kept plowing on no matter what happened to him."

—Virginia Davis McGhee

✦

"If you have spent two years in bed trying to wiggle your big toe, anything else seems easy."

—Franklin D. Roosevelt

✦

"I am not a quitter."

—Harry S. Truman on his approach to life

✦

Understanding that space and privacy were important for work, Alexander Graham Bell moved to the wide open fields of Nova Scotia. Knowing his own determination was his best ally, he hung a simple slogan on his laboratory wall to motivate himself: 'Keep on fighting."

✦

"Life is difficult."

—Scott Peck, *The Road Less Traveled*

✦

"That's the death knell. Who cares about what you used to do?"

—Jack LaLanne, age 90, on retirement

✦

"I spoke in Louisville on March 22, 2005, to the Kentucky Farm Bureau Insurance Convention. I met Leon Mayo, who sat next to Colonel Harland Sanders in 1971 at a luncheon. Leon said, 'I remember one thing the Colonel told me: "Don't ever quit." I can't pay him enough for that piece of advice. I've been in the insurance business for 30 years and you hear "no" a lot. You can't give up in this business or you'll get burned.'"

—Pat Williams

✦

"I kept right on."

—Ulysses S. Grant on his military strategy

"Quitting is a permanent solution to a temporary problem."
—Rich DeVos

✦

"You can recognize the pioneers by the number of arrows in their backs."
—Val Ackerman

✦

Harriet Tubman's motto was "Keep going." She said to the slaves when she led them toward freedom: "Children, if you are tired, keep going; if you are scared, keep going; if you are hungry keep going; if you want to taste freedom, keep going."

✦

"Shiloh underlined all the basic facts about the war—that it was being fought by men of enormous innate pugnacity; tenacious men who would quit a fight once begun only when someone was beaten."
—Bruce Catton

✦

"An inventor falls 999 times, and if he succeeds once he's in. He treats his failures simply as practice shots."
—Charles Kettering

✦

"The real glory is being knocked to your knees and then coming back."
—Vince Lombardi

✦

"I once talked to a guy who was one of Richard Nixon's football coaches. I asked him, 'Was Nixon any good?'

He said, 'No, he was the worst player I ever had.'

I said, 'Well, what's the story?'

He said, 'He showed up first for practice. Guys would run over his position and stomp him in the ground, and he always got back up. I finally put him in a game so he'd win a letter because the guy never quit. You could see that in the man. You could also see it in Ronald Reagan by the way he walked and handled himself.'"
—Roger Ailes

"What is the lesson of Ulysses S. Grant's life? Foremost of all is the lesson of tenacity."
—Theodore Roosevelt

✦

"Jesse was always a face-boy. When a problem came up, he always faced it."
—Jesse Owens' mother

✦

"Success without adversity is not only empty, it is not possible."
—Norman Schwarzkopf

✦

"The secret of business is to focus relentlessly on your unfair advantage—the thing you do that others don't."
—John Rollwagon

✦

"A desk is a dangerous place from which to watch the world."
—John Le Carré

✦

"You learn more from 10 days of agony than from 10 years of content."
—Sally Jessy Raphael

✦

"Nobody who ever gave his best regretted it."
—George Halas

✦

In 1979, at age 58, Indiana University swimming coach Doc Counsilman swam across the English Channel. At the time, he was the oldest person to accomplish this demanding feat. Doc's Channel swim took 13 hours and 7 minutes. His training included sitting with ice cubes in the bathtub to become used to the freezing water in the Channel. Later, Doc said: "If I hadn't tried to swim the Channel, I would have had a lot of regrets. If I tried and failed, I wouldn't have any regrets. There's nothing wrong with failing, and the swim only hurt once—from beginning to the end."

In 1937, Amelia Earhart disappeared on her attempted flight around the world. She told a friend before her departure: "If I should bop off, it'll be doing the thing that I've always most wanted to do."

✦

After the Japanese surrender, Douglas MacArthur became Supreme Commander of the Allied forces in Japan, and on South Korea's being invaded, Commander of the United Nations forces there. He was relieved of both commands on April 11, 1951 when it was feared his strategy would lead to general war with China and the Soviet Union. He immediately flew back to the United States, made a triumphant trip across the country, reminiscent of the triumph of a returning Roman general, and accepted the invitation to speak on April 19, 1951 before both Houses of Congress—an unheard-of procedure in American history. He said: "Once war is forced upon us, there is no other alternative than to apply every available means to bring it to a swift end. War's very object is victory; not prolonged indecision. In war, there is no substitute for victory. I am closing my 52 years of military service. When I joined the Army, even before the turn of the century, it was the fulfillment of all my boyish hopes and dreams. The world has turned over many times since I took the oath on the plain at West Point, and the hopes and dreams have long since vanished, but I still remember the refrain of one of the most popular barracks ballads of that day, which proclaimed, most proudly, that old soldiers never die; they just fade away. Like the old soldier of that ballad, I now close my military career and just fade away, an old soldier who tried to do his duty, as God gave him the light to see that duty. Goodbye."

✦

"These are not dark days: These are great days—the greatest days our country has ever lived."

—Winston Churchill

✦

Martin Luther, in 1521, in the town of Worms, before the Imperial Diet, uttered this memorable line in dramatic fashion: "Here I stand. I cannot do otherwise. God help me."

✦

"I know not what course others may take. As for me, give me liberty or give me death."

—Patrick Henry's closing words before the Virginia Convention of Delegates

"The one speech that will always resonate with me, and I was there and covered it, was the one he gave on June 12, 1987, at Brandenburg Gate in West Berlin: 'Mr. Gorbachev, open this gate! Mr. Gorbachev, tear down this wall!'"

—Lou Cannon on Ronald Reagan

✦

"To have courage for whatever comes in life—everything lies in that."

—Mother Teresa

✦

"Let us, therefore brace ourselves to our duties and so bear ourselves that if the British Empire and its Commonwealth last for a thousand years, men will still say, 'This was their finest hour."

—Winston Churchill

✦

"Let the word go forth, from this time and place, to friend and foe alike, that the torch has been passed to a new generation of Americans."

—John F. Kennedy

✦

"Years ago, General Dwight D. Eisenhower sat at a conference table, staring into some of the most intense faces he'd ever seen. He'd just unfolded the plans for D-Day. If successful, the Allies would win the war, but if they failed, Hitler would—for all practical purposes—rule the world and darkness would descend on the entire Earth. Eisenhower looked out at this diverse group: so many strong leaders, different opinions, large egos, and said, 'Men, it's one team, or we lose.'"

—David Foster

✦

"In a television documentary, I watched two rats solve a problem: how to bring an egg home to feed their offspring. I was amazed to see one rat grasp the egg with all four legs, then roll over onto his back while the other rat pulled him by the tail, dragging him until they reached their destination with the egg intact. Even the lowliest of critters knows that teamwork succeeds."

—Norman Lajoi

"It's been estimated that if a man could get all the muscles in his body to work together, he could lift over 25 tons (50,000 pounds). By comparison, the world record for a single lift, using the full capability of only one major muscle, is just over 1,000 pounds. The same principle holds true for partnerships. With a partner, a 25-ton dream may be attainable, but alone be simply unthinkable. Partnerships increase our strength."

—John Maxwell

✦

"A baseball team is like an organism which is constantly changing, one cell replacing another. You hang on to the old players too long and rot sets in."

—Whitey Herzog

✦

What happens to a dream deferred?
Does it dry up
Like a raisin in the sun?
Or fester like a sore--
And then run?

—Langston Hughes

✦

"For security reasons, the American Bald Eagle nests in high places such as rocky cliffs and tall trees. They have telescopic vision and are able to see a fish from two to three miles away. Their strong pinions enable them to attack their prey at speeds of 50 to 100 miles per hour."

—Julius Bosco

✦

Franklin D. Roosevelt accepted his party's nomination in 1936 by observing: "There is a mysterious cycle in human events. To some generations, much is given. Of other generations, much is expected. This generation of Americans has a rendezvous with destiny."

✦

"Ronald Reagan often said, 'America's best days are ahead, not behind.' He may not have had a lot of ideas, but he had that vision, and I think that was really his magic in a sense."

—Lou Cannon

"If an American, because his skin is dark, cannot eat lunch in a restaurant open to the public; if he cannot send his children to the best public schools available; if he cannot vote for the public officials who represent him ... then, who among us would be content to have the color of his skin changed? Who among us would then be content with the counsels of patience and delay? We face a moral crisis as a country and as a people ... a great change is at hand, and our task is to make that revolution peaceful and constructive for all."

—John F. Kennedy

✦

"We ought to live each day as if it were our last. Someday it will be."

—Billy Graham

✦

"If you are scared to go to the brink, you are lost."

—John Foster Dulles

✦

"Sam Walton had a big vision and then went out and outworked people. He went after it 24 hours a day. That's how he lived his entire life."

—Robert Lewis

✦

"Good business leaders create a vision, articulate the vision, passionately own the vision and relentlessly drive it to completion."

—Jack Welch

✦

Historian Gary Wills defined great leaders as those who have a vision to which followers respond; who organize a plan that followers make work; who have willpower so strong that followers let the leader's will replace their own; and who have determination, focus, a clear goal, and a sense of priorities. Wills noted: "To sound a certain trumpet does not mean just trumpeting one's own certitudes. It means sounding a specific call to specific people capable of response. We do not lack leaders. Various trumpets are always being sounded. Take your pick. We lack sufficient followers. That is always the real problem with leadership. Calls are always going down into the valley deep, but what spirits will respond?"

"The secret of success is persistence, and the secret of persistence is vision."
—Rick Warren

✦

"I was married to a man who never gave up."
—Dana Reeve on her husband, Christopher

✦

"He's like a turkey in a tobacco patch that sees the worm and knocks down 20 stalks to get it."
—Branch Rickey on manager Leo Durocher

✦

"Winning is the science of being totally prepared."
—George Allen

✦

"You can't go back and correct yesterday's mistakes. You can't waste time going over old losses. You have to look ahead."
—Bart Starr

✦

"Successful people hate to do the same things that failures hate to do. The difference is that successful people make themselves do what they don't like to do. The failures wait for someone to make them do it."
—Charlie "Tremendous" Jones

✦

"The first day Vince Lombardi met with us in Green Bay, he thanked the Packers organization for the opportunity, and then he said, 'Relentlessly chase perfection and you'll catch excellence. That's a whole lot better than being just good.' Then Coach Lombardi paused for emphasis and barked, 'I'm not remotely interested in being just good.'"
—Bart Starr

✦

"Winning isn't a part-time job. What's really important is trying to be the best. Don't ever substitute that thinking and say, 'Well, we'll win tomorrow.' You've got to do it now."
—Eddie Robinson

"Today, at 95, John Wooden is correctly viewed as a sweet, gentle grandfather figure. Don't be fooled, however. He didn't get to where he is in life without these two ingredients:

1. He was a fierce, competitive man at everything he did.
2. He had an intense desire to win."

—Bill Bennett

✦

"Keep sawing wood."

—Jim Finks on fighting, clawing, and scratching for success

✦

"It's easier to lose than win."

—Jerry Sloan

✦

"We were playing Denver at home in a big game. Our 89-year old owner, Wellington Mara, was dying of cancer and was in and out of consciousness. That morning, his son told him, 'Dad, we're playing Denver today.'

Mr. Mara softly said, 'I don't want to lose.' That was it, and he went back to sleep. We beat Denver in a dramatic finish. That night, Mrs. Mara told Wellington the team had won. He smiled. Two days later, Mr. Mara passed away, but the last words he spoke were about winning."

—Ernie Accorsi

✦

"If you want to avoid being crushed by your competition, you have to outthink, outplan, outwork, and outexecute them 52 weeks a year."

—Michael Bergdahl

✦

"There are several things worse than war, and they all come with losing one."

—Small sign at the entrance of 5th SFG Green Beret Headquarters, Nha Trang, Vietnam

✦

"We must do better than our best. We must do whatever is required to win."

—Winston Churchill

"When you talk about the greatest NBA players ever, the word 'relentless' will always come up."

—Carroll Dawson

✦

"I ain't never had much fun. I ain't never been two inches from a football. Some coaches want to go hunting or fishing or golfing. All I want to do is be alone ... studying how *not* to lose."

—Bear Bryant

✦

"I don't meet competition; I crush it."

—Charles Revson

✦

"Winning is not a sometime thing. It's an all-the-time thing. You don't win once in a while. You don't do things right once in a while. You do them right all the time. Winning's a habit. Unfortunately, so is losing. There is no room for second place. There is only one place in my game and that's first place."

—Vince Lombardi

✦

In his first speech after becoming Prime Minister, Winston Churchill told the House of Commons the objective was quite simple: "Victory. Victory at all costs. Victory in spite of all terror. Victory, however long and hard the road may be, for without victory there is no survival." In a radio broadcast, he told the British people, "I have nothing to offer you but blood, toil, tears, and sweat. We have before us an ordeal of the most grievous kind. We have before us many, many months of struggle and suffering."

✦

"Never walk by a problem. Fix it."

—Ray Kroc

✦

"If you're going to coach in the NBA or wherever, you better have a tremendous burning in your gut and love what you're doing; otherwise it just beats you down."

—Doug Collins

"I have worked for Sam Walton (Wal-Mart), Joe Albertson (Albertson's), and Howard Schultz (Starbucks). These three men share these three qualities:

1. They hunger for the business they founded. They never rest. They have an intense, daily passion for what they started.
2. They all stress the importance of not forgetting where you came from. Keep a sense of humility.
3. Grow big, but stay small (Starbucks has gone from one store to over 9,500 quickly). Avoid having a corporate mentality and stay engaged with your customers. Howard Schultz still keeps the key from the first store he opened in Seattle."

—Jim Donald

✦

"Two percent of basketball players are born with endless talent that would take a complete fool to mess up. The other 98 percent are going to succeed because of how much they put into it and how deep they dig into their souls."

—Bill Musselman

✦

"We have a sign at our facility that we see every day. At the top of it, it says, 'Do Your Job.'"

—Tom Brady

✦

"Boldness be my friend. Arm me, audacity, from head to foot."

—William Shakespeare

✦

"Dad used to say, 'Hit it hard, hit it hard. Don't worry about it, just hit it, go find it, and hit it again.'"

—Arnold Palmer

✦

"Harold MacMillan was prime minister of Great Britain from 1957 to 1963. He was once asked by a young man what the greatest challenge he faced in being a statesman was. 'Events, my dear boy, events,' MacMillan replied. 'Unforeseen events are a leader's greatest challenge.'

—Steve Farrar

"All the adversity I've had in my life, all my troubles and obstacles, have strengthened me ... You may not realize it when it happens, but a kick in the teeth may be the best thing in the world for you."

—Walt Disney

✦

"Look backward, move forward, but keep going."

—Harriet Tubman to slaves as she led them to freedom

✦

"When people quit what they love to do, that's the end."

—Wayne Newton

✦

"Winners have two things in common: definite goals and a burning desire to achieve them."

—Unknown

✦

"It's good to be smart; brilliance is even better, but persistence will trump them all if it comes down to that."

—Dan Rather

✦

"Self-motivation is the only thing there really is."

—Mike Ditka

✦

"Swim or sink, live or die, survive or perish—I'm with my country."

—John Adams at the start of the War of Independence

✦

"Cause of death: life."

—Tom Boswell at Bill Veeck's funeral

✦

"A life frittered away disgusts God; He loves those who run straight for the finish line."

—Proverbs 15:9 (The Message)

"Learning is not attained by chance. It must be sought for with order and attended to with diligence."

—Abigail Adams

✦

On December 22, 1944, Brigadier General Anthony McAuliffe answered a Nazi surrender demand with the famous one-word response: "Nuts!"

✦

"His competitiveness still drives him. He wants to land a number-one hit and has to compete with rockers one-third his age."

—Author David Buckley on Elton John at age 60

✦

"I rate the capacity of a man by, first, courage and ability; second, real experience under fire."

—Winston Churchill

✦

"Rally, brave men, and press forward! Your general will lead you! Jackson will lead you! Follow me!"

—Stonewall Jackson

✦

"Look, men. There is Jackson standing like a stone wall! Let us determine to die here, and we will conquer! Follow me!"

—Bernard Bee

✦

"Bobby Knight's greatest strength as a coach was his preparation. Give him a week to get ready for an opponent, and he'd have everything nailed down tight. That's how thorough he was. Coach wouldn't miss a thing."

—Mike Woodson

✦

"Talent, you either got it or you don't, but desire, that is something you can make up your mind about."

—Tommy Lasorda

"Being on the hot seat is what leading is about."

—Stephen H. Baum

✦

"He was always so prepared every day. He worked harder than the players. In fact, he worked harder than any coach I ever played for."

—Ollie Johnson on Hubie Brown

✦

"If we are ever unlucky enough to have it made, then we will be spectators instead of participants in life. It's the journey—not the arrival—that counts. Does the road wind uphill all the way? Yes, until the very end."

—Jim Finks kept these words written on a piece of paper in his wallet at all times

✦

"When I was covering the Celtics during the Larry Bird era, if I wanted to interview him before a game, I'd get to the old Boston Garden about 2 p.m. Larry would be out there alone, shooting by himself, working harder than anyone, and he was already a superstar. All the great ones are like that—Jordan, Magic, Kobe, and also Kevin Garnett."

—Sam Smith

✦

"Find a way to win."

—Quote in the 76ers' locker room

✦

"Persevere and get it done."

—George Allen

✦

"In business, the competition will bite you if you keep running. If you stand still, they will swallow you."

—William Knudsen, Jr.

✦

"I love running Berkshire Hathaway and if enjoying life promotes longevity, Methuselah's record is in jeopardy."

—Warren Buffett at age 77

"When a person begins to live out their passion, they become like a heat-seeking missile."

—Jentezen Franklin

✦

"Defeat awaits those who stray, dreaming of victories won—yesterday."

—Douglas MacArthur

✦

"Just keep going. Everybody gets better if they keep at it."

—Ted Williams

✦

"I'm not done yet. Hopefully, my good years are ahead."

—Tiger Woods at age 32

✦

"Every minute of each day, I'm training for life."

—Talonda Yates

✦

"As a leader, you must be willing to communicate, which means having some tough conversations. In great organizations there is a conflict, but it's not about us. It's not personal. You have to have difficult conversations in an effective way."

—J.P. Pawliw-Fry

✦

"I would like to see the wall come down today, and I call upon those responsible to dismantle it."

—Ronald Reagan on the 25th anniversary of the wall, 1986

✦

"I want it to be known throughout Montgomery and throughout this nation, that we are a Christian people, and we are determined here in Montgomery to work and fight until justice runs down like water and righteousness as a mighty stream."

—Martin Luther King, Jr.

"I never give up. Too many people give up."

—Larry Bird

✦

"Defeat, which disheartened most men, seemed to come as a tonic to George Washington."

—Alan Axelrod

✦

"There's nothing greater than the pleasure of talent and the drive to go along with it."

—Julie Krone

✦

"John was not the most skilled, but he was the most feared ... he never gave up."

—Otto Helwig, one of John McCain's teammates on the U.S. Naval Academy's boxing team

✦

"We will not tire, we will not falter, and we will not fail. Whether we bring our enemies to justice or bring justice to our enemies, justice will be done."

—George W. Bush on September 20, 2001

✦

"When Theodore Roosevelt died of a heart attack in January 1919, Vice-President Thomas Marshall remarked: 'Death had to take him sleeping. If Roosevelt had been awake, there would have been a fight.'"

—Paul F. Boller

✦

"Winston Churchill's greatest strength as a leader was his sense of fortitude. He refused to negotiate or compromise and conveyed to Great Britain and the world that we are going to win this war, come what may."

—Giles MacDonogh

✦

"Leadership is solving problems."

—Colin Powell

"A President is either constantly on top of events, or if he hesitates events will soon be on top of him. I never felt that I could let up for a minute."

—Harry S. Truman

✦

"Leaders don't ask others to do what they are unwilling to do themselves."

—Mike Huckabee

✦

"No one is a born leader. It is a skill, and like any skill you have to practice and work hard at it."

—Bobby Bowden

✦

"If you want a pleasant life, don't be a leader."

—Richard Brookhiser

✦

"Somebody may beat me, but they are going to have to bleed to do it."

—Steve Prefontaine

✦

"A champion is someone who gets up when he can't."

—Jack Dempsey

✦

"Days when you just don't have it, you don't mail it in, you don't pack it in, you give it everything you've got. You grind it out. I don't care what kind of game you have; you somehow try to find a way to get it done. You've seen me do it over the years. I should have missed many cuts by now, but you just somehow figure out a way. That's part of my attitude and belief—that you should always have the switch on. You can't turn it off and on."

—Tiger Woods

✦

"Eric couldn't put cream in his coffee without being intense."

—Billy Beane, Oakland A's general manager, on Eric Byrnes

"We fight, get beat, rise up, and fight again."
—Nathanael Greene

✦

At Detroit's Comerica Park, there is a tunnel leading to the batting cages. A sign there says: "If tomorrow you could not play, how hard would you play today?"

✦

"1. Take risks at every turn, and keep on reinventing yourself along the way.
2. Make your own breaks. There is no such thing as luck. Walt willed things to happen.
3. Have the courage of your convictions. This inspires others and forces them to do more than they thought they could."

—Don Peri, Disney historian, on life lessons from Walt Disney

✦

"The only thing that keeps a man going is energy, and what is energy but liking life?"
—Louis Auchincloss

✦

"You can't control your level of talent, but you can control your level of effort."
—Advice tennis player James Blake received from his father

✦

"You can't wait for inspiration. You have to go after it with a club."
—Jack London

✦

"To me, this is the first principle of life, the foundational principle, and a lesson you can't learn at the feet of any wise men: get up! The art of living is simply getting up after you've been knocked down. It's a lesson taught by example and learned in the doing."
—Joe Biden

✦

"Walt Disney was more comfortable with setbacks in his life than when things were going really well."
—Don Peri

"Problems are the price you pay for progress."
—Branch Rickey

✦

"Life's going to break your heart. Life is unfair."
—David Uth

✦

"Walt would come into a problem, and he would go right to the nut ... bing ... right there. We were wrangling over something and worrying. He'd come in and sit down and ... bing! Fantastic! That's what I call genius. We were in the presence of great genius."
—Dick Huemer on Walt Disney

✦

"No one ever saw him flinch."
—Timothy Dwight on George Washington's courage

✦

"Success seems to be largely a matter of hanging on after others have let go."
—William Feather

✦

"It's like driving a car at night. You never see farther than your headlights, but you can make the whole trip that way."
—E.L. Doctorow

✦

"You are not beaten until you admit it; hence, don't."
—George S. Patton

✦

"My mother would say every day, 'Go git 'em.'"
—Lance Armstrong

✦

After the first battle of Shiloh in 1862, General William T. Sherman said to General Ulysses S. Grant, "Well, Grant, we've had the devil's own day, haven't we?" Grant answered, "Yes, lick 'em tomorrow, though."

"I am grateful for all my problems. As each of them was overcome, I became stronger and more able to meet those yet to come. I grew on my difficulties."

—James Cash Penney

✦

"They all have a winning heart, and that keeps them going. They despise the thought of losing."

—Dan Jenkins, long-time sportswriter, on the common trait of the great athletes

✦

"I can't step up my preparation because I prepare myself as much as I can all the time."

—Kobe Bryant

✦

"There are no smooth paths, there never have been, and there never will be. You've got to bump on down the road to get where you want."

—Nicholas Aretakis

✦

"Over the years, I've heard many theories, often complex or convoluted, on what it takes to be an outstanding leader. Most of the theories seem to take a monumental work ethic for granted, as if it is assumed or something, as if people automatically know what it is and do it. I didn't assume it. The majority of people out there don't know what it is. They need to be shown, and you're the one who must show it."

—Bill Walsh

✦

"If you care about how you're perceived by others, including the public, it's good to remember the following: Criticism—both deserved and undeserved—is part of the territory when you're the one calling the shots. Ignore the undeserved; learn from the deserved; lick your wounds and move on. Sometimes you can't have the last word."

—Bill Walsh

✦

"You can't have a good football team unless you get a team committed to get a little bit better every day in practice. You've got to prepare yourself to practice well."

—Joe Paterno

"Most days it's about problem solving."
—Hillary Clinton on being Secretary of State

✦

"They had incredible capacities for hard work, activity, and achievement."
—Shawn Levy on the common traits of Frank Sinatra, Jerry Lewis, and Paul Newman

✦

"His was a case of brain hunger. It remained so until the end of his life."
—Father Cavanaugh at Notre Dame on Knute Rockne as a leader

✦

Speaker Joe Gandolfo motivates people to do what it takes to succeed by telling them about the swallows at San Juan Capistrano. Every year the swallows fly from Buenos Aires, Argentina, to this little town in southern California, arriving each year on March 19. They fly 6,000 miles to get there, mainly over water. Nobody knows how they do it. Swallows can't swim. They can't fly 6,000 miles non-stop either. So how do they do it? Each swallow carries a twig in its beak—a big burden for such a tiny bird. When the swallows get tired, they drop the twigs in the water, float on them and rest. They then fly some more. Swallows know they have to pay the price—carrying a heavy load—if they want to reach their goal. "The same goes for people," says Gandolfo. "You have to pay the price for success.

✦

"When you've got everybody pulling on the same end of the rope, it's easy to win."
—Aaron Rowand

4

Achieving Goals and Attitude

iStockphoto/Thinkstock

Davis Love, Jr., PGA golfer, once said, "Let your attitude determine your golf game. Don't let your golf game determine your attitude." One—perhaps the only—thing we can control in this life is our attitude; so, my friend, pick a good one!

Clear-cut, definite goals are powerful motivating forces. Reaching goals issues a rush of accomplishment and fulfillment that is extraordinarily gratifying. Motivator Zig Ziglar succinctly states, "Your attitude determines your altitude."

Profit from these statements about achievement and attitude.

"Fans, for the past two weeks you have been reading about a bad break I got; yet, today, I consider myself the luckiest man on the face of the Earth."

—Lou Gehrig

✦

"Companies that create the future are rebels. They're subversives. They break the rules. They're filled with people who take the other side of an issue just to spark a debate. In fact, they are probably filled with people who didn't mind being sent to the principal's office once in a while."

—Garry Hamel and C.K. Prahalad

✦

"Each success only buys an admission ticket to more difficult problems."

—Henry Kissinger

✦

"The mission of this Allied Force was fulfilled at 0241 local time, May 7, 1945."

—Dwight D. Eisenhower

✦

"Ronald Reagan knew that being President of the United States was not a management job. No one can manage a big bureaucracy like that. Reagan knew it was a leadership job."

—Robert Novak

✦

"If you're going to lead, you've got to be thinking further in advance than the people you are leading."

—Rick Warren

✦

"Pain is inevitable, but misery is optional."

—Tim Hansel, author

✦

"Whatever else history may say about me when I'm gone, I hope it will record that I appealed to your best hopes ... not your worst fears; to your confidence, rather than your doubts."

—Ronald Reagan

"Think of the happiest things, it's the same as having wings."

—Walt Disney

✦

"The story of the human race is the story of men and women selling themselves short."

—Abraham Maslow

✦

"Both optimists and pessimists contribute to our society. The optimist invents the airplane and the pessimist the parachute."

—Gil Stern

✦

"When this happens, when we let freedom ring, when we let it ring from every village and every hamlet, from every state and every city, we will be able to speed up that day when all of God's children—black men and white men, Jews and Gentiles, Protestants and Catholics—will be able to join hands and sing in the words of the old Negro spiritual: Free at last! Free at last! Thank God, almighty, we are free at last!"

—Martin Luther King, Jr.

✦

"If you don't know where you are going, you might wind up someplace else."

—Yogi Berra

✦

"If you make fun a part of you job, you're going to be successful."

—David Raymond

✦

"Good jobs don't open up. You take a bad job and make it a good job."

—Lou Holtz

✦

"All our fondest hopes will be realized tonight."

—A wire Charlie Chaplin sent to Walt Disney on the day of the *Snow White* premiere

Abraham Lincoln spoke of "the power of hope."

✦

"Hope that is seen is not hope; for why does one still hope for what he sees? But if we hope for what we do not see, we eagerly wait for it with perseverance."

—Romans 8:24-25 (NKJV)

✦

"Webster's tells us that hope is a desire for something with an expectation of its fulfillment. Hope is not wishful thinking. Hope lies between certain knowledge of something happening and wishing something would happen. It is the expectation of fulfillment that sets hope apart from wishful thinking. Hope is a confidence that something can happen if one works hard enough to make it happen. Hope, along with faith and love, are the greatest virtues a person can possess."

—Kevin Ryan

✦

"In our game, we play the ball as it lies."

—Bobby Jones, golfer, in a wheelchair crippled by a horrendous spinal disease, syringomyelia

✦

"I've learned the greatest lessons in my life through suffering and defeats. Adversity can produce blessings."

—Charles Colson

✦

"The only time you lose is when you quit."

—Mike Dunleavy

✦

"Walt Disney made a simple statement: 'You can lick 'em with product,' simply meaning that if you make the product good enough they cannot deny it."

—Ben Sharpstein

✦

"The single defining quality of leaders is their ability to create and realize a vision."

—Marshall Loeb

"He could see what was going to happen ten years down the road."
—Jim Steeg, former NFL executive, on Pete Rozelle

✦

"Over the long haul team chemistry is more valuable than talent."
—Glenn Wilkes, Jr.

✦

"The team, the team, the team is all that matters."
—Dick Tomey

✦

"In our pre-game and pre-practice huddles, we do not say, 'Defense!' or 'Win!' Instead, in union, we say, 'Together!' and we intend to play that way."
—Mike Krzyzewski

✦

"I had to understand that the most important thing was not *me*, but *us*."
—Terry Bradshaw on being the Steelers' quarterback

✦

"If you don't dream it, you can't become it."
—Magic Johnson

✦

"A house divided against itself cannot stand. I believe this government cannot endure half-slave and half-free. I do not expect the house to fall, but I do expect it will cease to be divided. It will become all one thing or all the other."
—Abraham Lincoln in his 1858 acceptance speech for the U.S. Senate

✦

"There is a man in the world who never gets turned down, whenever he chances to stray.
He gets the glad hand, in the populous town, or out where the farmers make hay;
He is greeted with pleasure on deserts of sand, and deep in the aisles of the woods;
Wherever he goes, there is a welcoming hand, he's the man who delivers the goods."
—Walt Whitman

"So first of all, let me assert my firm belief the only thing we have to fear is fear itself. Nameless, unreasoning, unjustified terror which paralyzes needed efforts to convert retreat into advance."

—Franklin Roosevelt

✦

"There's no such thing as an overachiever. We're all underachievers, each and every one of us."

—John Wooden

✦

"Now, I think I know how Lou Gehrig felt. It's not only a great day for me; it's a great day for all the Mantles. I wish my father could have been here. Thank you."

—Mickey Mantle's farewell speech, June 9, 1969

✦

"I've never made a drawing that I liked."

—Walt Disney

✦

"Red always consulted with us. He never gave us orders; then he'd make coaching decisions based on that information. So, we were part of the process. That's why it worked so well."

—Bill Russell on Red Auerbach

✦

"A bold heart is half the battle."

—Dwight D Eisenhower

✦

In January 1865, in an editorial titled "Have We a General Among Us?," the editors of *Harper's Weekly* dismissed General Ulysses S. Grant with a few sentences.

✦

"NBA lesson number one: Don't make today's loss the enemy of tomorrow's victory."

—Bill Bradley

"Do you know the hallmark of the second-rater? It's resentment of another man's achievement."

—Ayn Rand

✦

"I spoke to a Chrysler Auto Convention in Orlando in November 2004, and addressed the issue of competition and how to deal with it. After I finished, I heard the story of Charlie Foulke, a dealer in North Jersey. He was the dominant salesman in his region, but then a competitor hired a top car salesperson. When Charlie heard the news, he went home and told his wife, 'Honey, we just got a raise. I'm going to be selling a lot more cars.'"

—Pat Williams

✦

"I remember hearing the story of how the Roman emperors handled Roman generals returning victorious from battles. The generals were welcomed in grand parades that featured their soldiers, all the wealth they had acquired, and the prisoners they captured. Accompanying the generals in their golden chariots was a slave who, in the midst of the celebration, would whisper in the general's ear: 'Remember, you are a mortal man. All glory is fleeting.'"

—Harvey MacKay

✦

"When you are headed in the wrong direction, progress is turning around and going back."

—C.S. Lewis

✦

One ship sails east and another west
With the same winds that blow;
'Tis the set of the sails and not the gales
That decides the way we go.
Like the winds of the sea are the ways of fate
As they voyage along though life;
'Tis the will of the soul that decides its goals
And not the clamor or the strife.

—Ella Wheeler Wilcox

"In leadership, the troops better be sold on you. That means walking the walk and talking the talk in lockstep with each other."

—Jack Pardee

✦

"George Washington knew how to read people and get them to do what was needed, to get things done and goals reached."

—David Clary

✦

"I decided to be the best and the smartest."

—Oprah Winfrey

✦

"Tiger Woods has a laser beam focus that burns through titanium."

—Dan Bickley

✦

"Neither man nor nation can exist without a sublime idea."

—Fyodor Dostoyevsky

✦

"Ernie Banks once left the following message on my voice mail: 'In the absence of clearly defined goals, we become strangely loyal to performing daily acts of trivia.' Then, there was a pause, and Ernie said, 'Play two!'"

—Pat Williams

✦

"Joe doesn't think about the past or the future. He's just totally engaged in what is going on now, because that is the primary focus of his life. He just lives in the now."

—Tom Mitchell, a friend of Joe Montana

✦

"He has a focus that's almost maniacal."

—Mike Brey on Mike Krzyzewski

"If 400,000 fans went home during the Indianapolis 500 race, I'd never have known the difference because I was so focused on my driving."

—Janet Guthrie

✦

"He could see a nit on the telephone pole 500 yards away, and he just concentrated so much."

—Virgil Trucks on Ted Williams

✦

"Annika brings a level of intensity and focus we have not seen in any golfer other than Jack Nicklaus."

—Charlie Mechem on Annika Sorenstam

✦

"If I can't have fun doing something, what's the point of doing it?"

—Donovan McNabb

✦

"At the age of 28 and on the verge of losing the New York City mayor's race, he wrote a friend, 'I have had first-class fun.'"

—Karl Rove on Theodore Roosevelt

✦

"Life should be a world's fair of delights."

—Walt Disney

✦

"Do you know why we're so uptight in America? Because the Puritans came here and the really fun people all stayed behind."

—Roseanne Barr

✦

"I still haven't quite gotten over it that some men were willing to pay you for playing ball—a game which is so much fun."

—Connie Mack

Bob Hope in 1989, at age 86, when asked what he still looked forward to after a lifetime of fame, fortune, and praise: "More fun."

✦

"You need talent on a team, but make sure that that talent has self-esteem. Without it, insecurity will emerge and be destructive. You've got to know yourself and must be confident with yourself."

—Patrick Lencioni

✦

"Every day you aren't getting stronger and better, you are getting weaker and worse."

—D.A. Benton

✦

"Everyone who got where he is had to begin where he was."

—Robert Louis Stevenson

✦

"I visited the site of the Old Cattle Trail north of Dallas on October 7, 2003. At the site were many quotes from cowboys. This one hit me: 'If you have a hill to climb, waitin' won't make it smaller.'"

—Pat Williams

✦

"As one goes through life, one learns that if you don't paddle your own canoe, you don't move."

—Katharine Hepburn

✦

"I am seeking; I am striving; I am in it with all my heart."

—Vincent van Gogh

✦

"What makes an Olympian unique? You can be wealthy by accident. You can be beautiful by accident, but you can't be a champion by accident. It just doesn't happen. You must earn it, and when you do, the world recognizes you are a very special human being. Nothing is handed to a champion."

—Bart Conner

"Gather ye rosebuds while ye may; Time is still a-flying; these same flowers that bloom today; Tomorrow may be dying."

—Robert Herrick

✦

"Work can be more fun than fun."

—Noel Coward

✦

"I love the challenge of starting at zero every day and seeing how much I can accomplish."

—Martha Stewart

✦

"I was not born big or strong, but I did know what I wanted and worked at it every day."

—Theodore Roosevelt

✦

"I hate that feeling of going to bed at night when I don't feel like I pushed myself."

—Steve Nash

✦

"Things work out best for those who make the best of how things work out."

—John Wooden

✦

"If you don't see it on the field, don't wish for it to happen."

—Dave Bristol

✦

"When I was young, I was taught this doggerel: 'It's easy to be a starter, but are you a sticker, too? It's easy enough to begin a job. It's harder to see it though.'"

—Margaret Thatcher

✦

"Life is movement. It's the person who sits on the couch who's living dangerously."

—Grete Waitz

"Our parents really did have us convinced that even though I couldn't have a hamburger at Woolworth's, I could be President of the United States. I was taught to blast through the barriers. What's the alternative? Decrying the barriers? I tend to think that societies move largely through the force of individuals breaking barriers."

—Condoleezza Rice

✦

"The big secret in life is that there is no big secret. Whatever your goal, you can get there if you are willing to work."

—Oprah Winfrey

✦

"He has a John Stockton way about him. If something goes wrong, you don't see emotion on his face. He just keeps playing. I always have called it playing forward instead of playing backward."

—Jerry Sloan on Kirk Hinrich, formerly of the Bulls

✦

"On June 28, 2005, I took a tour of Washington D.C. We stopped at a little beverage stand to buy water. I started talking with the Vietnamese woman who operated the stand. In broken English, she said to me: 'America is the greatest country on Earth. If you work hard and study hard, you can accomplish anything you want.'"

—Pat Williams

✦

"I've never seen a jockey carry the horse across the finish line; the horse does the job."

—Larry Eustachy

✦

"Opportunity is missed by most people because it is dressed in overalls and looks like work."

—Thomas Edison

✦

"I seldom was ever off my seat on the bench during the game. I'd tell them, 'Don't look over at me. I prepared you during the week. Now do your job.'"

—John Wooden

"We could hardly wait to get up in the morning."
—Wilbur Wright

✦

"If you want to get something done, do it yourself."
—Margaret Thatcher

✦

"I firmly believe that any man's finest hour, the greatest fulfillment of all that he holds dear, is that moment when he has worked his heart out in a good cause and lies exhausted on the field of battle, victorious."
—Vince Lombardi

✦

"You do it by working. Working, just like I've always done."
—Walt Disney on how to make our dreams come true

✦

"This type of unity, this togetherness, this feeling that everyone is part of a team, is brought on by winning. Togetherness can be a lot of crud. You have to get the wins."
—Chuck Bednarik

✦

"We're all wired to detest losing."
—Brian Cashman

✦

"Finishing second is never fun."
—Tiger Woods

✦

"Winning, winning, winning, winning—that's my measurement of success: winning!"
—Hillary Clinton, during the 2008 Democratic primaries

✦

"Pessimism never won any battle."
—Dwight D. Eisenhower

"One time, I was on a flight with Johnny Unitas. I asked him to sign the book I was reading and said, 'Say something different, not just "Best wishes."' He thought for a minute and wrote: 'To Joy...Win! Johnny Unitas.'"

—Joy Millis

✦

"You don't know what you can do unless you try. Quit talking and start doing it."

—Walt Disney

✦

"They worked hard and played together."

—Alex English on the 1983 Philadelphia 76ers championship team

✦

"For me, playing is like religion."

—Kobe Bryant

✦

"I came to Hollywood in August 1923 with $30.00 in my pocket and a coat and a pair of trousers that didn't match. One half of my suitcase had my shirts and underwear and things ... the other half had my drawing materials. It was a cardboard suitcase at that."

—Walt Disney

✦

"If you're too big for a little job, you're too little for a big job."

—Tony Johnson

✦

"The fact remains, we're like those salmon, you know. You either get up the river or you don't."

—Katharine Hepburn

✦

"If you can't be a highway then be just a trail; If you can't be the sun, be a star; It isn't by size you win or you fail, Be the best of whatever you are."

—Duffy Daugherty to his Michigan State players

"A truly happy person is someone who never quite reaches the rainbow's end."
—Mary Kay Ash

✦

A St. Louis reporter asked Branch Rickey at the age of 82 his greatest thrill in baseball. Rickey replied: "Son, it hasn't happened yet."

✦

"Every day he woke up, he had one thing on his mind: What can I do to improve this day? Most people think that if you hit it big in business, you spend the rest of your life on the beach while other people run your company. All Sam was concerned about was improving himself or his company."
—David Glass on Wal-Mart founder Sam Walton

✦

"Your yesterdays got you where you are now. Today, you're enjoying it. Your tomorrows are still unknown. Today is tomorrow's yesterday. That means you must work now to secure your future success. It's wise regardless of what level you've attained to devote part of your present efforts to present requirements and part to your future."
—Gene Perret

✦

"You've got to work at living ... 99 and 9/10 percent of Americans work on dying! You've got to eat right, exercise, and have goals and challenges. Exercise is king; nutrition is queen. Put them together and you've got a kingdom."
—Jack LaLanne at age 90

✦

"If somebody had looked at the United States in 1954 and said that the Secretary of State would be a black woman, people would have said, 'No, really, are you kidding me?"
—Condoleezza Rice

✦

"People want to follow leaders who offer hope and direction."
—John Maxwell

✦

Over the entrance of his inferno, Dante hung a sign that said, "Abandon hope, all ye who enter here."

"I can't lose hope. I can't lose hope because when you lose hope you die."
—Martin Luther King, Jr.

✦

"Hope, hope, what can be accomplished without hope!"
—George Halas

✦

"You cannot give up hope ... the situation is hopeless ... but I might be wrong."
—Jacques Cousteau

✦

Sign at Killarney Baptist Church in Winter Park, Florida: "He who has hope has everything."

✦

"He always gave off the message that those were not the days. These are the days."
—George Shirk on coach Jack McMahon's view of life in the NBA

✦

"Hope is the only bee that makes honey without flowers."
—Robert Ingersoll

✦

"A campaign of hope beats a campaign of fear, every time."
—Howard Dean

✦

"The essentials of happiness are something to do, someone to love, and something to hope for."
—Unknown

✦

"There is one thing which gives radiance to everything. It is the idea of something around the corner."
—G.K. Chesterton

"There are no hopeless situations; there are only men who have grown hopeless about them."

—Clare Boothe Luce

✦

"It kills me that someday I'll have to die. I don't see how I'll ever get it all done."

—Steve Allen

✦

"The place you work will never be better than you make it."

—Charles Swindoll

✦

"An organization is the lengthened shadow of one man."

—Ralph Waldo Emerson

✦

"The small gravestone of Fanny Crosby, the blind gospel songwriter, said simply: "Aunt Fanny—she did what she could."

—Fred Smith

✦

"I forever remember Vince Lombardi barking, 'You don't do things right once in a while. You do them right all the time.'"

—Jerry Kramer

✦

"The only way to whip an army is to go out and fight it."

—Ulysses S. Grant

✦

"I leave this rule for others when I'm dead. Be always sure you're right, then go ahead."

—Davy Crockett

✦

"Leadership comes from the inside and is shown on the outside."

—D.A. Benton

"I believe in life with a large YES and a small no. I believe that life is good and that God is good."

—Rich DeVos

✦

"Great leaders like people and others recognize that. In fact, it goes way beyond liking. I have a hard time leading people I don't like or trust."

—Dick Vermeil

✦

"I know of no easy way to be president."

—Harry S. Truman

✦

"All of us are vulnerable to leadership."

—Tim LaHaye

✦

"I have it but I'll be darned if I can define it."

—George S. Patton on leadership

✦

"In the movie Robin Hood, Errol Flynn played Robin Hood. At one point he arrived in the forest and the merry men said, 'Robin Hood, you've come to join us.' Robin Hood replied, 'No, I've come to lead you.'"

—Phyllis George

✦

"I don't view myself as a manager, but as a leader."

—Terry Francona

✦

"In public life a leader must have a sense of optimism and hope. We all face problems that are so great that if the leader doesn't radiate optimism and hope, people will pick up on that and begin to believe it."

—Jeb Bush

"Power is nothing unless you can turn it into influence."
—Condoleezza Rice

✦

"Leadership is measured by results."
—Peter Drucker

✦

T-shirts worn by student council members at Springlake-Earth Student Council in Texas: "Leadership is not a state of mind. It's a way of life."

✦

"Red Auerbach has a philosophy of leadership: spread the credit and accept the blame."
—John Feinstein

✦

"I know no South, no North, no East, no West to which I owe any allegiance. My allegiance is to the American Union and to my State."
—Henry Clay of Kentucky

✦

John Lennon bought a bungalow in 1965 for his Aunt Mimi on the English Channel coast at Pools in Dorset. For her new home, he gave her a stone tablet inscribed with a quote of hers that he wanted her to never forget. It read, "A guitar's all right, John, but you'll never earn a living by it."

✦

"A sign of maturity is accepting deferred gratification."
—Adlai Stevenson

✦

"I was born weighing 135 pounds."
—Barbara Bush in response to a *Parade* article that put her weight between 135 and 145 pounds

"You're never too old to become younger."

—Mae West

✦

"Age is inevitable, but aging is not."

—Marv Levy at age 78

✦

"Praise God for the open doors no one can shut and for the doors he has closed that cannot be opened."

—Deloris Jordan

✦

"You must not miss your chance. Old Man Opportunity has long hair in front and he is bald behind. When he comes to you, you can snatch him and hold him tight, but when he is past he could be gone forever."

—Branch Rickey

✦

"Attitudes are to life as the angle of approach is to flying. Attitude will cause us to react and behave in a certain way."

—Chris Spicer

✦

"Be alive, man! You gotta love this game to play it. If you don't love this game, you'll never be great."

—Frank "Buck" O'Neill to his players while managing the Kansas City Monarchs

✦

"Optimists see the negative but don't fear, for they feel adequate to the challenge. False optimism is more denial than recognition."

—Fred Smith

✦

"Leaders must communicate unshakable and unbridled optimism."

—Bill Hybels

"Hope. What else is there in the world?"
—Frank "Buck" O'Neill

✦

"Optimism is an intellectual choice."
—Dana Schneider

✦

"She's hardwired to be happy and positive."
—Kiron Skinner on friend Condoleezza Rice

✦

"I am an optimist by occupational requirement."
—Joe Biden

✦

Philosophy at Ritz Carlton Hotels toward guests: "The answer is, 'Yes.' Now, what is the question?"

✦

"I tell people, 'If you don't want to get into positive thinking, that's okay. Just eliminate all the negative thoughts from your mind and whatever's left will be fine.'"
—Bob Rotella

✦

"Remember the five simple rules to be happy:

1. Free your heart from hatred.
2. Free your mind from worries.
3. Live simply.
4. Give more.
5. Expect less."

—Unknown

✦

"I don't care what you can't do. I want to hear what you can do."
—Walt Disney

"Ninety-eight percent of the day I'm positive. The other two percent of the time I work on being positive."

—Rick Pitino

✦

"Come to the park every day like you won yesterday. Maintain the same outlook every time you come to the ballpark. Be positive, because if you are down, everyone else will be."

—Chuck Tanner

✦

"In politics, optimists always trump pessimists."

—Kati Marton

✦

"To succeed, I believe it starts with enthusiasm."

—Ted Williams

✦

"I just try to come every day and have some fun."

—Rush Limbaugh

✦

"Ronald Reagan taught us to be optimistic. He taught us to look to the future. He taught me cheerful persistence."

—Newt Gingrich

✦

"He was the eternal optimist ... the glass is always half-full, not half empty. Since he felt that everything happens for a reason, he never saw things darkly."

—Nancy Reagan on Ronald Reagan

✦

"I'm just crazy enough to get up every morning saying to myself, with great enthusiasm, 'I'm sure the next big story, the biggest story I'll ever cover, is right there around the corner. It might happen today, and, boy, do I want to be there covering it.'"

—Dan Rather

"I never met anyone who was successful who was a pessimist. You have to be positive, or you'll never get anywhere."
—Bill O'Neil

✦

"Keep a green tree in your heart, and perhaps the singing bird will come."
—Chinese proverb

✦

"I believe optimism is the only philosophy of life that's compatible with sustained success and sanity."
—Sumner Redstone

✦

"Leaders have an intuitive sense that things will work out for the best. I do not see the dark side."
—Howard Schultz

✦

"Every great movement in the annals of history is a triumph of enthusiasm."
—Ralph Waldo Emerson

✦

"A wise man is the confirmed optimist."
—Andrew Carnegie

✦

"Optimism is a choice and one of the most powerful we can make."
—Ronald Reagan

✦

"He had the gift of greeting life with a glad heart."
—A California journalist on Francis "Lefty" O'Doul

✦

"Pessimists calculate the odds. Optimists believe they can overcome them."
—Ted Koppel

"My father had a policy of zero tolerance for despair or cynicism."
—Martin Luther King III

✦

"Psychologists have observed that people do not yawn when they think something bad is about to happen, so if you yawn this morning, I will take that as your anticipation that something good is going to happen this morning."
—Unknown

✦

"No pessimist ever discovered the secrets of the stars or sailed to an uncharted land or opened a new heaven to the human spirit."
—Helen Keller

✦

"Colin Powell is the most optimistic person I've ever met. He is congenitally upbeat."
—Richard Haas

✦

"Optimism is a force multiplier. I don't like wallowing with pessimists."
—Colin Powell

✦

"He always sees the brightest spot, even when things are the darkest."
—Jerry West on Bill Sharman

✦

"He always tries to find something positive in you before anything negative comes out."
—Eric Musselman on Jerry West

✦

"After the Vietnam War, thousands of Vietnamese people attempted to leave the country for a better life in the United States and Canada. A study was done to discover why some boats made it safely with no deaths and few illnesses. There was one common factor: one person in each boat took a position of leadership and led with a calm spirit, managing the ups and downs of this harrowing voyage. This person transmitted the thought that everything will be okay and didn't lose his poise and composure in the process."
—J.P. Pawliw-Fry

"I am still determined to be cheerful and to be happy in whatever situation I may be, for I have learned through experience that the greater part of our happiness or misery depends upon our dispositions, not upon our circumstances."

—Martha Washington

✦

"Optimists view setback as:

1. Not entirely due to them
2. Short-lived
3. Not their one defining quality."

—J.P. Pawliw-Fry

✦

"I still like waking up each morning. Just by waking up you got another shot at a miracle."

—Hank McGraw

✦

"A bad attitude is worse than a bad swing."

—Payne Stewart

✦

"I am, by nature, an optimist."

—John McCain

✦

The night before he was assassinated in Memphis, Tennessee, Martin Luther King, Jr. talked about the death threats he had recently received. Then he said, "Well, I don't know what will happen now. We've got some difficult days ahead, but it doesn't matter with me now because I've been to the mountaintop, and I don't mind. Like anybody, I would like to live a long life. Longevity has its place, but I'm not concerned about that now. I just want to do God's will, and he's allowed me to go up to the mountain. I've looked over, and I've seen the Promised Land. I may not get there with you, but I want you to know tonight that we, as a people, will get to the Promised Land. I'm happy tonight. I'm not worried about anything. I'm not fearing any man. Mine eyes have seen the glory of the coming of the Lord."

The next day he was shot.

"Met Life did a study over three years and discovered that optimists outsold the pessimists by 21 percent in year one and 57 percent in year two. In fact, in the second year, the extreme optimists outsold pessimists by 88 percent."

—J.P. Pawliw-Fry

✦

During World War II, Winston Churchill put up a sign in his underground hideout, in London, quoting Queen Victoria on the Boer War: "Please understand there's no depression in this house, and we are not interested in the possibilities of defeat. They do not exist."

✦

"Michael Jordan is always up."

—Luc Longley

✦

"I absolutely loved it. How could you do the things I did and not love it?"

—Sandy Koufax on baseball

✦

"When you're around Tina, you say, 'I want some of that energy that's coming off her.'"

—Oprah Winfrey on Tina Turner

✦

"To play the game is great, to win the game is greater, but to love the game is the greatest of all."

—Palestra plaque

✦

"If Walt Disney saw passion, he gravitated towards it because he knew passion produced greatness."

—Ron Stark

✦

"It is the greatest shot of adrenaline to be doing what you've wanted to do so badly. You almost feel like you could fly without the plane."

—Charles Lindbergh

"Passion is the lubricant of success."
—Brian Billick

✦

"Chuck Tanner's enthusiasm was off the charts. He never had a bad day. He made his players believe they were good. He'd tell them, 'Someone believes you can play or you wouldn't be here.'"
—Roland Hemond

✦

"Nothing is more contagious than enthusiasm."
—Mary Kay Ash

✦

"All I want is for the game to mean as much to the players as it means to me."
—Tom Coughlin

✦

In 2004, Arnold Palmer played in his 50th and final Masters at age 75. (Most days he's out hitting golf balls trying to find some way to play better.) He was asked if there was a single day that was his best on the golf course. "A single day," he repeated. "I've had 50 years of single days."

✦

"I love playing the game. It puts a smile on my face."
—Nomar Garciaparra

✦

"The thing that drives all real success is passion and enthusiasm for what you do."
—Don Shula

✦

"His blood temperature is 99.6, not 98.6 like everyone else. He's an emotional guy."
—John Bunting on Dick Vermeil

✦

"A battle is lost less through casualties than by discouragement."
—Frederick the Great

"I have written 340 articles on successful people over many years. The one common trait I have discovered with all of them is the passion they have for what they do."

—Michael Mink (*Investors' Business Daily* writer)

✦

"My sophomore year at Duke, Mike Krzyzewski stood in front of the team in those coaching shorts and a Duke shirt. He was talking about being a winner. He was so passionate about the topic you could see goosebumps appear all over his skin."

—Jay Bilas

✦

"I've never lost my enthusiasm."

—Larry King at age 70

✦

"It has never been a job for me, but a passion."

—John Chaney

✦

"Music to me is just like breathing. I have to have it. It's part of me, just as my liver or kidney is part of me."

—Ray Charles

✦

"I was totally in love with the game. That's my main message to kids today. If you're not in love with what you're doing, just move over and make room for somebody who is. If you can't enjoy it, it's ridiculous to play. I'd still be playing if I possibly could."

—Gordie Howe

✦

"He was a man who devoured life's smorgasbord in giant gulps. He had a beaming, let's have at them buoyancy."

—Cormac O'Brien on Theodore Roosevelt

✦

"When I retire someday to the ranch, I want to turn to my wife and say, 'My dance card was full. I lived life to the fullest.'"

—George W. Bush

"We are all worms, but I do believe I am a glowworm."
—Winston Churchill

✦

"In 1945, Winston Churchill was at dinner when a woman at the table asked, 'Now that it is all over, what was your worst moment in the war—the fall of France, the threat of invasion, the Blitz?'

"After a minute, he answered, 'Frankly, my dear, I enjoyed every moment of it.'"
—John Meacham

✦

"Give me a man who sings at his work."
—Thomas Carlyle

✦

"Satchel Paige died yesterday, but oh how he lived!"
—A newscaster

✦

"Had anyone ever grabbed life harder by the ears, shook it, pummeled it, and enjoyed it more?"
—Leigh Montville on Ted Williams

✦

"I'd rather be a failure at something I enjoy than be a success at something I hate."
—George Burns

✦

"It's a very short trip. While alive, live."
—Malcolm Forbes

✦

"It's important to feast from the plate of life with both hands."
—Charles Rosen

✦

"We shall be as a city upon a hill. The eyes of all people are upon us."
—John Winthrop in 1630, speaking to fellow Puritans on American soil

"At the 2004 Book Expo in Chicago, I did a signing of my Rich DeVos book. While waiting in the green room, I spotted Julie Andrews. For three years, I had been trying to contact her and talk about Walt Disney for my *How to be Like Walt* book. I introduced myself and asked, 'Julie, what is your most vivid memory of Walt Disney?'

She replied, 'His sparkling eyes.' With that, her handlers whisked her off to another assignment. I spent 10 seconds with her, but was as excited as a kid in a toy store."

—Pat Williams

✦

"That I'm the coach. If you lose the job someday, you make sure you lose it because you did things in all areas of your life. He'd give you three or four steps to get started, and then you were on your own. Once you caught on, there was no end to your journey."

—Tom Crean, Marquette coach, on what he learned most from Al McGuire

✦

"The key to leadership is the desire to make a difference. This creates high morale in any organization. If people in an organization think what they're doing doesn't make a difference, morale will be low."

—John Maxwell

✦

"We have to remember that here in this house, no man who sits here can ever afford to think himself first."

—Lyndon B Johnson

✦

"When they discover the center of the universe, a lot of people will be disappointed to discover they are not it."

—Bernard Bailey

✦

"People will run after you when they think you are important, so keep your feet on the ground."

—Susan Agnelli

✦

"He understood the players and could get peak performances out of them more consistently than other coaches. He got into their minds about improvement."

—Frank Broyles on Bear Bryant

"He's the most fundamentally optimistic person I've ever met. There really is a sense with him that every day is a new day. He always believes that whatever he's given he can make it better."

—An associate of Colin Powell

✦

"I have a new philosophy. I'm only going to dread one day at a time."

—Charles M. Schulz

✦

"The crew of Space Shuttle Challenger honored us by the manner in which they lived their lives. We will never forget them nor the last time we saw them, this morning as they prepared for their journey and waved goodbye, and slipped the surly bonds of Earth to touch the face of God."

—Ronald Reagan

✦

"Dave hired ordinary people and then found a way to get extraordinary results out of us."

—An executive on Dave Packard

✦

"We open four new stores every day, so we must be constantly training new leaders. We spend a lot of time and money on this. Our leaders must come from within our culture because we can't teach that to an outsider. How do we spot future leaders? They must have people skills. That's what our business is all about."

—Howard Schultz

✦

"Abraham Lincoln's main strength as a leader was he got things done and cared about people at the same time. That's a tough thing to do, but it's the mark of a great leader. Some people can do one or the other but very few can do both."

—Donald T. Phillips

✦

"Technique and ability alone do not get you to the top; it is the willpower that is the most important—it rises from your heart."

—Junko Tabei (1975) after becoming the first woman to climb Mount Everest

"Senator Paul Wellstone had the politician's great gift: an amazing memory for names. I saw him once pluck a vote with this gift. He answered questions for about 45 minutes in a room full of ordinary citizens whom he'd never seen before. He began his last answer this way: 'Your question reminds me of Mary's concern.' Mary, likely a rock-ribbed Republican, blushed a little and smiled. One more vote."

—Unknown

✦

"Everybody has a handicap. It's how you deal with it that makes a difference."

—Gail Devers

✦

"You can't take ghosts from last night's game into the next day. In baseball, if you can't turn the page and get to the next game, you're going to be in trouble."

—Mike Scioscia

✦

"The mark of a great quarterback was to win games and he never lost."

—Y.A. Tittle on Otto Graham

✦

"I don't think we're meant to live our lives over. One shot is all we get and we have to make the most of it."

—Herschel Walker

✦

"My goal is to take this American company and win every place in the world, every corner. So, I'm going to Asia next weekend for 10 days, and I'm selling my tail off. I'm selling engines in China, I'm selling medical equipment in Japan, and I'm going to India to sell."

—Jeffrey Immelt

✦

"There are no back moves on the chessboard of life."

—Aldous Huxley

✦

"If you're thinking about retiring, you've retired."

—Scotty Stirling

"The most important attribute an NFL head coach can have is the capacity to slam the door and pull down the shade on a tough loss and focus on the next game."

—Hank Stram

✦

"There are only the limits we place upon ourselves. It's when you look beyond those barriers that you see there are no limits."

—Thomas Edison

✦

"I've been around sports my whole life, so I've learned many of my lessons there. In sports, you don't talk about it; you do it. Just go out and show you can. Don't look at the other guy. The only one you have to please is in the mirror."

—Joe Garagiola

✦

"People always say that I didn't give up my seat because I was tired, but that isn't true. I wasn't tired physically or no more tired than I usually was at the end of a working day. No, the only tired I was, was tired of giving in."

—Rosa Parks

✦

"I wasn't going anywhere. I was giving up."

—Frank Sinatra describing himself at age 22

✦

"At the 2004 Disney Marathon, my daughter Karyn shared with me this Carl Bard quote that impacted her life: 'No one can go back and make a brand new start. Anyone can start from now and make a brand new ending.'"

—Pat Williams

✦

"I do not hunch my back with yesterday."

—Danny Thomas

✦

Inventor Charles Kettering had bad eyesight but looked at his poor vision as an aid in ignoring the constraining rules of his field: "It keeps me from reading all the theories that tell why things can't be done."

"To this day, I get messages about clothes that didn't look good or how I didn't sit in a lady-like position. She thinks that if she just says the right things, I'll get it right one day."

—Diane Sawyer at age 56 on her 82-year-old mom, Jean

✦

"I can't do anything about the past. I can only try to change the present and hope it carries over to the future."

—Dusty Baker

✦

"They were always thinking of the next thing to do. They didn't waste much time worrying about the past."

—Charlie Taylor, the Wright Brothers' chief mechanic

✦

"Remember this: Your brain is not a museum for the past or a lumber room for the present. It is a laboratory for the future even if the future is only five minutes ahead of you."

—John Frederick Charles Fuller

✦

On the day FDR died, Harry S. Truman wrote in his diary: "Went to bed, went to sleep, and did not worry any more."

✦

"I have peace with myself."

—John Wooden

✦

"Early in the war, I learned to save all my doubts about forthcoming operations for my pillow."

—Dwight D. Eisenhower

✦

"At my age, I didn't come to Washington to play politics as usual ... I came to Washington to try to solve problems, not to sweep them under the rug and leave them for those who will come later."

—Ronald Reagan

"Four little words sum up what has lifted most successful individuals above the crowd: a little bit more. They did all that was expected of them and a little bit more."

—Lou Vickery

✦

"All my life, the one thing I feared the most was mediocrity."

—Errol Flynn

✦

"Before I go on stage, I pump myself up like an athlete—emotionally, mentally. It's like a surgeon. I mean, these people come to see me and pay this kind of money, it can't be hit and miss. You know, you don't go to a surgeon and say this was an off day for him."

—Alan King

✦

"There's only one corner of the Universe you can be certain of improving, and that's your own self."

—Aldous Huxley

✦

"Whenever I go on a ride, I am always thinking of what's wrong with the thing and how it can be improved."

—Walt Disney

✦

"Quality is a question of expectations. If people are expected to make mistakes, they will, but if the goal of no defects is set from the start, people will work toward that goal, and quality will improve."

—Philip Crosby

✦

"My only goal is to be the best teammate anyone ever had."

—Jameer Nelson

✦

"I think if a player doesn't have respect for himself, he'll have a hard time getting respect from someone else."

—Gene Mauch

"Everyone wanted to please Coach Bryant. Coaches, players, alumni. They all wanted his approval and would do whatever it took to get it."

—Gene Stallings on coach Bear Bryant

✦

"I only regret that I have but one life to lose for my country."

—Nathan Hale's final words on September 27, 1776, after being captured by the British on Long Island while gathering intelligence and going to the gallows

✦

"Franklin D. Roosevelt was laid to rest in a courtyard of the house at Hyde Park. In a funeral service in the east room of the White House, Bishop Dunne led the mourners in hymns and prayer; then respecting the wishes of the First Lady, he recited the line that had rung through the chilly Capitol 12 years before: 'The only thing we have to fear is fear itself.'"

—Jonathan Alter

✦

"The lights are going out all over Europe. We shall not see them lit again in our lifetime."

—Sir Edward Grey

✦

"I'm still learning and trying to improve. When you start taking things for granted, you're through. I think I'm finally figuring out how to do this job."

—Bob Shepherd, New York Yankees' public address announcer for 55 years

✦

"In the name of the greatest people who have ever trod this Earth, I draw the line in the dust and toss the gauntlet before the feet of tyranny … and I say … segregation today … segregation tomorrow … segregation forever."

—George Wallace, Governor of Alabama, shocked the nation in his inaugural address (January 14, 1963)

✦

"We hereby proclaim the establishment of the Jewish State in Palestine to be called Israel."

—David Ben-Gurion, the new Prime Minister of Israel, on May 14, 1948

"My good friends, for the second time in our history, a British Prime Minister has returned from Germany bringing peace with honor. I believe it is peace for our time. Go home and get a nice quiet sleep."

—Neville Chamberlain, Prime Minister of Great Britain on September 30, 1938, in front of 10 Downing Street

✦

"Many years ago, the great British explorer, George Mallory, who was to die on Mt. Everest, was asked why did he want to climb it. He said, 'Because it was there.' Well, space is there, and we're going to climb it, and the moon and the planets are there and new hopes for knowledge and peace are there; therefore as we set sail, we ask God's blessing on the most hazardous and dangerous and greatest adventure on which man has ever embarked."

—John F. Kennedy

✦

"I've realized it's never going to be always up. A down's always coming around. It's just learning how to deal with it."

—Venus Williams

✦

"Ten strong horses could not pull an empty baby carriage if they worked independently of each other."

—John Wooden

✦

"I would take 12 guys who had a strong passion to play this game over 12 stars who don't respect the game."

—Michael Jordan

✦

"There's nothing worse than an all-star band with no teamwork."

—Les Brown

✦

"A sense of ownership is the most powerful weapon a team or organization can have."

—Pat Summitt

Near the end of his life, Winston Churchill said of Franklin D. Roosevelt: "We stood together, and because of that fact the Free World stands."

✦

Charles Lindbergh and his aircraft, *The Spirit of St. Louis*, were one. Together on May 21, 1927 they achieved what no one had ever accomplished, and from that point on Lindbergh always referred to the airplane and himself as "we."

✦

"You have to turn *to* one another when things get rough, not *on* one another."
—Johnny Davis

✦

"No one can do everything. Still, everyone can do something and together we can do anything."
—James Amrine

✦

"I've been in the NBA 28 years and worked for eight different teams. The biggest killers of a team's success are members of the 'whispering society.' These people gossip, gripe, undercut, complain, and end up tearing down the efforts of the team-builders."
—Johnny Davis

✦

"When somebody once asked me what I'd want written on my gravestone, I answered 'He was a great team player.'"
—Mickey Mantle

✦

"If you're not going to be a team player, fake it."
—Red Auerbach

✦

"Since quarterback Donovan McNabb was injured on November 17, the Eagles have been introduced before games as a group, not individually. It's a very cool thing. When Donovan went down, everybody said we were a one-man team. We knew different. We knew all along that we were a team, and we just decided that from here on out we were going to go out as a team."
—Brian Mitchell

"We preach team, team, team, team, team."
—Andy Reid

✦

"There's no 'me' in 'Mia' because in soccer and in life I could never do it alone."
—Mia Hamm

✦

"Everyone needs a team. You can't do anything by yourself."
—Michelle Akers

✦

"Apathy kills a football team more than turnovers."
—Mike Ditka

✦

"Unpleasant times can toss us some really tough sliders, curve balls, or hard tackles, but it's our decision how we respond. It says a lot about our attitude. After love, I consider attitude to be the most important word in our vocabulary. You'll pay a price for it later if you don't have the proper attitude."
—Bart Starr

✦

"The big thing is that regardless how things might go on a given night, the next day it's wiped out. It's a new day. To be able to handle that—especially to get a tough loss out of your system—is an art."
—Lee Elia on manager Lou Piniella

✦

"You don't really pay for things with money. You pay for them with time. In five years, I'll have put enough away to buy that vacation house we want. Then I'll slow down. That means the house will cost you five years and 1/12 of your adult life. Translate the dollar value of the house, car, or anything else into time, and then see if it's still worth it. Sometimes you can't do what you want and have what you want at once because each requires a different expenditure of time. The phrase 'spending your time' is not a metaphor. It's how life works."
—Charles Spezzano

"If you don't have an attitude of gratitude, all you have left is attitude."
—Kenny Luck

✦

"Tomorrow. What other recourse do you have?"
—Lee Mazzilli, former Orioles' manager, on the one positive during a rough stretch of the 2005 season

✦

"*Carpe Manana* means, 'Take hold of tomorrow.'"
—Jay Strack

✦

"If you want to live a happy life, tie it to a goal, not to people or things."
—Albert Einstein

✦

"Yesterday's science fiction is today's reality."
—Donald J. Palmisano, former American Medical Association president

✦

"Leaders are visionaries with a poorly developed sense of fear and no concept of the odds against them. They make the impossible happen."
—Robert Jarvik

✦

"Visions are born in the soul of a man or a woman who is consumed with the tension between what is and what could be."
—Andy Stanley

✦

"Dream big. Don't be just another guy going down the street and going nowhere."
—Al McGuire

✦

"Winning is still the most honorable thing man can do."
—Woody Hayes

"The biggest thing I've learned is to win all the games."

—Larry Coker

✦

"Don't disqualify yourself. Private victories must take place before public victories."

—Jay Strack's advice to young leaders

✦

"It's a winning business. Losing is not acceptable."

—Jody Conradt on the coaching profession

✦

"I never get bored with winning. It's a nice, secure habit. I win because I hate to lose, not because of the thrill of victory."

—Chris Evert

✦

"I despise it. It eats at me. I get physically sick."

—Pat Summitt on losing

✦

"The whole point of a presidential race is to win even if it's only by a fraction of a percentage point or one Supreme Court Justice. Winning has no margin of error."

—Maureen Dowd

✦

"I like points. I mainly like having more points than the other team when the game ends."

—Tony Dungy

✦

"Win today's game."

—Frank Frisch

✦

"Chemistry doesn't create wins. Wins create chemistry."

—Larry Bowa

"Losing is no fun. Winning solves all problems. It's not all that complicated."
—Dallas Green

✦

"Nobody understands how hard it is to win games in this league."
—Bill Walsh

✦

"Winning never gets old."
—Joe Torre

✦

"The hope of victory is essential."
—Douglas MacArthur

✦

"You have to play every game like it's opening day."
—Chuck Tanner

✦

"You win with people."
—Woody Hayes

✦

"I love the competition. That's what keeps me going."
—Annika Sorenstam

✦

"To be successful, you have to like to lose a little less than everybody else."
—Phil Jackson

✦

In January 1971, Notre Dame beat UCLA 89-82 to snap the Bruins' 88-game winning streak. After the game, a distraught Sidney Wicks said to Coach John Wooden: "I just can't believe we lost."

Wooden replied, "Then I suggest not to do it again."

Napoleon was asked, "Who do you consider to be the greatest generals?" He responded by saying, "The victors."

✦

"If you have to go into combat, it doesn't pay to come in second in our line of work."
—D. Michael Abrashoff

✦

"What do I miss? I miss the winning."
—Former Heisman Trophy winner Glenn Davis at age 79 on his career

✦

"There are only two possibilities: winning and misery."
—Pat Riley on coaching in the NBA

✦

"Show me a person without goals and I'll show you someone who's dead."
—George Allen

✦

"We never won as many as I wanted, which was all of them."
—Vince Lombardi

✦

"When I was in college, I found out that the MVPs and all-league teams and all that are hugely political. So I decided that if I win every game, that becomes historical fact, not anyone's opinion."
—Bill Russell

✦

"I've never figured out a way to deal with losing yet, so it doesn't sit well."
—Pat Quinn

✦

"Winning is what gives a coach authority in the NBA."
—Michael Wilbon

"You are talking about a guy who wouldn't let you be ordinary. That spilled over into everything ... that way of thinking. It affected all of us in so many ways."

—Jerry Duncan on his coach at Alabama, Bear Bryant

✦

"Success is peace of mind which is a direct result of self-satisfaction in knowing you did your best to become the best that you are capable of becoming."

—John Wooden

✦

"There's an elation in winning."

—Joe Paterno

✦

"If anything goes bad, I did it. If anything goes semi-good, we did it. If anything goes real good, you did it. That's all it takes to get people to win football games."

—Bear Bryant

✦

"His greatest gift as a leader was his ability to teach winning. His only goal in life was on the three-letter word: *Win!*"

—Paul Hornung on Vince Lombardi

✦

"Failure is the condiment that gives success its flavor."

—Truman Capote

✦

"I'm paid to be obsessed. I'm paid to win."

—Lance Armstrong

✦

"You're only a success at the moment that you do a successful act."

—Tex Winter

✦

"Just win and you'll become very smart."

—Marv Levy

"I want to be the best; maybe not the best coach, but the best winner. You can name me the worst coach if you give me 20 rings. I want to win."

—Doc Rivers

✦

"Don't lose."

—Bobby Cox, Braves manager, was asked the secret on his long and successful career

✦

Bill Parcells wore a t-shirt at the Dallas Cowboys' 2005 training camp that read: "Winning is a business."

✦

By what standards are we to be judged?
Intention may be noble.
Deeds may be glorious.
Effort may be outstanding.
Dedication may be praiseworthy.
Ability may be superior.
Results are everything!

—Unknown

✦

"I never in my life put on the uniform and didn't play to win, never."

—George Brett

✦

"As Peter Drucker believed, leadership is about results, but are they sustainable?"

—J.P. Pawliw-Fry

✦

The late Leonard Bernstein, composer and famed conductor of the world renowned New York Philharmonic, was asked what he believed to be the most difficult instrument in the orchestra to play. He responded, "Second fiddle."

✦

"I'm a win man myself. I don't go for place or show."

—Bear Bryant

"Winning is living. Every time you win, you are reborn. When you lose, you die a little."
—George Allen

✦

"He was strong-minded. He was intense every day that I worked with him for 13 years. His will to win would overtake the team."
—Dan Marino on Don Shula

✦

"It seems with every match I win, I get better looking to other people."
—Andy Roddick

✦

"I don't know of any ticker tape parades they have in the country for anybody other than war heroes, astronauts, or winning teams."
—Jerry Jones

✦

"You can't get it back, so why dwell on it? I come to the park and pretend we won."
—Bobby Cox on last night's loss

✦

"Coaching is a great profession when you win. It ain't worth a darn when you lose."
—Eddie Sutton

✦

"Losing feels worse than winning feels good."
—Joe Garagiola

✦

"Losing is never fun."
—Joe Paterno

✦

"I do have a strategy. We win. They lose."
—Ronald Reagan on destroying communism

"Coach Mike Krzyzewski at Duke uses failure better than anyone I've been around. His greatest victories have always come after his greatest failures."

—John Feinstein

✦

"I wouldn't give one iota to make a trip from the cradle to the grave unless I could live in a competitive world."

—Adolph Rupp

✦

"It's been my practice to try to get people that football meant something to, that winning meant something to; not only assistant coaches, but to secretaries, ticket takers."

—Bear Bryant

✦

"I think it's important to set lofty goals in your life, and the bigger the better. Goals make you compete and strive for excellence. Without goals, you won't get up when you get knocked down."

—Jerry West

✦

"I have won and I have lost, and winning is better."

—Bob Feller

✦

"It's about winning in this league. It's not about trying."

—Jeff Van Gundy

✦

"Losing is easy. It's not enjoyable, but it's easy."

—Bud Wilkinson

✦

"I love this game and I love competing. I love it when I get hit and when I hit back. I see kids playing video football games, and I want to scream at them, 'No, no, that's not football!' It's not the same."

—Steve Young

"Every effort in life is marked down as a win or a loss."

—Edward Bennett Williams

✦

"Big time college sports look like a lot of fun, but only when you win."

—Jerry Tarkanian

✦

"We have this immutable law in the NBA: there has to be a loss for every win."

—David Stern

✦

"My fondest memory of Joe? Super Bowl XXIII, the final drive. I'll never forget it. Just the way he ran onto the football field, came into the huddle, didn't say anything; just dropped down on one knee and called the play. I just knew inside that we would win that football game just because of his presence."

—Jerry Rice on Joe Montana

✦

"Win today and we walk together forever."

—Fred Shero just before winning the Stanley Cup

✦

"All of the glory—everything you had, everything that you won—is going to be small in comparison to winning this one."

—Vince Lombardi in the locker room before Super Bowl II in 1967

✦

"These are the boys of Pointe Du Hoc. These are the men who took the cliffs. These are the champions who helped free a continent. These are the heroes who helped win a war."

—Ronald Reagan on June 6, 1984, at Pointe Du Hoc, France with 62 World War II veteran American Rangers in attendance

✦

"Success is never final, but failure can be."

—Bill Parcells

"The news from France is very bad."

—Winston Churchill's opening words in his speech to his country after the fall of France

✦

On July 20, 1969, when he landed on the moon, Neil Armstrong reported to NASA: "Houston, Tranquility Base here. The Eagle has landed." That night at Arlington National Cemetery, an unknown person placed a bouquet on John F. Kennedy's grave with an unsigned note: "Mr. President, the Eagle has landed."

✦

"That's one small step for a man; one giant leap for mankind."

—Neil Armstrong

✦

"Once he drops his head, it's quiet. He does all the talking."

—Bob Vogel, former Colts tackle, on Johnny Unitas in the huddle

✦

"None of us is as good as all of us."

—Ray Kroc

✦

"Jose, my guide on October 24, 2008, in Mexico City, describing the up and down cycles of life in Mexico: 'When you are down you have to learn from it so when you get back on top again, you'll be smarter and know what to do.'"

—Pat Williams

✦

"I was raised in a household that taught us that everybody has the right to have a lot of fun."

—Rachael Ray

✦

"Ray Kroc and Walt Disney—the inventors of the Big Mac and Mickey Mouse respectively—were born in Chicago, 10 months apart, and served in the same Red Cross unit in World War I. Quite a state, Illinois."

—George Will

"Never grow accustomed to the emotions of continuous defeat."

—Branch Rickey

✦

"He perfected the art of gaining power by giving it away."

—Garry Wills on George Washington

✦

"Stripped to its essentials, leadership involves just three things: a leader, followers, and a common goal."

—Warren Bennis and Robert Thomas

✦

"I'd rather be the most hated winning coach in the country than the most popular losing one."

—Adolph Rupp

✦

"Don't let problems surprise you; expect them."

—John Maxwell

✦

"The thing I loved about Ted Williams was his glee. He had great glee."

—Jack Kerouac

✦

"True leaders get the players to give an A performance."

—Sam Walton

✦

"Do you know why I never have defeats? My reputation as a great general means too much to me ... You can't be a great general and have defeats."

—Bernard Montgomery

✦

"You could see how the focus in those eyes could lead marches that changed lives."

—Alan Alda on Martin Luther King, Jr.

"When Arnold Palmer was playing in a pro-am, he grew increasingly impatient with his amateur partner who was smacking the golf ball all over the fairway. 'For heaven's sake,' Palmer finally snapped, 'aim at something!'"

—Dick Jacobs

✦

"So, I close by saying that I might have had a tough break, but I have an awful lot to live for."

—Lou Gehrig

✦

"Get the ship into port and you worry about who the heroes were later."

—Frank Robinson on managing

✦

"He has the heart of a giant and that rare form of courage that allows him to kid himself and his opponent: cancer. He has the mental attitude that makes me proud to have a friend who spells out the word courage 24 hours a day of his life. I love Brian Piccolo and would like all of you to love him, too. Tonight, when you hit your knees, please ask God to love him."

—Gale Sayers, in New York (1969), when he received the George Halas Award as the NFL's most courageous player

✦

"He's the least backward-looking person I've ever known in my life."

—A senior staffer of George W. Bush

✦

"A leader must accomplish the difficult task of getting those on the team to believe that we supersedes me."

—John Wooden

✦

While honoring Steven Spielberg at the Kennedy Center on December 26, 2006, Liam Neeson said that when Spielberg was asked, "Which is your favorite ending?" he replied, "Hope."

"In a race, I go into autopilot."
—Danica Patrick

✦

"The only excuse for getting into a war is to win it."
—Douglas MacArthur

✦

"He was a successful president because of tunnel vision that kept his gaze on big goals."
—Robert Novak on Ronald Reagan

✦

"I became an optimist when I discovered that I wasn't going to win any more games by being anything else."
—Earl Weaver

✦

Winston Churchill arranged a meeting in 1954 with Billy Graham. After a few minutes, he confessed to Graham: "I see no hope for the world. I am a man without hope."

✦

"My optimism runs eternal. You just can't get rid of me, you know."
—Betty White at age 85

✦

"I started out as a truck driver and worked my way down to president."
—Guy Marlin

✦

"Managing is like holding a dove in your hand. Squeeze too hard and you kill it—not hard enough and it flies away."
—Tommy Lasorda

✦

"True leadership requires us to succeed. We must get results."
—Mike Huckabee

Sign above the entryway at Fort Monroe, Virginia: "Leadership excellence."

✦

"This is the voice of freedom. People of the Philippines, I have returned ... let no heart be faint."

—Douglas MacArthur

✦

"For reasons I have never been able to fathom, he always emerged the leader."

—Sara Delano Roosevelt on her son, Franklin

✦

"As head coach, you are somewhat of a dictator, but don't behave like one."

—Harry Gamble

✦

"The only problem I ever have in New York City is people. People present me with a constant headache ... we have too many slobs."

—John W. Lindsay

✦

"My fellow countrymen, today the guns are silent. A great tragedy has ended. A great victory has been won. The skies no longer rain death ... the seas bear only commerce ... men everywhere walk upright in the sunlight. The entire world is quietly at peace."

—Douglas MacArthur, speaking on the deck of the battleship *Missouri* in Tokyo Bay after the official surrender ceremonies that ended World War II

✦

"The one thing I know is that winning takes care of everything in this league."

—Mike Bibby

✦

"Winning is the most important thing in my life, after breathing. Breathing first, winning next."

—George Steinbrenner

"Winning cures the common cold."
—Ken Stabler

✦

"There's nothing like the moment when you've just won a game."
—Ernie Accorsi

✦

"We developed a relationship that is going to last a lifetime."
—Dwight Howard on his 2008 Olympic basketball teammates

✦

"I do not hunch my back with yesterday."
—Danny Thomas

✦

"Attitude is the mind's paintbrush. It can color any situation."
—Loring Forcier

✦

"Criticism is like being in the rain. Once you're wet, what's another drop?"
—Jack Kent Cooke

✦

"It's important to live in the is and not in the was."
—Colin Cowherd

✦

"Don't be afraid."
—George Washington to his doctor on his deathbed at Mount Vernon

✦

"I had zero control over getting cancer, but I have 100-percent control over how I respond to it."
—Kay Yow

On October 18, 1950, Connie Mack retired at age 88 as manager of the Philadelphia Athletics with these words: "I'm not quitting because I'm getting old. I quitting because I think people want me to."

✦

"I'm determined to be an optimist."
—Andrew Young

✦

"The leader has to be optimistic, simply because if he isn't, nobody else will be."
—Rudy Giuliani

✦

"You never give up just wanting to play and have fun the way that kids do."
—Jerry Seinfeld

✦

"I'm a pessimist by nature which is why I have spent my life as a journalist instead of trying to be a leader, which requires optimism."
—Robert Novak

✦

"He was a great leader because he was always optimistic and upbeat. He would say to us, 'Be positive! You can do it. We can win!'"
—Tony Muser on manager Chuck Tanner

✦

"What did I learn? I learned that what Chuck Tanner once said is true. Tanner managed my son, Dale, and those good Pittsburgh teams in the 1970s and always had a sunshine way, even when things got gloomy. 'There are three secrets to managing,' he said. 'The first secret is to have patience. The second is to be patient, and the third, most important secret is patience.'"
—Yogi Berra

✦

"I always felt that every job I had was too big for me."
—Lyndon B. Johnson

"If there is anyone out there who still doubts that America is a place where all things are possible, tonight is your answer."

—Barack Obama on November 4, 2008

✦

"I may not have won your vote tonight, but I hear your voices. I need your help, and I will be your president, too."

—Barack Obama

✦

"It is always against my nature to acknowledge problems, unless the problems really exist."

—Donald Trump

✦

"When you win, it's forever. It's forever, man, and that's a great feeling."

—Geoff Jenkins

✦

"We were doing teamwork."

—Laila Kindy, age 4, on putting together a toy with her cousins

✦

"I rate enthusiasm even above professional skill."

—Edward Appleton

✦

"As long as you're going to be thinking anyway, think big."

—Donald Trump

✦

"Long-range goals keep you from being frustrated by short-term failures."

—James Cash Penney

✦

"We must lead where we can, follow where we cannot."

—Thomas Jefferson

Tiger Woods was asked before the 2009 Masters, "Do you expect to win?" He replied, "Always."

✦

"Chances of things happening in this world without goals are slim."
—Bear Bryant

✦

"There is no way you can play this game with a busy mind—no way."
—David Ortiz

✦

"When you confront a problem you begin to solve it."
—Rudy Guiliani

✦

"Act enthusiastic, and you'll be enthusiastic."
—Dale Carnegie

✦

"Before you can inspire with emotion, you must be swamped with it yourself."
—Winston Churchill

✦

You know you and your crew should set goals to motivate yourselves and measure your progress, but how high should they be? Joe Farcht, a leadership consultant and amateur gardener, looks to his tomatoes for insight in this area. He used to set out four-foot stakes for his tomatoes to climb, but they would usually reach that height quickly—forcing him to tack on extension stakes to accommodate their vigor. One year he decided to get ahead of the curve. Instead of four-foot stakes, he set out eight-footers, thinking that he'd have plenty of room to spare. The tomatoes, however, had other ideas. They responded by accepting his growth challenge and took over the entire height of the stakes. With room to grow, healthy living beings will do the same. What tomatoes can accomplish, you and your staff can accomplish. Set some challenging goals and unite to reach them.
—Adapted from *Building Personal Leadership* by Joe Farcht (Genesis Publishing)

"Your boy, Lester, will never learn music."
—Les Paul's childhood piano teacher in a letter to his mother

✦

"Let's pretend."
—Walt Disney's favorite instruction

✦

"Athletes play better when they feel connected with their team."
—John Wooden

✦

"We want to be happy after the games."
—Chuck Daly on winning

✦

"When you're around him, everything is about today."
—John Mozeliak on manager Tony La Russa

✦

"We loved to win."
—Terry Bradshaw on the Steelers of the 1970s

✦

"A leader must have a vision, which is simply an elevated word for goal."
—Bill Walsh

✦

"I still believe that winning is the greatest feeling there is in coaching."
—Bobby Bowden

✦

"Follow the fellow who follows a dream."
—From the song "Look to the Rainbow" in *Finian's Rainbow*

✦

"You can accomplish anything in Washington if you give others the credit."
—Philip A. Hart

"He was passionate about what he did and just loved the business. He enjoyed all the different kinds of merchandise and got excited when he discovered new items for the stores."

—Jim Walton on his father, Sam Walton, as a leader

✦

"Winning is fun. That's all there is to it."

—Andy Pettitte

✦

I have awed at a solo performance,
And spectacular flashy display,
But I crave for the best
And my eyes are more blessed,
When an unselfish team makes a play.

A play that's so perfect and simple,
With the weaving of role with a role—
Every piece partly seen,
Like a fine-tuned machine,
And you notice not one, but the whole.

Like an orchestra tuned to perfection,
Where harmonious beauty is found,
Every note has a quest
To be part of the rest,
So the whole is a masterpiece sound.

Every wild one, once blinded by glory,
Is now cured and is one of the tame.
He receives his esteem,
As a part of the team,
And is eager to sacrifice fame.

It's amazing what teams have accomplished.
It's astounding how much they have done,
When the ultimate call,
Is when one is for all,
And the credit is reached for by none.

—Swen Nater

"By doing whatever I was asked to do, including making a pot of coffee to the best of my ability. I made the best coffee to be found."

—Madeleine Albright on how she went from a secretary in the White House to Secretary of State

✦

"I never saw so much love among a group as I saw back then. They wanted to play for each other."

—"Big Daddy" Lipscomb's wife on the Baltimore Colts of the 1950s

✦

"A career can be called a success if one can look back and say, 'I made a difference.'"

—Walter Cronkite

✦

"Boldness, be my friend. Arm me, audacity, from head to foot."

—William Shakespeare

✦

"Discipline is the bridge between goals and accomplishment."

—Jim Rohn

✦

"Don't fear failure. Success ruins more people."

—Janet Hill, Grant Hill's mother

✦

"I look for players who realize the world doesn't revolve around them."

—Pete Carril

✦

"Five seconds left in the game. Four left in the game. Do you believe in miracles? Yes! Unbelievable!"

—Al Michaels, 1980 Winter Olympics

✦

"I fly for the fun."

—Amelia Earhart

"Basketball's highest level comes down to one question: Can you make the choice that your happiness can come from someone else's success?"

—Bill Walton

✦

"Run it and let's get out of here."

—Vince Lombardi to Bart Starr before the last play of the famous 1967 Ice Bowl game

✦

"I disdain anything like duplicity."

—Thomas Jefferson in a letter to James Madison, August 3, 1797

✦

"No one man is greater than the team."

—Vince Lombardi

✦

"Play hard, play smart, play together."

—Mantra of the University of North Carolina basketball team

✦

"Okay, we're in great shape. We're exactly where we want to be because we are going to determine the outcome of this game. I'm serious. We're exactly where we want to be. This basketball game is ours. Michael, if you get it, knock it in." (*Hard Work* by Roy Williams)

—Dean Smith (down by one point), in the huddle prior to the final play of the 1982 NCAA title game

✦

"Wins—that's all that counts."

—Mike D'Antoni, NBA coach

✦

"Good managers have the ability to make players feel that 'we did it ourselves' when things go well. When things don't, the manager says, 'I'm to blame.'"

—Bill "Spaceman" Lee

"He was the perfect teammate. That's what he always wanted to be considered."

—Tony Kubek on Mickey Mantle

✦

"Same team that won yesterday is gonna win today."

—Roy Campanella

✦

"If they had told me I was the janitor and would have to mop up and clean the toilets after the show in order to play, I probably would have done it."

—Bruce Springsteen

✦

"Not everyone can be a chief executive officer, but all of us can be a different type of CEO: a chief example officer. Look for opportunities to be an example, and let it take place as a planned leadership approach."

—Ian Morrison

✦

"Motivation is a fire from within. If someone else tries to light that fire under you, chances are it will burn very briefly."

—Stephen R. Covey

✦

"I am convinced that the biggest challenge to leaders is maintaining a sense of humility. It's so easy to read our own press clippings too much."

—Bob Fryling

✦

"As a leader, Margaret Thatcher changed the definition of the possible. She understood that consensus is the enemy of leadership. As a leader, Mrs. Thatcher had the capacity to make tough decisions, to help people achieve their goals. Leadership is always about inspiring people to achieve their highest and best."

—John Ashcroft

✦

"I never quit trying. I never felt that I didn't have a chance to win."

—Arnold Palmer

"There are only two places in the league: first place and no place."
—Tom Seaver

✦

"He didn't have a whole lot of bad days."
—Chris Wheeler on Tug McGraw

✦

"When I was a senior at Christian High School in Grand Rapids, my religion teacher, Dr. Leonard Greenway, signed my yearbook: 'With talent and leadership potential for God's Kingdom.' I never considered myself a leader, but that little message registered with me as an 18-year-old and became my life's mission."
—Rich DeVos

✦

"His philosophy was that adversity is just another opportunity."
—John McLendon on James Naismith, inventor of basketball

✦

"When I was 42, I was Tom Brady's back-up quarterback with the New England Patriots. Tom was the best teammate I ever had. One game I made a suggestion about a pass pattern that might work. It did work, and we scored on the play. Tom ran right over to me on the bench and said, 'You called it. That's your touchdown.' That's how Tom was in those days. He always told the other guys what they did to make the play work out successfully. He was the ultimate teammate."
—Doug Flutie

✦

"Friendship takes a lot of effort if it's going to work."
—Bill Russell

✦

"Teamwork divides the tasks and multiplies the success."
—Theme for a technology convention in St. Petersburg, Florida, April 17, 2010

✦

"If it doesn't win football games, then don't do it."
—George Allen

"Do what I tell you, and do it to the best of your ability. No moaning, groaning, complaining, whining. No excuses. Just get it done. Play hard, have fun, be unselfish, take responsibility. Remember always, it's not about you."

—Geno Auriemma

✦

"You're my fullback."

—Paul Brown, Cleveland Browns' coach to rookie fullback, Jim Brown after a long run in the first pre-season game in 1957

✦

"Never measure the height of a mountain until you have reached the top; then you will see how low it was."

—Dag Hammarskjöld

✦

"Bear Bryant possessed a clear sense of the goal and never wavered from that. It was defined very clearly—win a national championship. We didn't think about winning the first game. We wanted to win the last game and the one before it and the one before it. We worked back from our overall goal. And roadblocks were not problems, but just obstacles to overcome. The goal was in front of us and the question was, 'How are you going to reach it?'"

—Jack Smalley

✦

"He was a great teacher, but you didn't know that you were being instructed."

—Jimmy Krapf on Bear Bryant

✦

"Say 'yes' as often as you can. Saying 'yes' begins things. Saying 'yes' is how things grow."

—Michael Hogan

5

Truth or Consequences—Character

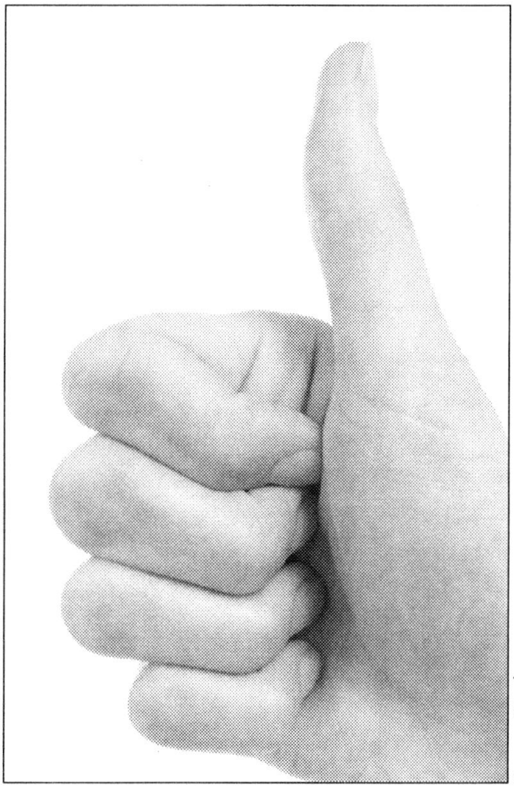

BananaStock

John Maxwell, best-selling author, on the subject of leadership, says, "You can only go as high on the leadership ladder as your character will allow."

Dallas Green, when managing the Philadelphia Phillies in the late 1970s, constantly clamored for "character people" on his team. "Given a choice of hiring a super talent with low character, or a person with above-average talent with high character, the wise executive chooses the latter. Honesty, integrity, responsibility, work ethic, courage, and perseverance characterize life's true winners," he said.

Take a character inventory as you consider these statements.

"He could act no part but his own. He copied no one, either in manner or style."
—Joshua Speed, Abraham Lincoln's friend

✦

"The only thing that walks back from the tomb with the mourners and refuses to be buried is the character of a man. What a man is survives him."
—J.R. Miller

✦

"Early on, I received a fine piece of advice about dealing with young people. It came from Dean Elizabeth Hamilton, speaking at a Miami University Chapel Program when I was a student. She said, 'The eternal verities will always prevail. Such things as truth, honesty, and good character will never change, no matter how people and times change.'"
—Paul Brown

✦

"Character is the single-most important asset of a president."
—David McCullough

✦

"Know who you are. Accept who you are. Be who you are."
—Charles Swindoll

✦

"Maybe I overuse the word 'character,' but I believe you win with 'character' players."
—Dick Vermeil

✦

"It's character, just character. He stands like a rock in memory now."
—Eric Sevareid on Harry S. Truman

✦

"Telling the truth is a skill. Those who don't do it habitually lose the ability."
—David Brooks

✦

"I have no pretense to absolute goodness, but if I have one virtue, it's honesty."
—Martin Luther King, Jr.

"The footsteps of a child are most likely to be the ones the parents thought they covered up."

—James Dobson

✦

"I pledge to show up in my life as myself, not as an imitation of anyone else."

—Maria Shriver

✦

"Please call me the founder."

—Lamar Hunt, correcting a Kansas City Chiefs' official who described him as the team's owner

✦

"He has the power of drawing the hearts of men toward him … He merely has to smile at you, and you trust him at once."

—Bernard Montgomery on Dwight D. Eisenhower

✦

"You cannot maintain your integrity 90 percent and be a leader. It's got to be 100 percent."

—Leonard Roberts

✦

"The word integrity means 'oneness.' A person's words, thoughts, and actions are one."

—John Maxwell

✦

"What did you come into the world with and how do you get the most out of it? Don't try to be what you can't be."

—Jim Ferrell, CEO of Ferrell Gas

✦

"The humble person has access to God's wisdom and God's favor."

—Pat Robertson

"After practice in 1992, when I was an assistant for the Olympic Dream Team, Michael Jordan said, 'Coach, I would like to do about a half an hour of individual work, and I was wondering if you could please work with me.' After the workout, Michael shook my hand and said, 'Thanks, Coach.' Michael Jordan had just called me 'Coach' and had said 'Please' and 'Thank you.' Everyone on Michael's team is treated with respect."

—Mike Krzyzewski

✦

"If you want to know the real secret of Walt's success, it's that he never tried to make money. He was always trying to make something that he would have fun with or be proud of."

—Ward Kimball, animator, on Walt Disney

✦

"Humility must always be the portion of any man who receives acclaim earned in the blood of his followers and sacrifices of his friends."

—Dwight D. Eisenhower

✦

"Thank you, prison."

—Aleksandr Solzhenitsyn, Russian intellectual, after being released from the horrible Siberian work camp where Joseph Stalin sent him.

✦

"Thomas Jefferson had the ability to understand what was going on in the minds of other people. That was his greatest strength as a leader."

—Charles Cerami

✦

"I wasn't sure then, but he seemed to get along with all the other players, and he seemed to take his work seriously. He was the kind you could have a lot of confidence in."

—Tim Mara on hiring Steven Owen as New York Giants' coach in 1932

✦

"The power of Mr. Lincoln is not his presence or his speech, but in the honest and gloriously refreshing sincerity of the man."

—Horace Greeley on Abraham Lincoln

The Face in the Glass

When you get what you want in your struggle for self,
And the world makes you king for a day,
Just go to the mirror and look at yourself
And see what that face has to say.
For it isn't your father or mother or wife
Whose judgment you must pass,
The person whose verdict counts the most in your life,
Is the one staring back from the glass.
Some people might think you're a straight-shooting chum,
And call you a great gal or guy,
But the face in the glass says you're only a bum,
If you can't look it straight in the eye.
That's the one you must please, never mind all the rest,
That's the one with you, clear to the end,
And you know you have passed your most dangerous test,
If the face in the glass is your friend.
You may fool the world down the pathway of years,
And get pats on the back as you pass,
But your final reward will be heartache and tears,
If you've cheated the face in the glass.

—Unknown

✦

"His honesty, integrity, and admiration for mankind."

—Mamie Eisenhower on why Ike should be remembered

✦

"He is too honest to make a penny outside his salary."

—Mary Lincoln on her husband, Abraham

✦

"Leadership means doing what's right, even when it's not easy."

—Joseph Lieberman

✦

"Do what's right; avoid what's wrong."

—Lou Holtz's guiding life philosophy

"I'm going to do what I think is right, and if people don't like me for it, that's just the way it is."

—George W. Bush

✦

"Put it this way: if you think you should not be doing it, don't."

—Emeka Okafor

✦

"My religious belief teaches me to feel as safe in battle as in bed. God knows the time for my death. I do not concern myself about that, but to be always ready, no matter where it may overtake me. That is the way all men should live, and then all would be equally brave."

—Stonewall Jackson

✦

"Frederick Douglass always had the courage to stand up for his beliefs—well, not always; once it took all his strength to sit for those beliefs. He was in a railroad car and was asked to leave because he was black. He wouldn't budge. Some white men tried to make him go. Douglass held on while they pulled the seat out of the floor of the car. He kept his seat."

—Joy Hakim

✦

Rosa Parks worked for the Montgomery Fair Department Store for $25.00/week as a tailor's assistant. On the Cleveland Avenue bus on December 1, 1955, the driver James Blake said, "You all make it light on yourselves and let me have those seats."

Three black patrons moved.

Blake to Parks: "Are you going to stand up?"

Parks: "No, I'm not."

Blake: "Well, if you don't stand up, I'm going to call the police and have you arrested."

Parks: "You may do that."

Two policemen came on the bus and arrested Rosa Parks.

✦

"Most forms of courage aren't especially visible. Most courage, in fact, is quiet. Often it is the refusal to do something, and such refusals may happen out of sight in private moments and hidden places."

—Frank Deford

"With self-discipline, most anything is possible."
—Theodore Roosevelt

✦

"If you don't want anyone to know it, don't do it."
—Dale Carnegie

✦

"Discipline is not the enemy of enthusiasm."
—Principal Joe Clark in the movie *Lean on Me*

✦

"In reading about the lives of great men, I found that the first victory they won was over themselves. Self-discipline with all of them came first."
—Harry S. Truman

✦

"The secret of discipline is motivation. When a man is sufficiently motivated, discipline will take care of itself."
—Sir Alexander Paterson

✦

"The tougher you are on yourself, the easier life will be on you."
—Zig Ziglar

✦

"Douglas Southall Freeman ends his four-volume work on Robert E. Lee with a touching scene. General Lee was wrinkled and gray and stooped over, very close to death, when a young mother came to see him with her infant cradled in her arms.

When Lee reached out for her baby, she responded by placing the infant in Lee's still-strong arms. The great general looked deeply into the child's eyes, and then slowly turned to the mother and said, 'Teach him he must deny himself.'"
—Charles Swindoll

✦

"It takes one kind of courage to face a duelist, but it's nothing like the courage it takes to tell a friend no."
—Harry S. Truman

"Life is mostly froth and bubble. Two things stand in stone. Kindness in another's trouble. Courage in your own."

—Unknown

✦

"Where do we get such men?"

—Ronald Reagan, quoting from James Michener's *The Bridges at Toko-Ri*

✦

"He was the best pro football coach ever, and one of the reasons was his extraordinary knowledge. I can't ever remember him being wrong."

—Gene Stallings on coach Tom Landry

✦

"Josiah was eight years old when he became king. He ruled for thirty-one years in Jerusalem. He behaved well before God. He kept straight on the path blazed by his ancestor David, not one step to the left or right."

—2 Chronicles 34:1-2 (The Message)

✦

"Most of all, in anything that has been accomplished through my life, it has been solely God's doing and not mine, and He, not me, must get the credit."

—Billy Graham

✦

"Character is the will to do what is right as defined by God, regardless of personal cost. It involves doing what's right because it's the right thing to do, and there is a standard that is permanent—an unwavering benchmark by which we can measure our choices."

—Andy Stanley

✦

"I'm most proud of being who I am and not who everybody thinks I should be."

—Ken Griffey, Jr.

✦

"Nixon doesn't always think that honesty is the best policy, but he does think that it's a policy."

—One of Richard Nixon's aides

"My dad is aware of who he is—a frail human being. He still thinks of himself as a farm boy from North Carolina."

—Ruth Graham, Billy Graham's youngest daughter

✦

"Children are facing temptations and pressures we never had to face. Instead of "Thou shalt not,' it is, 'Why Not?'"

—Ruth Graham

✦

No disobedience.
No dishonesty.
No disrespect.
No defiance.

—Jim Henry, *The Four Ds of Raising Children*

✦

"No earrings, no tattoos. My mom always told me and my brother that she's the only one in the house waking up in the morning and putting earrings in."

—Chris Paul

✦

"I know not what course others may take, but as for me, give me liberty or give me death."

—Patrick Henry

✦

"'Tis better to be alone than in bad company."

—George Washington

✦

"Fun. Papa was fun."

—Theodore Roosevelt's youngest son, Quinten, when asked by a White House journalist to describe the president in one word

✦

In 1942, Franklin D. Roosevelt wrote Winston Churchill: "It is fun to be in the same decade with you."

"He stuffed 20 pounds of life into a five-pound sack. His life was a charm bracelet of good times."

—Steve Rushin on Catfish Hunter

✦

"The crazy thing is that he's exactly who he says he is."

—Ryan Dobson on his father, James Dobson

✦

"I am real good being me."

—Pete Carroll

✦

"Do you want to know what's hip? Hip is being what you are. What's unhip is trying to be something you are not."

—Bill Gaither

✦

"The nicest compliment anybody ever pays us is when they meet us at a cocktail party and say, 'You're just like you are on TV.' That's really important. A lot of people in this industry are afraid to be themselves on camera."

—Matt Lauer

✦

"Celebrity is a mask that eats into the face."

—John Updike

✦

"He manages his team, he manages us, he manages reporters ... I've never seen anything like it in my life. The thing I like best about him is that he's so genuine. There's not a bit of phoniness there—no artifice."

—Andy MacPhail on Dusty Baker

✦

"Always be a first-rate version of yourself instead of a second-rate version of somebody else."

—Judy Garland

"You've got to be original because if you're like someone else, what do they need you for?"

—Bernadette Peters

✦

"With Reagan, what you saw is what you got."

—James Baker on Ronald Reagan

✦

"You know, you've made this day a special day by just being you. There's only one person in the whole world like you. And people can like you exactly as you are."

—Fred Rogers (Mister Rogers) closed his programs with these same words for more than 30 years

✦

"My dad doesn't have a public face and another face in private. He has the same face all the time, which means he's a real person."

—Ruth Graham, Billy Graham's daughter

✦

"It's not hard being a ballplayer—when you're a ballplayer."

—Honus Wagner

✦

"When you're on for two hours, five days a week, if you try to be something you are not, it will show through."

—Tom Brokaw

✦

"I marvel that she's the same whether talking to the President of the United States or to a homeless person on the street. She doesn't change. That's true authenticity."

—Stedman Graham on Oprah Winfrey

✦

"Billy Graham is the only one that God could really use because he is the only one who is truly humble enough."

—A friend of Billy Graham

"I've come to appreciate his quality. He's not two people; he's his own man. He is the same wherever you meet him."

—Robert Perm, a friend of Billy Graham

✦

"He's the same in private as he is publicly. There are not two Billy Grahams. He shows us it can be done."

—Greg Laurie on Billy Graham

✦

"The Billy Graham you see in public is the same Billy Graham you see at home. I have been around people in the public eye who turn into different people when the cameras turn off. That's not the case with my father."

—Franklin Graham

✦

"No one's perfect, and of all people I know he's not, but he's closer than anyone else I know, and by that I mean he really does live in congruence with the philosophy he espouses."

—Andy Hill on John Wooden

✦

"I attribute my success in life to this: I never gave or took an excuse."

—Florence Nightingale

✦

"You can fiddle with your income tax, you can have body odor, you can do anything; but if you cheat at golf, nobody wants you."

—Peter Alliss

✦

"In a satirical work published in 1873, Mark Twain and his next door neighbor, Charles Wagner, gave the era the name it deserved—*The Gilded Age*. 'What's the chief aim of man?' Twain once asked. 'To get rich. In what way? Dishonestly if we can, honestly if you must.'"

—James M. Perry

"What upsets me is not that you lied to me, but that from now on I can no longer believe you."

—Friedrich Nietzsche

✦

"Be honest with people. One lie can doom you."

—Whitey Herzog

✦

"Better to be poor and honest than a rich person no one can trust."

—Proverbs 19:1 (The Message)

✦

"I don't think Sandy ever told a lie in his life."

—Emil Joseph "Buzzie" Bavasi on what made Sandy Koufax different from everyone else

✦

"The problem with lying is that no one ever trusts your word again."

—Kathleen Parker

✦

"I have tried so hard to do right."

—Grover Cleveland on his deathbed in 1908

✦

"The man is incapable of telling an untruth."

—Art Modell on Wellington Mara

✦

"If ever there was an honest man on the face of the Earth, it was Abraham Lincoln."

—General Ambrose Burnside to his staff in 1862

✦

"Their life supports what their lips purport."

—Dr. Gil Peterson on leaders with integrity

"It's the only leadership I can offer, and it's the only type of leadership worth having."
—Tony Blair on honesty in leadership

✦

"A great president. He said exactly what he was going to do, and he did it."
—Harry S. Truman, paying tribute to James K. Polk by ranking him as one of the country's top eight presidents

✦

"The ultimate test of honesty came when a man said to me, 'You can shoot dice with me over the phone.'"
—Thomas "Hollywood" Henderson

✦

Upon the death of General Jeb Stuart on May 11, 1864, Robert E. Lee paid him the ultimate compliment for a cavalryman, when, in a shaken voice, he affirmed that Stuart "never brought me a piece of false information."

✦

"Because he is such an infernal liar."
—Ulysses S. Grant on why he favored the impeachment of Andrew Johnson

✦

"I will keep my word until the stones melt."
—Delshay of the Toronto Apaches, in a report to the U.S. Secretary of the Interior, 1871

✦

"Mother always told me if you tell a lie, always rehearse it. If it don't sound good to you, it won't sound good to no one else."
—Satchel Paige

✦

"I have long considered my ability to keep my word the chief gem of my character."
—Abraham Lincoln

"To be handcuffed by a lie is the worst of all imprisonments."

—Ravi Zacharias

✦

"Nice goes a long way in life and in politics."

—Bill O'Reilly

✦

"There is only one way to deal with Barbra Streisand; tell her the truth. If you don't tell the truth, you're going to have problems."

—Jule Styne, composer of *Funny Girl*

✦

"I know only one method of operation: to be as honest with others as I am with myself."

—Dwight D. Eisenhower

✦

"Honesty is the first chapter in the book of wisdom."

—Thomas Jefferson

✦

"He that loseth his honesty hath nothing else to lose."

—William Penn

✦

"I pray Heaven to bestow the best of blessings on this house and on all who shall hereafter inhabit it. May none but honest and wise men ever rule under this roof."

—John Adams, in his first days as president, to his wife Abigail; these words are carved in the State Dinning Room mantel in the White House

✦

"I'm trying to become more honest. If you can just get honest, maybe you can take that last breath without it catching in your throat."

—Hank McGraw, Tug's brother

"I may not be the smartest guy, but I know how to be honest."
—Tom Monaghan, former owner of Domino's

✦

"He was so honest with everyone. People always knew where he stood with him. They may not have liked it, but players and staff always respected that."
—David Shula on his dad Don Shula

✦

"You can't put yourself in the water unless you trust them and they trust you."
—Dawn Brancheau on the dangers of being a trainer of killer whales at Sea World

✦

"He always told the truth. He didn't lie to you."
—Cookie Rojas on manager Whitey Herzog

✦

"The role of the president, as far as I am concerned, is to stand up and tell the truth."
—George W. Bush

✦

"He was almost a monomaniac on the subject of honesty."
—Mary Lincoln on Abraham Lincoln

✦

"I always tell the truth the first time and do not need a good memory to remember that."
—Sam Rayburn

✦

"Sacrifice your life rather than your word."
—Stonewall Jackson

✦

"Unscrupulous people fake it a lot; honest people are sure of their steps."
—Proverbs 21:29 (The Message)

"Honesty was the linchpin of Orville Wright's moral universe."

—Mark Bernstein

✦

"He is so honest, he is slow to believe that others are not equally so."

—Joshua Speed, Abraham Lincoln's friend

✦

"I was always honest with my players. They knew they could talk to me at any time and I'd never lie to them. That built up the trust they had in me."

—Whitey Herzog

✦

On the morning of July 3, 1775, General George Washington first met his army on a muddy parade ground in Boston. He reviewed the troops, delivered a short speech, and read Psalm 101. Verse seven reads: "No one who practices deceit will dwell in my house; no one who speaks falsely will stand in my presence." (NIV)

✦

"Lying is not illegal. It is often wicked, usually immoral, and sometimes cowardly, but it is not against the law. Perjury—lying under oath—is illegal. Most of us can forgive wrong actions; it's lying about them that we find hard to accept."

—Joy Hakim

✦

Once the game is over, the king and the pawn go back in the same box.

—Italian proverb

✦

"I never felt as an artist that I was a good artist. I was never happy with anything I did as an artist."

—Walt Disney

✦

"Humility always has been a priority with God. Even today, it is a true sign of greatness."

—Tim LaHaye

"I'm more comfortable with people just calling me Wayne, not 'The Great One.' There've been a couple of stretches in my career where I probably could have been called 'The Good One' or 'The Mediocre One.'"

—Wayne Gretzky

✦

"Not every man can carry a full cup. Sudden elevation frequently leads to pride and fall. The most exacting test of all to survive is prosperity."

—Oswald Chambers

✦

"The measure of a man is the way he bears up under misfortune."

—Plutarch

✦

"Arrogance is a quality of tyrants, and humility is a quality of heroes."

—Jack Higgs

✦

"Though high in position, the humblest could approach him and feel at home in his presence."

—Frederick Douglass on Abraham Lincoln

✦

"Humility, properly placed, is the only sure foundation of leadership."

—Theodore Roosevelt

✦

"I define humility as understanding that God is God and you are not."

—Ray Pritchard

✦

"Pride lands you flat on your face; humility prepares you for honors."

—Proverbs 29:23 (The Message)

✦

"Life is a long lesson in humility."

—James M. Same

"If human pity could have rescued him from the sad part of his life, the glorious part that followed would have been lost."

—Paul E. Billheimer on St. Joseph

✦

"I believe that the first test of a truly great man is his humility. I do not mean by humility doubt of his own powers, but really great men have a curious feeling that the greatness is not in them but through them and they see something divine in every other man."

—John Ruskin

✦

"No one who knew George Washington well was surprised. Everyone else in varying degrees was astonished at the singular failure of the corruption of power at work. Indeed, it was a rare moment in history. In London, George III questioned American-born painter, Benjamin West, what Washington would do now that he had won the war.

'Oh,' said West. 'They say he will return to his farm.'

'If he does that,' said The King, 'he will be the greatest man in the world.'"

—Paul Johnson

✦

"He was the most humble man I've ever known. Sam never knew he had money, and he acted that way his whole life."

—David Glass on Sam Walton

✦

"Humility does not mean you think less of yourself. It means you think of yourself less."

—Ken Blanchard

✦

"A sense of humility is a quality I have observed in every leader I have deeply admired."

—Dwight D. Eisenhower

✦

"The integrity of the man."

—George C. Marshall on Harry S. Truman's strength

"The author, Jim Collins, has determined the two main ingredients of successful leaders are will and humility. Humility is the main thing God uses to qualify you to lead. Leaders can be made if they possess a humble spirit."

—Ken Blanchard

✦

"I'm not sure I ever figured out this celebrity business. Why in the world would I get an invitation to Elizabeth Taylor's wedding? I still can't believe it was news that I get my hair cut at the barbershop in Bentonville. Where else would I get it cut? Why do I drive a pick-up truck? What am I supposed to haul my dogs around in? A Rolls-Royce?"

—Sam Walton

✦

"To maintain your perspective, work hard on humility."

—Colin Powell

✦

"Humility is like underwear—you should have it, but don't let it show."

—Jim Henry

✦

"I'm just a regular guy as far as I'm concerned."

—Denzel Washington

✦

"Those whom the gods would destroy they first make proud."

—Ancient proverb

✦

"It's all right to be Goliath, but always act like David."

—Phil Knight

✦

"The elder President Bush praised Ronald Reagan's humility in his eulogy. In 1981, Reagan was recovering from the gunshot wound he received during an assassination attempt. Just days after the surgery that repaired his life-threatening injuries, his aides discovered him on his hands and knees in his hospital room wiping water from the floor. Bush said of Reagan, 'He was worried that his nurse would get in trouble.'"

—Charles Swindoll

"In 1949, I was the shortstop for the Boston Braves. We were in Pittsburgh one day at old Forbes Field. Our regular manager, Billy Southworth, was away from the team that day, and Johnny Cooney was the manager. Late in the game, he took me out for a pinch-hitter, and I went wild. I took my bat and started smashing a wheelbarrow in a little room behind the bench. Every time I hit that thing, it sounded like a shotgun going off. I really put on a scene. After the game, I was sitting in front of my locker, and Eddie Stanky, my teammate, sarcastically said, 'Babe Ruth! So, you're Babe Ruth? You're too good to be taken out for a pitch-hitter?' I wanted to punch Eddie's head off, but he taught me a great lesson in humility that day."

—Alvin Dark

✦

"On his way to a reception held in his honor, Ulysses S Grant got caught in a shower and offered to share his umbrella with a stranger walking in the same direction. The man said he was going to Grant's reception out of curiosity; he had never seen the general. 'I always thought that Grant was a much overrated man,' he said. 'That's my view also,' Grant replied."

—*The Little, Brown Book of Anecdotes*

✦

"To understand this story, you have to understand Sam Walton's personal lifestyle. Even though he was a billionaire many times over, you wouldn't know it if you met him on the street. He drove that old white pick-up truck, and he lived in a humble house in Bentonville that almost anyone with a job could have afforded. His home phone number was even published in the local phonebook. He was a common, self-made man who stubbornly refused to change his simple lifestyle throughout his life. Sam Walton ultimately died of bone cancer, but in those final weeks he continued to work in a weakened state, lying down in that hospital bed while he wrote notes with an anti-gravity pen on his clipboard. Imagine the influence of his behavior on all of the Wal-Mart employees. There is no way an associate would even think about calling off sick with a cold or a case of the sniffles when the company chairman was fighting cancer and continuing to provide leadership to the organization. The sight of him lying there in his office in the final days of his life continuing to work from a hospital bed is an inspirational image burned forever into my memory."

—Michael Bergdahl

✦

One day, President Lyndon B. Johnson was preparing to board a helicopter and he headed toward the wrong one. An aide pointed him in the right direction, saying, "This is your helicopter, Mr. President." President Johnson responded, "Son, they're all my helicopters."

"Though one of the most vilified American presidents, Abraham Lincoln remained sensitive to newspaper rejection. Critical journalists he saw as 'villainous reporters' who 'persistently garbled' his words, but 'commendation in newspapers,' he admitted in 1862, was 'all that a vain man could wish.' Lincoln was not a particularly vain man, but when he dressed for the last time before going to Ford's Theatre on April 14, 1865, he put in his pockets nine newspaper clippings he thought worthy of saving. Not surprisingly, several praised him lavishly."

—Harold Holzer

✦

"Leadership is not something automatically conferred by title or by rank. Leadership is influence. It is a matter of ability, not position. To state it simply, leadership is influence. The real leader is an example to follow."

—John MacArthur

✦

And men shall tell their children, Tho all other memories fade,
That they fought with Stonewall Jackson, In the old "Stonewall Brigade."

—Unknown

✦

"If you touch it anywhere, you set the whole thing trembling. As we move around this world, and as we act with kindness perhaps, or with indifference, or with hostility toward the people we meet, we too are setting the great spider web a-tremble. The life that I touch for good or ill will touch another life and that another until who knows where the trembling stops or in what far place and time my touch will be felt. Our lives are linked. No man is an island."

—Frederick Buechner, comparing the world to a great spider web

✦

"When I was 15 years old, I heard Martin Luther King, Jr. speaking over the radio. It was as if he were addressing me directly, and I thought, 'John Lewis, you can do it!' I was so inspired by Dr. King I knew I couldn't sit on the sidelines. I started working with Dr. King when I was 19."

—John Lewis

✦

"Leadership rises or falls to the level of the leader's integrity."

—John Maxwell

"One day, when Mahatma Gandhi was on a train pulling out of the station, a European reporter running alongside his compartment asked him, 'Do you have a message I can take back to my people?" It was a day of silence for Gandhi, part of his regular practice, so he didn't reply. Instead, he scribbled a few words on a piece of paper and passed it to the journalist: "My life is my message."

—Lance Secretan

✦

"Choose integrity over popularity and you will always be cool."

—Carlos Santana

✦

"If you have integrity, nothing else matters. If you don't have integrity, nothing else matters."

—Alan Simpson

✦

"I look for three things: The first is personal integrity; the second is intelligence; and the third is a high energy level, but if you don't have the first, the second two don't matter."

—Warren Buffett on hiring decisions

✦

"If you ask my fellow coaches, I always followed the NCAA rules. I never cheated. I've never done anything illegal or unethical because I wouldn't get any pleasure out of winning if I did that. I guess I'll be remembered as an honest guy who worked hard."

—Charles "Lefty" Driesell

✦

"His whole career in one sentence? Integrity. Through the ups and downs, he never wanted to sacrifice that for another win or two."

—Jay Paterno on his father, Joe

✦

Colonel Harland Sanders, who founded the restaurant chain that became the Kentucky Fried Chicken empire, served as its public spokesperson for years after he'd sold the company. In the process, he became familiar to people around the world. When he was once asked about what it was like to have one of the best-known faces in the world, he replied, "You don't mind being known if you're behaving yourself."

"You are born with three things: intelligence, endurance, and the opportunity to build integrity. You decide how much intelligence and endurance you are going to use. You build integrity every single day with the choices you make."

—Bob Kerry

✦

"In 2005, integrity was the most sought-after definition in Merriam-Webster's online dictionary. Of all the entries in the dictionary, people wanted to know the definition of integrity more than any other word. The phenomenon seems to reflect a strong interest in integrity, as well as significant confusion about its meaning."

—*Outreach* (March/April 2006)

✦

"Integrity. Integrity."

—Rosemary Kerry's last words to her son, Senator John Kerry

✦

"Individual integrity also makes group integrity, and this is essential to a company. It is the guidance and control system that directs company performance."

—Henry Ford II

✦

"We have not passed that subtle line between childhood and adulthood until we move from the passive voice to the active voice—that is, until we have stopped saying, 'It got lost,' and say, 'I lost it.'"

—Sydney Harris

✦

"He who walks with integrity walks securely."

—Proverbs 10:9 (NKJV)

✦

George Washington refused to appoint "any person in whose integrity he had not confidence."

✦

"God can't stand deceivers, but oh how he relishes integrity."

—Proverbs 11:20 (The Message)

"I would walk a million miles with someone who had job performance problems, but wouldn't take the first step with someone with an integrity problem."

—Sam Walton

✦

"I have known him from 1779, and I can say, conscientiously, that I do not know in the world a man of purer integrity."

—Thomas Jefferson on James Madison

✦

"As I look over Ronald Reagan's years in the public limelight, I think the secret of his success is his enormous personal integrity."

—Charles Z. Wick

✦

"There are a lot of things in life over which we have no control; however integrity is one area over which each of us has 100-percent control."

—Elizabeth Dole

✦

"The sign of a great man is that the closer you get, the greater he seems."

—Chofetz Chaim

✦

"It takes 20 years to build a reputation and five minutes to ruin it. If you think about that, you'll do things differently."

—Warren Buffet

✦

"It was the integrity of the man that would stand down the ages more even than the courage of his decisions."

—George C. Marshall on Harry S. Truman

✦

"Glass, china, and reputation are easily cracked and never mend well."

—Benjamin Franklin

"Integrity implies a reasonable consistence between beliefs and actions."

—Dennis Bakke

✦

"He had an iron discipline between the foul lines and none outside it."

—Roger Kahn on Pete Rose

✦

"Integrity is a combination of the words, *integritas* and *integer*. It refers to this putting on of armor, of building a completeness, a wholeness, a wholeness of character. How appropriate that the word integrity is a derivative of two words describing the character of a member of the profession of arms."

—John DiFrances

✦

"Character!"

—J.P. Morgan, financier, when once asked what he thought was the best bank collateral

✦

"When you combine your public life with your private life, you start living a life of integrity."

—Les Steckel

✦

"Integrity is what we do, what we say, and what we say we do."

—Don Galer

✦

"Live a life of integrity even if it means getting fired."

—Sallie Krawcheck

✦

"Integrity says you keep your word. You do as you say you will do. If you fail at that, your integrity acknowledges the failure and you make it right. Without it, you drift into compromise. With it, you stand in confidence. Integrity helps us stand fast."

—Charles Swindoll

"If you walk the walk you actually become the walk."
—Paul Dietzel

✦

"Once you lose your integrity, you can never get it back."
—Tommy B. Franks

✦

"Integrity is being true to your God-given values at all times."
—Richard Exley

✦

"Integrity has no sliding scale. You either have it or you don't."
—Rosemarie Grego

✦

"Integrity was very important. He worshipped at the throne of integrity."
—A Focus on the Family associate of James Dobson

✦

"Having integrity means more to us than simply the absence of deception. It means we are completely forthright in all our dealings. We say what needs to be said, not simply what people want to hear."
—Scott Cook

✦

"Character is what you are deep down inside you. Reputation is what other people think you are. When your character and your reputation are the same, you are a person of integrity."
—Harry Piland

✦

"I try not to do anything that my father would not be proud of."
—Bill Russell

✦

"Integrity is honesty with a little oomph."
—Pat Williams' son Michael at age 19

"Integrity and firmness is all I can promise. These never shall forsake me, although I may be deserted by all men."

—George Washington at the start of his presidency

✦

"You can be successful and be honest. You can be successful and be ethical. You can be successful and keep your values. In other words, you can be successful and stand for what's right."

—J.C. Watts

✦

"My dad was a man of integrity. His toes always pointed in the same direction as his tongue. In other words, he walked his talk."

—Pat Croce

✦

"You'll never ever find that even the liberal media has been able to find Jim in a lie."

—H.B. London, friend of James Dobson

✦

"Monroe was so honest that if you turned his soul inside out, there would not be a spot on it."

—Thomas Jefferson on James Monroe

✦

"His honesty, integrity, and admiration for mankind."

—Mamie Eisenhower, long after Ike's death and shortly before hers, when asked what she'd like people to remember about Ike

✦

"Integrity is honesty in action. You cannot be a leader of some integrity. It's like being pregnant—you either are, or you are not."

—Blythe McGarvie

✦

"To be a successful coach, you must have intelligence, passion, and integrity. You can't top that trio."

—Ron Wolf

"Integrity conveys a sense of wholeness that can be found in the serenity of a person who is confident in the knowledge that he or she is living right. Integrity requires three essential steps:

- Discerning what is right and what is wrong.
- Acting on what you have discerned, even at a personal cost (a person of integrity is steadfast and keeps commitments.)
- Saying openly that you are acting on your understanding of right from wrong. This person is unashamed of doing the right thing."

—Stephen Carter

✦

To remind myself of my responsibility to live without wax, with sincerity and integrity, I took the liberty of rewriting Edgar A. Guest's poem, *Sermons We See*, to apply to setting an example as a real winner for my children and grandchildren:

I'd rather watch a winner, than hear one, any day.
I'd rather have one walk with me, than merely show the way.
The eye's a better pupil and more willing than the ear.
Fine counsel is confusing, but example's always clear.
The best of all the coaches are the ones who live their deeds.
For, to see the truth in action, is what everybody needs.
I can soon learn how to do it, if you'll let me see it done.
I can watch your hand in action, but your tongue too fast may run.
I'd rather see a sermon than hear one any day.
I'd rather one should walk with me than merely show the way.
Fine counsel is important, but example's always clear.
The best of all the preachers are the men who live their creeds.
For to see the good in action is what everybody needs,
I can soon learn how to do it if you'll let me see it done.
I can watch your hands in action, though your tongue too fast may run.
And the lectures you deliver may be very wise and true,
But I'd rather learn my lesson by observing what you do.
For I may misunderstand you and the fine advice your give,
But there's no misunderstanding how you act and how you live.

—Pat Williams

✦

"The foundation of leadership is character, not charisma."

—Rick Warren

"I am not the Catholic candidate for president, but the Democratic Party's candidate for president who happens to be a Catholic."

—John F. Kennedy

✦

"Most good leaders have a problem with pride. They have to battle it all the time to prevent having a big head."

—John Adams, Sunday school teacher

✦

"The greatest crisis in America today is a crisis of leadership, and it is rooted in a crisis of courage and a crisis of convictions."

—John Perkins

✦

"A leader does not have the luxury of self-pity. He must be the first believer."

—Vince Lombardi

✦

"If all goes right, dozens of people will claim the credit, but if it goes wrong, you'll be the only one to blame."

—Kay Sommersby, Dwight D. Eisenhower's driver and confidant, on the eve of D-Day

✦

"When in command, I take charge."

—Norman Schwarzkopf

✦

Sister Teresa Marie at the high school Johnny Unitas attended in Western Pennsylvania was the first person to read inspiration into his last name. When they met she remarked, "Unite us. You must be a leader."

✦

"Leaders cannot rise above the limitation of their character."

—John Maxwell

"Love and truth form a good leader; sound leadership is founded on loving integrity."
—Proverbs 20:28 (The Message)

✦

"Tom Landry led by example. He did what was right, even though it wasn't always popular. He never threw you a curve ball. He walked the talk."
—Mike Ditka

✦

"The keys to leadership are simple:
- Take care of the troops;
- Keep your mouth shut and do your job, every day;
- Don't worry about your next job."

—Colin Powell

✦

"What made Johnny Unitas the greatest quarterback of all time was not his arm or his size. I've always said the purest definition of leadership was watching Johnny Unitas get off the team bus when the Colts were on the road."
—Ernie Accorsi

✦

"To be an effective leader, check your ego at the door. You can reclaim it later."
—Alan Axelrod

✦

"No man will make a great leader who wants to do it all himself or get all the credit for doing it."
—Andrew Carnegie

✦

Reginald Jones, longtime CEO of GE, died at his Greenwich, Connecticut, home on December 30, 2003 at the age of 86. His wife, Grace, wrote down his final words as he whispered, "Leadership requires ethics, morals, and values." He smiled at Grace and took his final breath, and he was gone.

✦

"Leadership means you lose your right to be selfish."
—John Maxwell

"One summer, as a teenager, I played baseball for an American Legion team. We were in a tournament down in the bootheel of Missouri and stopped at a restaurant. We had a couple of black players on the team, and the restaurant refused to serve them. I stood up and said, 'Let's get out of here.' Everyone followed me out the door."

—Bill Bradley

✦

"Credit-hogging doesn't lead to healthy team dynamics. Credit-hogging is the beginning of the end for the leader. God opposes the proud, but loves the humble."

—Bill Hybels

✦

"Should my success be less than I desire and expect, the least I can say is the fault is not with you."

—Ulysses S. Grant in a letter to Abraham Lincoln (spring of 1864)

✦

"Henry has some sort of magnet. He could draw people to him; that was the funny thing about him."

—A contemporary of Henry Ford

✦

"I spent 16 years with Tom Landry. He was a great role model because he didn't just talk the talk. He always walked the walk and lived out his Christian faith."

—Dan Reeves

✦

"After Dwight Eisenhower's death in 1969, cartoonist Bill Mauldin drew a U.S. military cemetery with hundreds of crosses and Stars of David sketched in the background. In the foreground were the simple words, 'It's Ike himself. Pass the word!' That tribute spoke volumes—about leadership, about greatness, and about West Point's most distinguished graduate."

—Daniel Christman

✦

"He was a good one. To know Ray is to love him. He was a great guy, a great man. You wouldn't know Ray had fifteen-cents if you were around him all the time."

—Emil Joseph "Buzzie" Bavasi on Ray Kroc

"Reggie White. What else can you say? He is, by far, the best leader and the best defensive player I've ever played with. He is the ultimate leader. I've never been big on getting up and talking at player meetings, as you know, but Reggie was the master of it. He would be rolling along and telling us what we should and shouldn't do, and he'd look at me every so often and say, 'Isn't that right, Brett?' I'd say, 'Sure is, Reggie.' What else am I going to say? It's Reggie White. Like I'm going to argue with him."

—Brett Favre

✦

"Only a leader with strong character and a strong sense of security can feel so certain of the blamelessness of his heart that he invites the scrutiny of his peers. C.S. Lewis called this quality, 'Leaders with chests.' Lewis likened the properly ordered soul to the human body; the head (reason) must rule the belly (the sensual appetite) through the chest (character and spirit). The chest is the indispensable liaison between reason and the appetites. Without a strong 'chest,' men would succumb to excuses, relativism, and compromise. Lewis called those with no character or integrity, 'men without chests.'"

—John Maxwell

✦

"The supreme quality for leadership is, unquestionably, integrity. Without it no real success is possible no matter whether it's on a football field, in an army, or in an office."

—Dwight D. Eisenhower

✦

"Loyalty is the vital virtue."

—Rudy Giuliani

✦

"They were old enough to know the difference between right and wrong."

—Eddie Collins on his teammates on the 1919 Black Sox

✦

"Achingly painful, too, for the aging president were the personal denunciations of him. Newspapers, he complained, attacked him in indecent terms as could scarcely be applied to a Nero, a notorious defaulter, or even to a common pickpocket. Every manner of malicious falsehood had been invented to 'wound my reputation and feelings.'"

—James MacGregor Burns on George Washington

"When I'm upset, I wait."
—Mother Teresa

✦

"He never acted like a general or a president. He always acted like just another person."
—Robert Balfour, former aide to Dwight D. Eisenhower

✦

"There aren't two Billy Grahams. The man you see in a huge stadium is the same one you'd see one-on-one on his front porch. He is a truly humble man whose motto has been, 'Suit up, show up, and let God do the rest.' Faithfulness is the centerpiece of Mr. Graham's ministry."
—Larry Ross

✦

"As early as 1777, an anonymous writer in the *Pennsylvania Journal* had responded to an attack on the general: "If there are spots on his character, they are like the spots in the sun, only discernible by the magnifying powers of a telescope. Had he lived in the days of idolatry, he would have been worshipped like a God."
—Stanley Weintraub on George Washington

✦

When Don Moser, an employee of Michelin Tires, met the company's founder, Francois Michelin, he said, "It's nice working for you." Mr. Michelin replied, "And me for you."

✦

"You never know who is watching you and the imprint you are having on their life. In 1985, I was a lowly assistant at LaSalle under head coach Speedy Morris. We were playing North Carolina at the Palestra that year, and before the game Dean Smith comes over to our bench, shakes our hands, and says to me 'Fran, have a good game.' My immediate thought was 'How did he know my name?' Well, obviously, he went through the LaSalle press guide and learned all our names."
—Fran Dunphy

✦

A London reporter told an executive committee member of the Billy Graham Evangelistic Association: "We have searched for any trash we can find in Billy Graham's life to do a big expose. We can't find a thing so we just gave up digging."

"Not many years ago, Daddy placed a call to one of my sister Gigi's friends whom he had met previously. Getting the friend on the line, my father began the conversation this way: 'Hello. This is Billy Graham. Do you remember me?' I love that anecdote. It illustrates who my father really is—a man who doesn't think of himself as any more important than the next person. Not that he is naive about his influence in the world. He simply doesn't presume others know him or think he's exceptional."

—Ruth Graham, Billy Graham's daughter

✦

"I don't have to prove to anybody that I can work 16-hour days if I can get it done in eight. I have no food preference and no drink preference. A cheeseburger will be fine. I like Holiday Inns."

—Colin Powell on his no-frills approach as Secretary of State

✦

"There is no one in the world quite like you. Don't water your own wine."

—Red Barber's advice to a young Vin Scully

✦

"The human tongue has done more damage and caused more heartaches than any other source of trouble. What we say cuts far deeper than any knife or sword. I had a physician tell me not to be hesitant about calling the tongue the strongest muscle in the body. 'Anatomically, it's true,' he said. 'The muscle makeup of the tongue would qualify it as certainly one of the strongest if not the strongest muscle in the human body.'"

—Charles Swindoll

✦

"Six days after the D-Day invasion, George Marshall traveled to Europe to visit his troops and inspect the massive army that he had, as Winston Churchill said, 'called into being.' During a private moment with Dwight Eisenhower, Marshall asked his protégé a candid question: 'Eisenhower, you've chosen all these commanders or accepted those we sent from Washington. What's the principal quality you look for?' Without a moment of hesitation, Eisenhower responded, 'Selflessness.' Upon reflection, Eisenhower later admitted that Marshall 'himself gave me that idea.'"

—Jack Uldrich

✦

"Our kids need heroes. Our kids need somebody to look up to, and y'all are it."

—Reba McEntire

"Respect your teammates. Respect your coaches. Respect yourself. Respect your family's name."

—Doc Rivers on his respect rules

✦

"Like my grandfather used to say, 'The only thing we really owe each other is mutual respect.' Pretty simple, isn't it?"

—Vida Blue

✦

"He was first in war, first in peace, and first in the hearts of his countrymen."

—Congressman Henry Lee speaking at George Washington's funeral service in Philadelphia

✦

On June 6, 1944, after General Dwight D. Eisenhower watched the first convoy of troops getting ready to depart for Normandy, he scratched out a little note to himself about what he'd say if the invasion failed: "Our landings have failed ... the troops, the air, and the Navy did all that bravery and devotion to duty could do. If any blame or fault attaches to the attempt, it is mine alone."

✦

"Boys, if you ever pray, pray for me, now. When they told me yesterday what had happened, I felt like the moon, stars, and all the planets had fallen on me."

—Harry S. Truman to the press, after becoming president

✦

"I would think I would have a good chance to get a job anywhere if it weren't for an hour-and-a-half of my life."

—Mike Price, former Alabama coach, on wanting to coach college football again

✦

"Dr. King believed our Civil Rights efforts had to be a team effort if we were going to be successful. He stressed that we had to work together. He was the least egotistical member of the team. He always submerged himself in order to relate to others. He gave away all his speech money and his Nobel Prize winnings."

—Andrew Young on Martin Luther King's leadership skills

"I used to visit Ronnie in the Oval Office almost every week. Whenever he would go out to Camp David, he would collect sacks of acorns and bring them back to the White House. Right outside the Oval Office is a veranda. Ronnie would sprinkle the acorns out there for the squirrels. There were glass doors leading outside, and sometimes you'd hear this noise and it would be a squirrel scratching at the door. While Ronnie would keep talking, he'd reach into his desk and grab some more acorns, go over and open the door, and throw them out into the veranda for the squirrels."

—A.C. Lyles, producer and longtime friend of Ronald Reagan

✦

"Because there is no fourth class."

—Albert Schweitzer when once asked why he traveled third class wherever he went

✦

"Your conversation is your personal advertisement, for every time you open your mouth you allow others to look into your mind."

—John Schuerholz

✦

"Of all the men I ever met, he seemed to possess more of the elements of greatness, combined with goodness, than any other."

—William T. Sherman on Abraham Lincoln

✦

"If you are to succeed in Washington DC—or in life—your word must be your bond."

—Elizabeth Dole

✦

"Trust is the lubrication that makes it possible for organizations to work."

—Warren Bennis

✦

"You are your record."

—Bill Parcells

✦

"He was more fun than a goat."

—John Hay on Theodore Roosevelt

"To be persuasive, we must be believable. To be believable, we must be credible. To be credible, we must be truthful."

—Edward R. Murrow

✦

"His cardinal mistake is that he isolates himself and allows nobody to see him, and by which he doesn't know what is going on in the very matter he's dealing with."

—Abraham Lincoln wrote General David Hunter about General John C. Fremont

✦

"I knew wherever I was that you thought of me, and if I got in a tight place you would come if alive."

—William T. Sherman's famous tribute to Ulysses S. Grant after the Battle of Shiloh

✦

"Unless you have ruthless integrity, you can't really lead."

—Mark Eppler

✦

"When you played for Don Shula of the Dolphins, you knew he was in charge."

—Kevin Reilly

✦

"We have a lot of millionaires in our company, but they better not act like millionaires or they won't be here!"

—Ray Kroc

✦

"Thank you, Mr. Robinson … Character."

—Billboard at the Chicago Marathon about Jackie Robinson

✦

"As we say in the infantry, this is a guy you take on a long patrol."

—Colin Powell on being a soldier of honesty and integrity

✦

"I remembered how my father listened with rare empathy to everyone."

—Joseph P. Kennedy II on his father, Robert F. Kennedy

"I want you to say that I tried to love and serve humanity."

—Martin Luther King, Jr. on how he'd like to be remembered

✦

"He was always doing something for someone else."

—Jackie Robinson when Branch Rickey died

✦

"That I'd made some contributions to my country, to those who are less well off."

—Robert F. Kennedy when asked by David Frost how he would like to be remembered

✦

"Character counts in the presidency more than any other single quality."

—David McCullough

✦

"We all know about Honest Abe, but keep in mind that it was also Honest George Washington. You can rummage around in his closet all day, and you won't find any skeletons."

—David A. Clary

✦

"Character is the basis of genuine leadership."

—Fred Smith, Sr.

✦

"A strict disciplinarian, the mother of George H.W. Bush had established rules that guided her son's life:

- 'Don't walk ahead'
- 'Don't use I'
- 'Don't be a braggadocio'
- 'How did the team do?'"

—Timothy Naftali

✦

"Courage is contagious. If a leader shows courage, others get the idea."

—David McCullough

"I neither can nor will make any retraction since it is neither safe nor honorable to act against conscience. Here I stand. I can do no other. God help me. Amen."

—Martin Luther (April 1521) before a German court in Worms

✦

"Leadership is always about character."

—Warren Bennis and Robert Thomas

✦

"Your words matter. Everything you say is on the record."

—Rick Warren

✦

"I'm just who I am. What you see in front of you, that's what you get."

—Tiger Woods

✦

"He is the truest friend. He has the farthest vision. He is the greatest man I've ever known."

—Winston Churchill on Franklin D. Roosevelt just before the end of World War II

✦

"John Winthrop, the leader of the Puritans who settled in Boston, described their mission in a famous sermon: 'We shall be as a city upon a hill. The eyes of all people are upon us.'"

—Noah D. Oppenheim

✦

"That they talk straight to the American people and don't lie (you will get found out). Be a leader of honor and possess a certain vision. Have a sense of what's important 30 years from now and what's essential down the road."

—Douglas Brinkley, historian, on what Americans want in their presidents

✦

"They were looking for someone who wouldn't flinch, and that was me."

—Paul Tibbetts on why he was selected to pilot the B-29 Enola Gay to drop the atomic bomb on Hiroshima

"Your companions are like buttons on an elevator; they will either take you up or they will take you down."

—Sign in the hallway at Andrews Academy, Michigan

✦

"I have been your faithful servant, so far as it lay within me to be. I have endured."

—George Washington after the Revolutionary War

✦

"I'm a Ford, not a Lincoln."

—Gerald R. Ford on humility

✦

"The first key to greatness is to be, in reality, what we appear to be."

—Socrates

✦

"I suppose you know Abraham Lincoln is my hero. He was a man of the people who always felt with and for the people, but who had not the slightest touch of the demagogue in him."

—Theodore Roosevelt wrote to John Hay

✦

"I shall endeavor to do my work honestly. Honesty and decency and administrative efficiency are the prime requisites for a legislator."

—Theodore Roosevelt at the start of his political career

✦

"An actor knows two important things—to be honest in what he's doing and to be in touch with the audience. That's not bad advice for politicians, either."

—Ronald Reagan

✦

"Tony's a guy who recruits by character ... hires coaches who have character. When he leaves a city, the city's better after he left it then when he came. I believe the tongue in his mouth and the tongue in his shoes always go on the same direction. He walks the walk and he talks the talk. He's the real deal."

—Ken Whitten on Tony Dungy

"You can't erase character problems."

—Gerald R. Ford

✦

"I hope history remembers me that I was a dedicated, hard-working, honest person who served constructively in Congress and in the White House."

—Gerald R. Ford

✦

"Billy, I can trust you, and you can trust me."

—Abraham Lincoln to his new partner William Herndon in 1844

✦

"You show me loyalty, and I will watch your back forever."

—Tommy Lasorda

✦

"People who cheat cannot get away with it. It may take some time but eventually they will be caught."

—Marion Jones

✦

"There's only one way to develop trust. You need to experience it, need to see it, and need to live it."

—Urban Meyer

✦

"No matter what happens, sooner or later character in leadership is revealed."

—David Rothkopf

✦

"Joe treated everybody with respect whether you're a batboy, coach, or trainer. He does everything the right way."

—Larry Bowa on Joe Torre

✦

"He was a minority with a majority vision."

—Jesse Jackson on Martin Luther King, Jr.

"Lord, help me be a simple man in a complex world."
—Clint Hurdle

✦

"My mother's optimism ran as deep as the cosmos."
—Ronald Reagan

✦

"George Armstrong Custer was an American hero to me and thousands of other kids who read, watched, and, therefore, bought into the stories we were told. The fact that a closer examination of Custer reduces his valor to a series of broken treaties and promises is beside the point. The relevance here is that Custer was outmaneuvered and killed by the Sioux at the Battle of Little Big Horn.

"Custer had been warned by the Sioux many times. After his death, he was found with blood coming out of each ear. It was clarified later that the Indians punctured both ear drums so that he would be able to listen better in the next life."
—Keith Glass

✦

"I've known Tony for a decade, and he never talks about himself or his accomplishments. He's always giving credit to others."
—Mark Merrill, Tony Dungy's friend

✦

"Lincoln is the rare person who improves the closer he is scrutinized."
—An Abraham Lincoln presenter

✦

"All great leaders are humble. Instead of talking about their accomplishments, leaders are looking to give the team the credit."
—John Maxwell

✦

"He's a world-class listener … the best one-on-one man I have ever met."
—Frank Gifford on Pete Rozelle

✦

"If you add to the truth, you subtract from it."
—The Talmud

"Unlike a lot of politicians I've met, Bobby didn't look over your head when you talked to him. He truly listened to people."

—Frank Gifford on Bobby Kennedy

✦

"People edged their chairs to the radio. There is a man leaning across his desk, speaking clearly and cordially, so that you and I will completely understand."

—John Dos Passos on Franklin Delano Roosevelt

✦

"He may not be much of a debater, but with a prepared text he's the best speaker I've ever seen. I'm beginning to think that, in this respect, he dwarfs both Roosevelt and Kennedy."

—Tip O'Neill, House Speaker, on Ronald Reagan's eloquence

✦

"He had enthusiasm, that optimism, that capacity for empathy that made so many ordinary people love this rich man and stick with him."

—Columnist Richard Cohen on Franklin D. Roosevelt

✦

"If you hang out with a group of people in a certain place, you're bound to end up doing the things they do."

—Josh Hamilton

✦

"If you're doing the right things, it doesn't matter how bright the lights are. If you're doing the wrong thing, it only takes a flashlight."

—Tyrone Willingham

✦

"If the foundations are destroyed, what can the righteous do?"

—Psalm 11:3 (NKJV)

✦

"Integrity means total congruence between who we are and what we do."

—Kevin Cashman

"On meeting Tony, I was reminded that most of the great people are nice to be with because they don't have anything to prove."

—Paul McCartney on Tony Bennett

✦

"The quality I most admire in my grandfather is his humility. More than any person I know, he has more reason to not be humble with all his accomplishments, but 'Daddy Bill' views himself as just a country preacher from Charlotte, North Carolina."

—Tullian Tchividjian, Billy Graham's grandson

✦

"Anybody who runs for public office today has got to know his or her life will be an open book. I've decided that if you want to run for public office, you have to decide at the age of five and live your life accordingly."

—Helen Thomas

✦

"He was a great man and also a good man, and that is a rare combination in history."

—John Kaminski on George Washington

✦

"Press Maravich lacked any talent for duplicity."

—Mark Kriegel

✦

"My nature is honest and free from guile."

—George Washington

✦

"Brooks Robinson never asked anyone to name a candy bar after him. In Baltimore, people name their children after him."

—Gordon Beard

✦

"Good moral character is the first essential in a man."

—George Washington

"Rules cannot take the place of character."

—Alan Greenspan

✦

"He is brutally honest with you all the time. You always know where you stand with him because he doesn't sugar-coat things or con you."

—J.J. Reddick on Coach Mike Krzyzewski at Duke

✦

"He has remained true to himself despite his success and fame. The Rick Warren you see on television is the same man who lives next door. I've known him for 17 years, and he hasn't changed yet."

—Robyn Henk on Rick Warren

✦

"I can meet your friends without even meeting you and tell you what kind of person you are."

—Ed Young, Jr.

✦

"You are the country to these men. They have fought for you."

—Henry Wise to General Robert E. Lee on the morning of Lee's surrender

✦

"The supreme quality for leadership is, unquestionably, integrity. Without it no real success is possible."

—Dwight D. Eisenhower

✦

"When he rides by, the boys never cheer him, but pull off their hats and worship."

—A Confederate soldier on General Robert E. Lee

✦

"A kindly, just, and beloved officer, wise in counsel, resolute in action, courageous unto death. Seriously wounded, he refused to relinquish his command until, mortally wounded, he fell leading his comrades to victory. His last words were, 'Take care of my men.'"

—Major Murray Davis statue in Kansas City

"The goal of any man or woman who would be President of the United States must be to emulate the very first president, both as a manager and a symbol."

—Alan Axelrod

✦

"None of them believed they were irreplaceable. They were constantly looking for others who were younger to train and empower. These great leaders felt that nothing they had was theirs; it was all a gift."

—David P. Zanotti, president of the American Policy Roundtable, on the common traits of America's greatest leaders

✦

"George Washington possessed the gift of silence. This I esteem as one of the most precious talents."

—John Adams

✦

"George Washington understood that when it was not necessary to speak, it was necessary not to speak. Washington adopted a strategy for keeping his mouth shut."

—Richard Brookhiser

✦

"He was a man who was willing to listen to what players had to say."

—Frank Gifford on Vince Lombardi

✦

Calvin Coolidge was once described as "an eloquent listener who could be silent in five languages."

✦

"He really listens to you when you disagree, and I mean *really listens*."

—An advisor on Barack Obama

✦

"Modesty marks every line and feature of his face."

—Abigail Adams on George Washington

"His character was, in its mass, perfect."
—Thomas Jefferson on George Washington

✦

"I tried never to forget who I was and where I'd come from and where I was going back to."
—Harry S. Truman

✦

"It is unhealthy to marinate in your own press clippings."
—Sam Walton

✦

"The President of the United States hears a hundred voices telling him he is the greatest man in the world. He must listen carefully to hear the one voice that tells him he's not."
—Harry S. Truman

✦

"Humility invites people to your side; they want to help you—something every manager from CEO to night-shift supervisor needs."
—John Baldoni

✦

"Biblical humility is simply saying, 'God, I need you.' You don't just say it once. You say it every day."
—Lance Pitman

✦

"We are all guilty. We ought to plead guilty and not to exculpate ourselves by throwing the blame on others."
—William Wilberforce on Great Britain's slave trade

✦

"He was not liked by people because he did not like people."
—Bryce Harlow, close associate of Richard Nixon

✦

"Be swift to hear, slow to speak, slow to wrath."
—James 1:19 (NKJV)

"He's the greatest listener in history. He derives what he needs to know by listening, then he puts it into action."

—Michael Lombardi on Bill Belichick

✦

"It's easy to talk to him. He can listen."

—Russian President Dmitri Medvedev on Barack Obama

✦

"The absence of arrogance."

—Katharine Graham when asked what is the most important leadership quality

✦

"I stopped putting God first. I put Him in the middle of my life."

—Larry Osborne

✦

"Leadership is always about character."

—Warren Bennis

✦

"A great teammate."

—The first line on Mickey Mantle's plaque at Yankee Stadium

✦

"A story about FDR comes to mind: crowded, grieving masses surged along Constitution Avenue in April 1945, waiting for his funeral cortege to pass by. As his hearse neared, a well-dressed, middle-aged man standing in the throng fell to his knees, sobbing desperately, until finally regaining his composure. A stranger by his side asked, 'Did you know the president?' The man could barely reply, 'No, but he knew me.'"

—Warren Bennis

✦

"He was an excellent horseman at West Point, setting a jump record that stood for 25 years. Whenever he was reminded of the feat, Grant would invariably smile and defer to his mount: 'York was a wonderful horse.'"

—Jean Edward Smith on Ulysses S. Grant

"If I told him this week, 'Walter Cronkite died,' he'd laugh and say, 'Walter who? Never heard of him."

—Tom Brokaw on Walter Cronkite

✦

"Humility is not denying the power you have. It is realizing that the power comes through you, not from you."

—Fred Smith

✦

"A leader has responsibilities to be who he says he is."

—Roger Staubach

✦

"Nothing about me personally."

—Dwight D. Eisenhower's rule of dealing with the media during World War II

✦

"I believe that character-based leaders tend to seek and attract character-based employees in sports, in business, or anywhere else."

—Bill Walsh

✦

"He put one at once at ease, and we talked for a good time."

—Colonel Oliver O. Howard on his Maine regiment meeting Abraham Lincoln in the spring of 1861

✦

"Last January, ESPN television ran a compelling feature about Indianapolis Colts' quarterback, Peyton Manning, who had just been named the NFL's Most Valuable Player but the feature was not about football. Instead it explained that for several years when certain competitors Manning admired were retiring from the NFL, he took time to handwrite a note to them, congratulating them on their careers and their character. Each recipient who was interviewed expressed deep appreciation that one of the greatest players of all time would do that. It was a great reminder of the power of the written word."

—Bill Crowder

Bob Ward, a limo driver in Cincinnati, tells this story about Colin Powell: "The General landed at a small airport in a private plane. When he got in my car he said, 'Before I go to my hotel, I need to make a stop at the Sherman House.' I had to call my dispatcher to find the place. I'd never heard of it. The dispatcher said, 'Oh, it's a very bad neighborhood.' I did find the location and discovered the Sherman House was a home for homeless military veterans. I went in with General Powell and he spoke to these men for about 20 minutes. He got them laughing and showed them a real good time. Then I took him to his hotel. General Powell was in Cincinnati to give a corporate speech. I think his service of kindness to those homeless veterans was his most important mission."

✦

Bob Ward also tells a story about driving Bob Dole: "Mr. Dole was very interested in my thoughts about issues affecting the country. He asked me some questions and was genuinely focused on what I told him. When I got to the airport, I said to Mr. Dole, 'I just want to thank you for all the contributions you have made to this country. You are a great American and I am proud to have met you.' Mr. Dole got very emotional and I thought he was going to cry. He said, 'Rarely do I ever hear anyone say that. You have greatly encouraged me.'"

✦

"He knows what it means to say 'please' and 'thank you' and to wait in line. There's nobody like him."

—Mike Kryzyzewski on Grant Hill

✦

"I'm big on personal trust and loyalty. Once you damage that, it's pretty much over."

—Kevin Garnett

✦

"I often ask former UCLA players why they go to Vip's to have breakfast with Coach Wooden. They reply, 'Because he is fun to be with.'"

—Gary Cunningham

✦

"Integrity means a lot, and one broken promise will stay with you in professional football."

—Forrest Gregg

"Subordinates can advise, urge, help, and pray, but only one man, in his own mind and heart, can decide, 'Do we or do we not'?"

—Dwight D. Eisenhower in a letter to his wife, Mamie (February 15, 1945)

✦

"There are three qualities a great leader must possess: conscience, courage, and great goals in life so you can achieve your true purpose."

—Helen Thomas

✦

"Sometimes basketball players are like little puppies, and we want our owners to pat us on the head and tell us, 'Good job.' I know even when I make a mistake, I like for my Dad to say that sometimes. 'It's okay, and we'll get 'em next time."

—Dwight Howard

✦

"His greatest strength as a leader was his consistency in every area of his life. He was the same every day which meant his players and staff knew what to expect."

—Jim Meyers, longtime Dallas Cowboys assistant under Tom Landry

✦

"They do not truly love who do not show their love."

—Shakespeare

✦

"Doing the right thing, rather than the tempting thing, is what character is all about."

—*USA Today* editorial, December 4, 2009

✦

"Great leaders rally people to a better future. Leaders are fascinated by the future and never satisfied with the present. The friction between what is and what could be burns them, stirs them, and propels them forward."

—Marcus Buckingham

✦

"People will forget what you said, people will forget what you did, but people never forget how you made them feel."

—Maya Angelou

"If you purport to be something, you'd better make sure you're living up to the message."

—Roger Staubach

✦

"The most important thing about a commander is his effect on morale."

—William Slim

✦

"By George, we did it! Leadership."

—A billboard in Orlando with a picture of George Washington on his horse

✦

"He came over to me in spring training and said, 'Hi, I'm Mickey Mantle,' as if I didn't know. He'd been my hero since I was little."

—Roy White

✦

"Tell the truth when you can, and when you can't, don't tell a lie."

—Bill Moyers

✦

"Bill Clinton has a surplus of emotional connectivity. I've seen him cast a spell of personal intimacy with dozens of people in a room, sequentially, men as well as women. He can always (as if performing a parlor trick) remember something you told him in a previous conversation and lead you to believe he had been thinking about it ever since."

—Walter Isaacson

✦

"He's a fine judge of a fly ball. He fields grounders like an infielder. He never makes a wrong throw and if he comes back to the hotel at three in the morning when we're on the road and says he's been sitting up with a sick friend, he's been sitting up with a sick friend."

—Casey Stengel in a 1949 profile of Tommy Henrich in *The New Yorker*

✦

"You couldn't break his concentration at home plate with a hot poker. He never let up. He was the most intense player I ever saw."

—Vic Raschi on Ted Williams

"When tempted to do anything in secret, ask yourself if you would do it in public. If you would not, be sure it is wrong."

—Thomas Jefferson

✦

"I was the Yanks number-one pick in 1975. The next year I was in Triple-A at Syracuse under manager Bobby Cox. You could tell then that he was a future Hall-of-Famer. He was very demanding, but never demeaning. He was critical, but always supportive. As a result, you wanted to play as hard for him as you did for yourself."

—Gil Patterson

✦

"Integrity is the essence of everything successful."

—Richard Buckminster Fuller

✦

"He could be tough and demanding on his players, but your friend at a time of need. Not every manager can do both; it's very hard to do. That was TK's real gift."

—Frank Viola, pitcher, on Minnesota Twins' manager, Tom Kelly

✦

"The buck stops here."

—Harry S. Truman's desk sign in the White House

✦

"Character is a must, but the overriding component is good judgment. Good judgment comes from good character. It enables one to choose right from wrong in any situation."

—General Hal Moore

✦

"1945 taught me that a president is either constantly on top of events or, if he hesitates, events will soon be on top of him. I never felt that I could let up for a single moment."

—Harry S. Truman

✦

"I'm an eternal optimist."

—Ronald Reagan

"Grant is the first general I've had! He's a general! He's the quietest little fellow you ever saw ... I believe two or three times he's been in this room a minute or so before I knew he was here ... The only evidence you have that he's in any place is that he makes things git!"

—Abraham Lincoln on Ulysses S. Grant

✦

"George Washington spoke to 500 officers threatening mutiny. He pulled out a pair of glasses and read from a letter: 'Gentlemen, you must pardon me, for I have grown not only gray but blind in the service of my country.' The officers were stunned. Many openly wept. The mutiny was disbanded."

—John R. Miller about events of March 14, 1783 at Newburgh, New York

✦

"I surrendered as much to Lincoln's goodness as I did to Grant's armies."

—Robert E. Lee

✦

"Nearly everything depends on the commander. If the men have confidence in him and in his movements, they will stand by him to the end. They will actually come to feel safer in following him no matter where he leads, than in breaking away from him. No matter how brave men are, they will not fight if they feel that they are in doubtful and unskilled hands. If a general can only inspire his own men with the feeling that he knows what he is about, he will have good fighters. He can put them anywhere, on any field, and in the face of any fire."

—General James Longstreet

✦

"He'd come out on the field during batting practice and start walking around the field talking to his players. He'd start with Alan Trammel and then go to Lou Whitaker; then he'd go right over to any player who was struggling. Sparky would pump that guy up and convince him he was a great player. In fact, he'd have everyone of his players convinced they were outstanding and vital to the success of the team. That was his greatest strength as the leader of the ballclub."

—Dickie Noles on former Detroit manager Sparky Anderson

✦

"Leadership is more about what you do than what you say."

—Reggie Jackson

"Once, when Ronald Reagan completed a questionnaire form about attending an event at his alma mater, Eureka College, under present employment he wrote, 'Governor of California.' What a mark of humility."

—Joseph Garcia

✦

"He emphasized the team concept over individualism and discarded players who wouldn't buy into that."

—John Eisenberg on Vince Lombardi

✦

"Yogi Berra always reflected that truth that says you play a game much better if you enjoy it."

—Allen Barra

✦

"I am quite positive I must give the order ... I don't like it, but there it is ... I don't see how we can do anything else."

—Dwight D. Eisenhower at 9:30 p.m. on June 5, 1944

✦

"Jim went out of his way to talk to his players and his coaches. He'd ask questions like, 'What do you think?' or 'How can we do this better?' That made you feel like you were really part of the team."

—Jim Eisenreich on Jim Leyland, manager of the 1997-98 Florida Marlins

✦

"Leaders tell us not what is but what can be."

—Herb Brooks

✦

"He's just miserable if he's not doing anything."

—Rosalyn Carter on Jimmy Carter at age 85

✦

"The greater you are, the more you must practice humility."

—Ben Sira

"There is no 'I' in *team*, but there is an 'M' and 'E,' and that spells *me*!"
—Cartoon by Randy Glasbergen

✦

"He knew the strength of the phrase, 'What do you think?' He made you feel very secure."
—Gene Tierney, actress, on John F. Kennedy

✦

"If you see a leader walking slowly through the crowd, that's a sign they love people."
—Jay Strack

✦

"One night after an award dinner, Coach thanked everyone for coming, said good night, and added, 'I know none of you would be here if we hadn't won all those games.'"
—Steve Jamison on John Wooden

✦

"In this game, if you try to be somebody other than who you are, you're going to get exposed."
—Joe Torre

✦

"The most important single ingredient in the formula of success is knowing how to get along with people."
—Theodore Roosevelt

✦

"So many people have said to me, 'I only met Coach once but I feel like I knew him.' I reply to them, 'You did.'"
—Andy Hill after John Wooden's death on June 4, 2010

✦

"People with integrity have nothing to hide and nothing to fear. On the other hand, people without integrity always have something to hide. Those become deep secrets which haunt the leader who struggles with integrity issues."
—Warren Wiersbe

6

Helping Others

Seiya Kawamoto

At the end of the day, the only thing that lasts is the impact we have had on other people. Each day should begin with the question: "What can I do today to make a difference in someone's life who can't possibly ever repay me?"

Philosopher/writer Ralph Waldo Emerson phrased this sentiment beautifully: "One of the great compensations of this life is that one cannot help another without helping oneself."

Go ahead and devour this helping of helpings. The rewards of having a servant's heart are far beyond riches and fame.

"Coaching is all about relationships. You must know who your players are and what they need. They all need the three As: attention, affirmation, and affection."

—Les Steckel

✦

"Ralph Houk's best quality is that when he's not building you up, he's leaving you alone."

—Jim Bouton

✦

"Respect is the starting point for all human interaction."

—Wesley K. Clark

✦

"When I hear the word respect, I think of treating everyone the same."

—Mike Krzyzewski

✦

"You are wearing either a bib or an apron. You are either a servant or a celebrity, so put on the apron, leaders. That apron should say: shaped to serve. You have no idea what happens when you serve others. You are sending a message that won't be missed."

—David Uth

✦

"Do you want to stand out? Then step down. Be a servant. If you puff yourself up, you'll get the wind knocked out of you. But if you're content to simply be yourself, your life will count for plenty."

—Matthew 23:11-12 (The Message)

✦

"The best leaders are actually servants. Unselfishly they give of themselves to accomplish objectives, regardless of the sacrifice or cost."

—Charles Swindoll

✦

"The day your soldiers stop bringing you their problems is the day you've stopped leading them."

—Colin Powell

"I stand before you, not as a prophet, but as a humble servant of you, the people. Your tireless and heroic sacrifices have made it possible for me to be here today. I therefore place the remaining years of my life in your hands."

—Nelson Mandela to the massive crowds who greeted his freedom on the day he was released from prison

✦

"Servant-leadership can't be inactive. Servant-leadership is active. It's not just a mantra. It's really doing and being the kingly leader that Jesus would have us model. Serving leadership is not about me. It's about giving myself absolutely to my mission."

—Israel Gaither

✦

"From now on, any definition of a successful life must include serving others."

—George H.W. Bush

✦

"The measure of a man is not how many servants he has, but how many people he serves."

—D.L. Moody

✦

"The mark of a good leader is loyal followers; leadership is nothing without a following."

—Proverbs 14:28 (The Message)

✦

"True leadership must exist for the benefit of the followers, not the enrichment of the leaders. I think John Adams, our second president, best exemplifies these two points. He doesn't get the praise and recognition of Washington and Jefferson, but Adams was a great leader."

—Harvey Mackay

✦

"People don't leave organizations. They leave people."

—J.P. Pawliw-Fry

"We believe that love and marriage is above all else about making each other better."
—Mike and Mickie Krzyzewski

✦

"And now these three remain: faith, hope and love. But the greatest of these is love."
—1 Corinthians 13:13 (NIV)

✦

"Red had the unique ability to make every one of his players feel important. You always felt better about yourself after you left his office. He had a positive personality and would say, 'We are counting on you,' things like that. Red cared about his guys and he let you know he cared. From the outside, his people skills looked hideous, but from the inside, they were beautiful."
—Kevin McHale on Red Auerbach

✦

"The key to leadership is caring for the lowest people in your organization."
—Ken Hatfield

✦

"I don't do it for God, the president, or even my country. I do it for the guy next to me."
—Richard Padron, Sgt. First Class on his career in combat with the Army

✦

Unable to withstand the wrenching moans of the wounded and dying Union soldiers at Fredericksburg, Virginia, 19-year-old Confederate Sergeant Richard Kirkland asked permission to go to the Yankees' aid. Brigadier General Joseph Kershaw acquiesced, but refused to allow the white flag that would ensure Kirkland's safety. When they saw him springing over the wall, the Federals at first fired upon Kirkland until they realized his intent. Cheers then rang out from both sides as the "Angel of Mary's Heights" offered water to one adversary after another.

✦

"Vince Lombardi was the greatest teacher I'd ever encountered on or off the field. No detail was too small for him to master and then drill into us. He taught us things over and over until they became instinct."
—Pat Summerall

"Listen and learn before you talk and teach."

—Jean Pawlowski

✦

"Good teams become great ones when the members trust each other enough to surrender the 'me' for 'we.'"

—Phil Jackson

✦

"Team over self is why we won."

—Coach Tom Coughlin on the 2007 New York Giants' Super Bowl season

✦

"I wish I could explain to everybody what a real close family all of us on this ball club are. We love each other."

—Willie Stargell on the 1979 Pirates

✦

"As a team, we're all inside a bubble. Each of us has so much room to operate. You have to carve out your space and recognize that, because of someone else's needs, you might have to compromise a bit."

—Ray Allen

✦

"Leadership is not magnetic personality. That can just as well be a glib tongue. It is not 'making friends and influencing people.' That is flattery. Leadership is lifting a person's vision to higher sights, the raising of a person's performance to a higher standard, and the building of a personality beyond its normal limitations."

—Peter F. Drucker

✦

I am here to serve, not show off.
I am here to inform, not to impress.
I am here to do good, not to look good.
I am here to make a difference, not a name.

—Sam Horn's Speaker's Mantra

"Coach Joe Gibbs was a great collector of people. He knew how to empower them and then enable them to become leaders. Joe's main mission was to get these people to self-motivate themselves. He did that by giving them enough instruction, teaching, and love. Joe knew nothing about auto racing, but went out and started the Joe Gibbs Racing team and did the same thing there that he did with the Redskins."

—Jeff Bostic

✦

"I just love teaching. The gym's my classroom. That's what keeps me in coaching."

—Pat Summitt

✦

"Teaching is causing people to learn."

—Howard Hendricks

✦

"I've said this before—the measure of any teacher, provided he's not an egomaniac, is to see anybody that he taught do better than he did."

—Pete Carril

✦

"When he talks to us, it's not so much like a coach who's demanding something from us. It's more like a father who loves us."

—Patrick Ghee on Wake Forest coach Jim Grobe

✦

"We didn't realize that what he was doing to us he was really doing for us."

—Willie Davis on Vince Lombardi as a disciplinarian

✦

"True heroism is remarkably undramatic. It's the urge to serve others at whatever cost."

—Arthur Ashe

✦

"Teachers can only teach so much. Really good teachers teach you how to teach yourself."

—Jack Nicklaus

"In my many years in the game, my greatest satisfaction as a coach was teaching. In my heart, I truly believe that coaching is for today, but teaching is forever."

—Pete Newell

✦

"I taught John quite a bit the first couple of years. I think he'd tell you that himself; then he started teaching me."

—Wilbur "Weeb" Ewbank on Johnny Unitas

✦

"The best teachers teach life lessons."

—Mark Macon

✦

"Teaching is the key to coaching."

—Larry Brown

✦

"Cal Ripken, Sr. was a great teacher. He taught Cal not only how to play but how to act."

—Bud Selig

✦

"Best teacher I've ever had. He taught it so well you ran to class every day."

—Charlie Coles on a football theory class taught by coach Bo Schembechler

✦

"People learn the most when teaching others."

—Peter Drucker

✦

"A coach is a teacher. He has to pound the lessons into the players by rote, the same way you teach pupils in the classroom. They call it coaching, but it is really teaching. You do not just tell them; you show them the reasons why it is so and you repeat and repeat and repeat until they are convinced, until they know."

—Vince Lombardi

"Every mother is like Moses. She does not enter the Promised Land. She prepares a world she will not see."

—Pope Paul VI

✦

"Small things done with great love will change the world."

—Steve Sjogren

✦

"Be on your guard; stand firm in the faith; be men of courage; be strong. Do everything in love."

—1 Corinthians 16:13-14 (NIV)

✦

"I am but a small pencil in the Almighty Hand of God writing a love letter to the world."

—Mother Teresa

✦

"God will let thousands of dollars flow through your hands if you do not let much stick."

—Dwight L. Moody

✦

"Hope is an infectious disease, and Ronald Reagan was a carrier."

—Nancy Gibbs

✦

"I wanted to give people hope."

—Mel Gibson to Diane Sawyer when asked why he made *The Passion of the Christ*

✦

"I've always maintained that the one thing a quarterback brings to every football team is hope."

—Marty Schottenheimer

✦

"You know how good teams win? By staying together."

—Juwan Howard

"Blessed are the poor in spirit, for theirs is the Kingdom of Heaven.
Blessed are the meek, for they will inherit the Earth.
Blessed are those who hunger and thirst for righteousness, for they will be filled.
Blessed are the merciful, for they will be shown mercy."

—Matthew 5:3, 5-7 (NIV)

✦

"Four score and seven years ago, our fathers brought forth upon this continent a new nation, conceived in liberty and dedicated to the proposition that all men are created equal."

—Opening of Lincoln's address at Gettysburg

✦

I watched the flag pass by one day, it fluttered in the breeze.
A young Marine saluted it, and then stood at ease.
I look at him in uniform, so young, so tall, so proud.
With hair cut square and eyes alert, he'd stand out in any crowd.
I thought how many men like him had fallen through the years.
How many died on foreign soil, how many mothers' tears?
How many pilots' planes shot down? How many died at sea?
How many foxholes were soldiers' graves? No, freedom isn't free.
I heard the sound of "Taps" one night, when everything was still.
I listened to the bugler play and felt a sudden chill.
I wondered just how many times that "Taps" had meant "Amen."
When a flag draped a coffin of a brother or a friend.
I thought of all the children, of the mothers and the wives.
Of fathers, sons, and husbands, with interrupted lives.
I thought about a graveyard at the bottom of the sea.
Of unmarked graves in Arlington, no, freedom isn't free.

—Unknown

✦

"In all my years of coaching, I never had any rules. I had one standard: 'Don't let your teammates down.'"

—Bruce E. Brown

✦

"To grow your business, bury your ego. Don't be the star. Be the star-maker."

—Bud Hadfield

"Have you ever noticed that even the Lone Ranger had Tonto? He would have been more honest to call himself the 'almost Lone Ranger.' He must have known that a campfire with one can be lonely and depressing, but a campfire with two is lively and fun. That's just the way God made things for us."

—David Jeremiah

✦

"John Wooden's philosophy of life is simple: Be the best you can be, and help others do the same."

—Steve Bisheff

✦

"Unfailingly courteous to fans, Jay Leno always signs autographs, poses for pictures, and somehow finds time to call many of the people who write to him. 'I called one woman,' says Jay, 'and I asked, "Is Susan there?"'

'No. Who's this?'

'This is Jay Leno.'

'Well, this is her mother. Whaddya want?'

'She wrote me a letter,' I replied.

'Oh, well,' she answered. 'She writes to every crackpot on television.'"

—Russell Miller

✦

In 1980, the Cleveland Browns were driving for a winning touchdown in a first-round playoff game against Oakland. Quarterback Brian Sipe had pulled miracle plays all year, and tried to win the game with an out pass to Ozzie Newsome. The pass was intercepted, and the Browns lost on a viciously cold, windy day. As Sipe trudged off the field, his coach, Sam Rutigliano, rushed out to meet him and said, "Brian, I love you."

✦

"I love the story of how Vince Lombardi just killed Jerry Kramer in practice and never let up on him. Kramer was at the breaking point after practice one day, sitting in front of his locker. He thought, 'Today's the day I hit him in the mouth.'

"Just then, Lombardi walked over to Kramer and said, 'Kramer, you're going to be one of the finest guards in the history of the National Football League.' That moment was the turning point in Jerry's career."

—Ernie Accorsi

"The two most influential people in baseball to me were Leo Durocher and Gene Mauch. Here's what they taught me: When you're wrong, admit it and correct it. When you're right, don't get cocky and take yourself too seriously. Here's a prayer I tried to live by as a manager: 'Lord, when I'm wrong, make me willing to change. When I'm right, make me easy to live with. So strengthen me that the power of my example far exceeds the authority of my rank.' I always tried to remember that you manage by influence and not by authority."

—Alvin Dark

✦

"I am advising the former President, the Governor of Florida, and the President of the United States. I guess you could say I rule the world."

—Barbara Bush, former First Lady, on her personal political power

✦

"John McNamara, because he helped me get through the death of my mother."

—Wade Boggs on which of his managers had the biggest impact on his life

✦

"The mediocre teacher tells. The good teacher explains. The superior teacher demonstrates. The great teacher inspires."

—William Ward

✦

"A true leader inspires others to lead themselves."

—Ari Kaplan

✦

"If your actions inspire others to dream more, learn more, do more, and become more, you are a leader."

—John Quincy Adams

✦

"Out of all the rigidities and mistakes of my past, I've learned one final lesson, and I'd like to see it engraved on the desk of every business leader, teacher, and parent in America: The greatest leaders don't rule. They inspire."

—Robert Mondavi

"He lost a lot of games but never lost the team."

—Art Rooney, Steelers owner, on coach Chuck Noll, after his first season as a coach when the Steelers won only one game

✦

Ruth Graham once said to Dr. V. Raymond Edman, former president of Wheaton College, "Wheaton trains leaders." Edman replied, "No, Ruth, not leaders but servants."

✦

"I have seen competent leaders who stood in front of a platoon, and all they saw was the platoon, but great leaders stand in front of a platoon and see it as 44 individuals, each of whom has aspirations, each of whom wants to live, each of whom wants to do good."

—Norman Schwarzkopf

✦

"His greatest leadership strength was his people skills. He understood people and what made them tick. We all knew Coach Bryant cared about us."

—Ozzie Newsome on Bear Bryant

✦

"Leadership is like the abominable snowman whose footprints are everywhere, but who is nowhere to be seen."

—Warren Bennis

✦

"Vince Lombardi led by example, and that's the greatest form of leadership. I spent nine years with him and heard his teachings over and over. Still, I couldn't wait to go to his meetings. His energy and enthusiasm just radiated through the air and uplifted you every day."

—Bart Starr

✦

"People want leadership, and in the absence of genuine leadership they'll listen to anyone who steps up to the microphone. They want leadership. They're so thirsty for it. They'll crawl through the desert toward a mirage, and when they discover there's no water, they'll drink the sand."

—*The American President*

"I'm a teacher. I've always wanted to have an impact."

—Joe Paterno

✦

"A real leader is a person who can get other people to go places they can't or won't go by themselves."

—Jerry West

✦

"The great leader is seen as a servant first, and that simple fact is the key to his greatness."

—Robert K. Greenleaf

✦

"There can be no definition of a successful life that doesn't involve service."

—George H.W. Bush

✦

"Red Auerbach had a philosophy of leadership: spread the credit and accept the blame."

—John Feinstein

✦

"When God measures the greatness of a leader, He puts His tape measure around the heart, not the head."

—John Maxwell

✦

"Leaders explain. They teach, and they sell. Those words sound too mundane to describe the lofty task of leadership, but if leaders aren't teaching and selling, they're not leading."

—John W. Gardner

✦

"When those disciples were sitting in the boat and all they saw was calm, they didn't need Jesus, did they? But when the storm hit, that's when they needed leadership."

—Tyrone Willingham

"Do right, do your best, show you care."
—Lou Holtz's three rules for leading men

✦

"Leadership is helping other people grow and succeed. Leadership is not just about you. It's about them."
—Jack Welch

✦

"X's and O's are overrated. That's why Coach Bryant was the best. He knew how to handle people."
—Charlie McClendon on Bear Bryant

✦

"The growth and development of other leaders is the highest calling of leadership."
—John Maxwell

✦

"Before you are a leader, success is all about growing yourself. When you become a leader, success is all about growing others."
—Jack Welch

✦

"People are not the means to your leadership end; they are the end."
—Greg Norris

✦

"I was 13 years into my own career at GE before I learned the key lesson of leadership—it's no longer about your success, but about the success of others."
—Jack Welch

✦

"Good leaders are open and make a religion out of being accessible."
—Jack Welch

✦

"Leadership is about giving, not getting. Leaders lose the right to be selfish."
—John Maxwell

"Leadership is the ability to get someone to do something they don't particularly want to do in a way that will benefit everybody."

—Gene Stallings

✦

"Bear Bryant was the best leader I was ever around. He was in command of everything. He could get more out of an individual than even that person thought he had. Whatever you had, Bear would get it out of you, and more."

—Bobby Bowden

✦

"Leadership isn't creating gifts in people. It's recognizing giftedness, then nurturing and developing it and giving it focus and direction."

—Al Mawhinney

✦

"A leader takes people where they want to go. A great leader takes people where they don't necessarily want to go but ought to be."

—Rosalyn Carter

✦

"You only manage the unable and the unwilling. Everyone else you lead."

—Doug Jones

✦

"The truth is that everything in leadership comes back to relationships."

—Donald T. Phillips

✦

"I just go around lighting fires under other people."

—Henry Ford

✦

"My ability to get along with people is my greatest strength as a leader. I don't dwell on people's weaknesses. I look to the positive aspect of their lives."

—Jerry West

"The Army is all about leadership, and one of the things they teach you is that leadership is convincing people they can do something they really can't."

—John Feinstein

✦

"Leadership is an art and that involves more than just *motivating* people. It means *inspiring* them—a more powerful word. A leader must inspire his followers."

—Colin Powell

✦

"The earmark of a leader is his willingness to serve others. More than anything, that provides deeper and longer lasting meaning and value to life."

—J.P. Pawliw-Fry

✦

"Leadership is a privilege to better the lives of others. It is not an opportunity to satisfy personal greed."

—Mwai Kibaki

✦

"The job is a teaching job."

—Ernie Accorsi on NFL coaches

✦

"There is a huge thrill in watching someone achieve what they didn't think they could do. It's better than doing it yourself. I work in Washington where power is everything. I have learned, however, that you acquire power by giving it away. You also acquire leadership by giving opportunities to others. As a leader of thousands of people, I don't drag others along. I let them pick me up, but I must be smart enough to ask them for their help."

—Douglas Holtz-Eakin

✦

"He never criticizes those closest to him. He'll only praise the qualities that he likes and admires. People feel safe around him because of this and try to live up to what he wants."

—Alice Schroeder, biographer, on Warren Buffett

"When I first came to this business, it was the issues. It's not. It's people. It's people, and I understand that."

—Senator John Kerry on his profession

✦

"The great leader realizes he doesn't know it all, but he's big enough to be okay with that. He then reaches out to others to tap that pool of knowledge. A leader needs to create a container of safety and inspiration so that people will feel they can add to the team and help the leader lead. The greatest failure in leadership is the feeling you have to know it all which, of course, is an impossibility. The second greatest failure is refusing to tap the resources of the people around you and take advantage of their knowledge and experience."

—J.P. Pawliw-Fry

✦

"They still want to be able to sit down with you and you tell them what you feel about them."

—Joe Paterno on the difference of players from different eras

✦

"He takes the time to listen and hear, which is a lost art. Coach has the patience to talk with and to people and not at them."

—Seth Greenberg on John Wooden

✦

"I believe that unarmed truth and unconditional love will have the final word in reality."

—Martin Luther King, Jr. accepting the Nobel Peace Prize in 1964

✦

"I'm proud of you."

—Fred Rogers' usual statement to his friends and associates

✦

"Nothing else can quite substitute for a few well-chosen, well-timed, sincere words of praise. They're absolutely free and worth a fortune."

—Sam Walton

"Praise, praise, praise."

—Gertrude Stein when asked by a friend what it was that writers wanted most

✦

"If you want a good definition of the word 'encourage,' think of the word 'courage.' To encourage means to put courage in. Conversely, to discourage means to draw courage out."

—Robert Morris

✦

"Flatter me and I may not believe you. Criticize me and I may not like you. Ignore me and I may forgive you. Encourage me and I will not forget you."

—William Arthur Ward

✦

"On the nights I didn't do well, Tony would leave a note in my locker, 'You're the best, Eck.' You have no idea how much that meant to me."

—Dennis Eckersley on Tony La Russa

✦

"He was a hero-worshipper and he got us to worship with him. ... Oh, if you could hear him talk about George Washington."

—Stephen Ambrose on his professor, William B. Hesseltime, who inspired him to become an historian when he was a pre-med student at the University of Wisconsin in the mid-1950s

✦

"Management is easy. Leadership is motivating people, turning people on, getting 110 percent out of a personal relationship."

—Colin Powell

✦

"The ability to elevate men around you is a quality that is way too underrated."

—Jayson Stark

✦

"When a leader senses what the people want and need, they'll always stay with him."

—Harry S. Truman

"Leadership's about persuasion and bringing people along. That's true in almost every situation."

—Lawrence Summers

✦

"I coach by encouragement."

—Roy Williams

✦

"He made you feel like a giant."

—Mark Koenig, Yankees' player, on manager Miller Huggins

✦

"A great leader is not necessarily one who does the greatest things. He is the one who gets the people to do the greatest things."

—Ronald Reagan

✦

"The art of choosing men is not nearly so difficult as the art of enabling those one has chosen to attain their full worth."

—Napoleon

✦

"I have always said that if I were a rich man, I would employ a professional praiser."

—Osbert Sitwell

✦

"I never criticize my players until they're convinced of my unconditional confidence in their abilities."

—John Robinson

✦

"He always encourages me."

—Andrea Mitchell on her husband, Alan Greenspan

✦

"There is a common sign of people in need of encouragement—they are breathing."

—Truett Cathy

"I was watching the Giants play at San Diego when the Maras told me that Vince Lombardi was dying in a Washington hospital and wouldn't last the week. I drove right back to L.A. and flew all night to Washington and went right to the hospital. I met Mrs. Lombardi and we went in to see the coach. That was the only time I ever saw him not in control. You should've seen the smile when he saw me. He whispered, 'Willie, you were a great player. That was the best deal I ever made.' He started to cry and I did too. I was only in the room about two minutes. Mrs. Lombardi led me out and said, 'He gets very emotional when the old Packers come to visit.' I went outside to get a cab to go back to the airport. A bunch of reporters were standing outside and as the cab started to pull away, one said, 'Willie, why did you fly all the way across the country to see Coach Lombardi?' My answer was, 'Because the man made me feel important.' I paused and added, 'I love the man.'"

—Willie Davis

✦

"My philosophy has always been, 'I don't coach football *players*. I coach *people* who play football for a living."

—Dick Vermeil

✦

"God designed you to make a difference. You were not put on this planet to take up space."

—Rick Warren

✦

"He is a man who passionately loves his players and gets emotionally attached to them. He cares very deeply."

—Kurt Warner on Dick Vermeil

✦

"Good leaders make people feel that they're at the very heart of things—not at the periphery."

—Warren Bennis

✦

"He believed in the family concept with his team and he lived it. He and his wife Carol got close to every player and their families."

—Carl Peterson on Dick Vermeil

"There are other coaches who know more about X's and O's, but I've got an edge. I know more about football players than they do."

—Vince Lombardi

✦

"He was a father figure who cared about his children. He wanted us to grow up to be responsible men. Sparky wanted bright and happy futures for us because he cared about us."

—Lou Whitaker on manager Sparky Anderson

✦

"The manager maintains, the leader develops. The manager accepts reality, the leader investigates it. The manager focuses on systems and structure, the leader focuses on people."

—Warren Bennis

✦

"When I told General Tommy Franks that my son David is a Marine and was in combat at the start of the Iraq invasion in 2003, the General said to me, 'You tell your son that someone else loves him besides you.' Both of us lumped up when he said that."

—Pat Williams

✦

On the night of June 4, 1968, Robert F. Kennedy won the Democratic Primary in California. As he walked through the kitchen at the Ambassador Hotel following his victory speech, he was shot by Sirhan Sirhan. As he lay on the floor, his wife, Ethel, leaned over him. He asked, "Is everybody else all right?" Those were the last words he spoke.

✦

"Life is for service."

—Fred Rogers

✦

"Know that you are in the people business. You must love people and build right stuff into their lives because you genuinely care for them. Years from now, you want your players to say, 'He really listened to me and cared about me as a person.'"

—Ed Young

"That meant more to me than the game itself because I idolized him as a kid. For him to call me and tell me what a great game it was and how proud of me he is, that meant more to me than 81 points."

—Kobe Bryant on a phone call he received from Magic Johnson in the locker room after his 81-point game for the Lakers in January 2006

✦

"The photographers and cameramen flew in the back-up plane during the campaign. Every one of them would've taken a bullet for Bobby Kennedy because he knew the names of all of them. They all loved him because they knew he cared."

—George Mitrovich, press aide to Senator Robert F Kennedy in 1968

✦

"I am the minister of the people. I am out helping people. Please leave a message."

—Voice mail of Jose B. Fernandez, dean of the College of Arts and Humanities of the University of Central Florida

✦

"Anyone in a supervisory position must get across to people you care for them. I wanted my players to know I cared for them personally. I think they subconsciously work harder to please you if they know you care for them."

—John Wooden

✦

"Carve your name on hearts and not on marble."

—Unknown

✦

"I played for Dick Vermeil for two years at UCLA in the mid 70s. Thirty-years later, my mother was receiving Christmas cards from Dick and his wife, Carol."

—Randy Cross

✦

William Gladstone and Benjamin Disraeli were both prominent statesmen in Great Britain in the 1800s. When Gladstone entered a room, the feeling was that he was the most important person in the room. When Disraeli entered the room, he made you feel like you were the most important person in the room.

"You don't manage people. You manage things. You *lead* people."

—Grace Hopper

✦

"You can easily judge the character of others by how they treat those who can do nothing for them or to them."

—Malcolm S. Forbes

✦

"Everything in leadership goes back to relationships."

—Mike Krzyzewski

✦

"People."

—Harry S. Truman to John Gunther on what he liked most

✦

"They're not employees, they're people."

—Peter Drucker

✦

"Look at him late in the game when the Braves are behind. He'll be up on the dugout step pulling for his players right up to the last out. That's why they love him."

—Dave Bristol on Bobby Cox of the Braves

✦

"Aim at the elevation of people. Oppose whatever tends to degrade them."

—Abraham Lincoln

✦

"Life is a people business."

—George Kell

✦

"Leadership is all about people because if it wasn't for people, leadership would be pretty easy."

—Dick Abell

"At his peak, Tommy's players loved him so much they'd go through a wall for him. His players would go and give him that extra effort. Tommy was like a loving parent to them."

—Karl Kuehl on Tommy Lasorda

✦

"Vince Lombardi's greatest strength as a leader was his understanding of the individual. He treated everyone as an individual. He always kept the communication lines open. If he had a problem with a player, he didn't let it fester"

—Jerry Kramer

✦

"Coach Bryant had the ability and the presence that made everyone strive to please him: *everyone*."

—Mal Moore, who coached under Bear Bryant

✦

"The saintly McKinley was so selflessly devoted to his wife that even as he lay dying from an assassin's bullet, he whispered to those next to him, 'My wife, be careful how you tell her, oh, be careful."

—Michael John Sullivan on President William McKinley

✦

"Leadership, like coaching, is fighting for the hearts and souls of men to get them to believe in you."

—Eddie Robinson

✦

"Mission first; people always."

—Leo S. Brooks

✦

"He is a fair man and gives equal opportunities to everyone. He has genuine love for his players. One night, my wife and I invited Carol and him to our home for dinner. We broke out a bottle of wine, and Dick proposed a toast to us. He said, 'I've been in this game for years, and this is the first time a player has ever done this.' Then he started crying. After all these years, I still get a call from Dick every Christmas day."

—Bill Bergey on Dick Vermeil

When Ronald Reagan was president, a young man wrote to him about not having a suit to get married in. Reagan sent him one of his own. A soldier from California asked Reagan to send his wife flowers for their anniversary. Reagan delivered them in person.

✦

"You sound like you were really getting to know every single man in your platoon. That's the real secret of leadership."

—Dwight D. Eisenhower in a letter to his son, John, at West Point (November 2, 1944)

✦

"He would fuss at you and could beat up on you, but deep down you knew that he genuinely cared about you. He'd show it to you in a multitude of different ways."

—C.M. Newton on Bear Bryant

✦

"Relationships, relationships, relationships."

—Isiah Thomas on Chuck Daly's greatest strength as a leader

✦

"She could not pass a starving person without feeling hunger."

—Adlai Stevenson on Eleanor Roosevelt

✦

"He's very good with the group. He has the ability to make great demands of the players, but still has empathy for them. He's aware of what they're going through and talks to the guys and pays attention to them. Bill is very good at getting his players and coaches to see it as *us*."

—Dick LeBeau on Bill Cowher

✦

"In 1963, I was a young coach just starting out. John Wooden was doing a clinic outside of Philadelphia, and I went armed with pads and pens to write down all his X's and O's. Coach spent 70 percent of his time talking about relationships, and I left kind of disappointed. As I got older, I realized Coach Wooden had nailed it. Coaching is at least 70 percent about relationships with people and probably more."

—Charlie Woollum

"Die when I may, I want it said of me by those who know me best that I always plucked a thistle and planted a seed where I thought a flower would grow."

—Abraham Lincoln

✦

"Admiral Lord Horatio Nelson, victor at Trafalgar (October 22, 1805), in a battle that shaped history and enshrined his name among its greatest warriors, and his philosophy of leadership: 'Men treated well serve well.'"

—Jay Tolson

✦

Two important Civil Rights leaders flew to the Atlanta airport to meet with Martin Luther King, Jr., but as they approached King, a janitor began speaking with him. Disgruntled, one leader said to the other, "I haven't come a thousand miles to wait for a common porter." The other replied, "When he does not use his power to recognize the needs of a common porter, I will not come even one mile to see him."

✦

"Every player on that team thought Herb liked him best."

—Jim Craig on Herb Brooks' secret with the 1980 Olympic hockey team

✦

"A platoon leader doesn't get his platoon to go by getting up and shouting and saying, 'I am smarter, I am bigger, I am stronger, I am the leader.' He gets men to go along with him because they want to do it for him and they believe in him."

—Dwight D. Eisenhower

✦

"I played for Tony Dungy when he coached the [Tampa Bay Buccaneers], and I was impacted by the way he led. Tony led in a respectful way. He had an authority without degrading the men he was leading. Tony didn't have to curse you or trash you to get his point across. I believe a great leader guides you to victory, but after it's all over, you still appreciate and respect the person for not just what he helped you accomplish, but how he did it."

—Shaun King

✦

"Leadership is salesmanship. Getting people to say, 'C'mon, we can do this.'"

—William Cunningham

"I get better results by selling my ideas than by telling people what to do."

—Alfred Sloan

✦

"Reaching beyond yourselves."

—Orlando billboard about Mother Teresa

✦

"It's a race to the bottom, and it comes from your interest in other people more than your own self-interests."

—Tom Taylor on the concept of being a servant-leader

✦

Julia Ward Howe, author of the "Battle Hymn of the Republic," once asked Senator Charles Sumner of Massachusetts if he could give some assistance to a family in need. Senator Sumner said, "I'm sorry, Mrs. Howe, but I can't. I have become so busy. I can no longer devote any time to individuals."

Mrs. Howe said, "That's pretty amazing, Senator. Not even God is that busy."

✦

"In the early days of the Republic, leaders like George Washington signed their letters, 'Your most humble and obedient servant.'"

—Robert E. Greenleaf

✦

"Great leaders are servants first."

—Charles Swindoll

✦

"*Ut Prosim* [That I may serve]"

—Virginia Tech motto

✦

"This is how people out there approach success. For them, it's all about position, status, power, and titles. That's not how it's supposed to be with you. Success is in the opposite direction: serving, waiting tables, meeting each others' needs."

—Jedd Medefind and Erik Lokkesmoe on Jesus' view of success

"Everyone can be great because everyone can serve."

—Martin Luther King, Jr.

✦

"Life's most urgent question is: 'What are you doing for others?'"

—Martin Luther King, Jr.

✦

"I am reminded of a saying we have in the army: 'Officers eat last.' Taking care of your soldiers is an act of stewardship."

—Colin Powell

✦

"And so, my fellow Americans, ask not what your country can do for you, ask what you can do for your country. My fellow citizens of the world, ask not what America will do for you, but what together we can do for the freedom of man."

—John F. Kennedy

✦

"I thought if the colored guy could help the team, he deserved the chance to try. I'm not a philosopher, but I suppose I was trying to make the world a little better. That's what you're supposed to do with your life, isn't it?"

—Pee Wee Reese, at the end of his life, reflecting on playing baseball with Jackie Robinson

✦

"He was buried at Cypress Cemetery near the border of Brooklyn and Queens under a modest stone and an epitaph he had written for himself: 'A life is not important except in the impact it has on other lives.'"

—Roger Kahn on Jackie Robinson

✦

"1. On whose needs are you focused?
2. Are you consistent in doing the right thing?
3. Are you serving others?

The questions should have been answered like this: 1. Others; 2. Yes; 3. Yes."

—Gary Richmond's maturity test

"In sign language, the gesture for a servant is hands out in front with palms up, moving back and forth between the signer and the signee. This simple motion communicates powerful component qualities about a servant and servant-leadership: trusting, being open, offering help, caring, and being willing to be vulnerable.

"Two questions need to be continually asked and answered if we are to model servant-leadership:

- Does my pattern of leadership significantly differ from the world's?
- Does the focus of my leadership cast the spotlight on me or on others?

"Always remember that in Christian leadership, people aren't the means to an end, people are the end."

—Greg Morris

✦

"I've learned from personal experience that what Jesus taught me was true: the greatest sense of fulfillment we can find here on Earth comes not from fame or fortune but from serving and doing things for other people."

—Deloris Jordan

✦

"The other day, we read one of those Ronald Reagan stories that bring a tear. It came from retired pilot Michael Glynn, telling the *Los Angeles Times* what it was like to fly the president's helicopter during Reagan's White House years. One of Glynn's colleagues was piloting Marine One in Paris when Reagan silently boarded the chopper after a hard day of talks. As the chopper revved up, the pilot felt a hand on his shoulder and turned to see the president. 'I just have to apologize,' Reagan said. 'I didn't even acknowledge you when I walked on board.'"

—Unknown

✦

"After games, Red would always come around to see you and he'd always say something positive. It didn't matter if you'd played two minutes or 30 minutes. He'd say, 'That rebound you grabbed was the turning point of the game,' or 'We wouldn't have won without that loose ball you got.' You might've done a lot of things wrong, but Red would always point out a good thing. When he was finished, your confidence was sky-high and you felt you could take on the world."

—Wayne Embry on Red Auerbach

"The only ones among you who will be truly happy are those who have sought and found how to serve."

—Albert Schweitzer

✦

"The greatest leaders are those who serve others. A good leader exists for the people, not the other way around."

—Rick Warren

✦

"Tell them not to talk too long, and I hope someone would mention that Martin Luther King, Jr. tried to give his life serving others."

—Martin Luther King, Jr. on instructions for his funeral service

✦

During the Civil War, Sojourner Truth went to meet Abraham Lincoln in Washington to discuss the freeing of the slaves. Lincoln said he had "done nothing himself," and added he "was only a servant of the country."

✦

"My last conscious thoughts will be of the Corps, and the Corps, and the Corps."

—Douglas MacArthur in his West Point address on "Duty, Honor, Country"

✦

"Business is a matter of human service."

—Sign in the office of Milton S. Hershey

✦

"Whoever desires to become great among you, let him be your servant."

—Matthew 20:26 (NKJV)

✦

"The first thing I want the pitchers to know is this is not about me."

—Jason Varitek

✦

"I never put my team's welfare above the individual's."

—Dean Smith

"Mr. Graham is a servant-leader because he has an enlarged heart—a big heart for people. With Billy, it is never about power and prestige. It's always about others."

—Cliff Barrows, Billy Graham team member for almost 60 years

✦

"Those pep talks of his! I was 36 years old and thought I had a little sophistication, but when I heard those pep talks, I'd cry and go out and try to kill people. Nobody else could do that to me."

—Emlen Tunnell on Vince Lombardi

✦

"The test of our progress is not whether we add more to the abundance of those who have much. It is whether we provide enough for those who have too little."

—Franklin D. Roosevelt as he pushed for minimum wage in 1938

✦

University of Notre Dame football player George Gipp died on December 13, 1920 at the age of 25 at St. Joseph's Hospital in South Bend, Indiana. In 1928, Notre Dame was having a tough season and about to play Army in Yankee Stadium. After the pre-game warm-ups, Coach Knute Rockne huddled his players on the cold, clammy locker room floor. He waited until the room was silent, lowered his head and began to speak slowly about Gipp's last words at his bedside: "I've got to go, Rock. It's all right. I'm not afraid. Sometime, Rock, when the team is up against it, when things are wrong and the breaks are beating the boys, tell them to go in there with all they've got and win just one for the Gipper. I don't know where I'll be then, Rock, but I'll know about it, and I'll be happy." Rockne continued, "The day before he died, George Gipp asked me to wait until the situation seemed hopeless, then ask a Notre Dame team to go out and beat Army for him. This is the day and you are the team." Notre Dame was charged up and held on to win 12-6.

✦

"I do love to teach—I miss my kids. In a class of 20, there are always two or three for whom the lights go on."

—Condoleezza Rice

✦

"Make sure you let the other guys carry the cup."

—Denis Potvin on Al Arbour's advice after winning the Stanley Cup

When Ray Berry coached the New England Patriots, he took pictures of all the ball boys who assisted the team. At a team meeting, he distributed the photos and told each player to learn the boys' names. "The boys know who you are," Berry told the team. "I want you to know them. Everybody's important." Make a list of the "ball boys" in your organization, those vital but sometimes overlooked contributors to your team. Make sure all of your 'players' know these people and their value.

✦

"He was not a star player, but he was a star teammate."

—George Halas on Brian Piccolo of the Bears

✦

"The eagerness to lose oneself in the group for the good of the group: in other words, think of others first."

—John Wooden on teamwork

✦

"If you're lucky enough to do well, it's your responsibility to send the elevator back down."

—Kevin Spacey

✦

"The secret of a leader to get people to join his team can be found in a single sentence: 'I can't do it without you.' Leaders can become great only when they realize that they are the ones who need people."

—John Maxwell

✦

"To get the most out of being a member of the team, it is absolutely necessary to establish yourself as an integral part of the unit. That is your responsibility, not anyone else's."

—Bill Russell

✦

"I am a member of a team and I rely on the team. I defer to it and sacrifice for it because the team, not the individual, is the ultimate champion."

—Mia Hamm

"Nobody—not Wilt, not Bill Russell, not Michael Jordan, not Babe Ruth—nobody alone ever wins a team game. Only the team can win. You can only win as a team. You can only lose as a team."

—Leonard Koppett

✦

"The strength of the team is you and the strength of you is the team."

—Written by Doc Rivers on the blackboard in the Orlando Magic practice locker room

✦

"Perhaps my favorite historical anecdote is the story of the night in 1945 when General Eisenhower was walking along the banks of the Rhine River, thinking of the crossing in which he would lead the Allied armies. He met a soldier and asked him why he wasn't sleeping. The young G.I., who didn't recognize Ike, said 'I guess I'm just a little nervous.'

'So am I,' said Eisenhower. 'Let's walk together, and perhaps we'll draw strength from one another.'"

—Elizabeth Dole

✦

"No one who is thinking of himself can rise to true heights. You never thought of yourself."

—Secretary of War Henry Stimson to George C. Marshall on May 8, 1945, the day Germany surrendered

✦

"There is a soul to an army as well as the individual man, and no general can accomplish the full work of his army unless he commands the soul of his men, as well as their body and their legs."

—William T. Sherman

✦

"As a team, you have to strangle the nature of selfishness. When you control it, you can be great, but when it raises its nasty demon head, it can kill you."

—Coach George Karl on success in the NBA

✦

"When you pass the ball, you're a good team. When you don't, you're not."

—John Wooden to a UCLA team

"A manager has to be an understanding person. I loved my players. I wanted them to play to their full potential. Every time I hug my players, it's to show them that."

—Tommy Lasorda

✦

"A flake of snow is very small,
'Tis lost to sight quite quickly:
But many flakes combined will fill,
The roads and pathways quickly,
United we can face the fight,
Without distress or fuss:
A little less of you or me,
A little more of us."

—William T. Card

✦

"Martin Luther King could talk to Ph.D.s and no Ds and bring them all together for the same cause."

—Donald T. Phillips

✦

"We play as a unit. We always try to think of passing the ball before shooting."

—John Wooden

✦

"We're still a team today. We're all in our 60s and 70s and still put the team first. We never wanted to let our teammates down, and we still don't. Coach Lombardi instilled that in us by putting us through the fire when we played for him."

—Jerry Kramer in a 2006 radio interview on the Packers of the 1960s

✦

"The two most important lessons on leadership that I learned came from my years in the Marine Corps:

1. The troops fight for each other and not for their country, flag, or officers. In that regard, they're like NFL players. When the chips are down, these guys are playing for their teammates and nobody else.
2. Officers eat last."

—Al Lerner

"The best teams usually win because their star doesn't act like one."

—David Whitley

✦

"We could learn a lot from crayons. Some are sharp, some are pretty, some are dull, some have weird names, and all are different colors, but they all have to learn to live in the same box."

—Unknown

✦

"He genuinely cares about you, and his players know it. That's why his relationships last. There's a great bond of trust there."

—John Bunting on Dick Vermeil

✦

"A very important part of leadership is lifting people up and making them realize that they're better than they are."

—Walter Rodgers

✦

"Stay together. Trust each other, and be good teammates to one another."

—Ernie Accorsi's advice to NFL players

✦

"He's a born teacher, and that's critical to his success. He loves to teach."

—David Halberstam on Bill Belichick

✦

"For the people around you to really believe you can help them out of the woods, they've got to see you come to work with a smile on your face and attack problems. Working out a problem is a way to grow, an opportunity to get better, and an opportunity to teach and to coach."

—Dick Vermeil

✦

"He wasn't just about football. He was about human beings."

—Doug Williams on coach Eddie Robinson

Franklin D. Roosevelt and Winston Churchill met for the first time, face-to-face, on August 9, 1941, aboard the American cruiser *Augusta* in Placentia Bay, Newfoundland. Roosevelt said, "At last, we've gotten together."

✦

"Top leaders downplay how important they are. They put their mission and other's needs ahead of themselves. The results vault those leaders to greatness."

—John Maxwell

✦

"When you're a leader, you have to remember that you work for them, not the other way around."

—Lingyun Shao, former military nurse

✦

"You have to coach 'em as though he was the boy who was going to marry your daughter. You can't coach 'em if you don't love 'em."

—Eddie Robinson

✦

"With a heart full of love and gratitude, I now take leave of you."

—George Washington in a tearful farewell to officers

✦

"I've changed. I've let my guard down. I make it a point to talk to my players more. I hug them more. I'm in their world more and I've never enjoyed coaching more."

—Gary Pinkel

✦

"A group in Winston-Salem attempted to reach Dr. Maya Angelou to see if she would cook dinner as a fundraiser for the March of Dimes. They never got through to her so someone in the group asked if I would call her because I know her. I did call Dr. Angelou and asked if she would cook the meal as an auction item.

"She said, 'Yes' immediately, and I replied, 'Dr. Angelou, I hope you don't feel I'm using our friendship on this request.'

"She said to me, 'Mr. McGregor, if one cannot be used, it only means one is useless.'"

—Gil McGregor, New Orleans Hornets' broadcaster

"The secret of motivating others is providing them with hope."

—John Maxwell

✦

"I want to be known as one who stretched others."

—Fred Smith, Sr.

✦

"Ralph taught me that if you treat players like human beings they will try to play like Superman. He taught me how a pat on the shoulder can be just as important as a kick in the butt."

—Tommy Lasorda on Ralph Houk

✦

"I do like to infect people with enthusiasm. I am avid about being avid."

—Alan Alda

✦

"He was emphatically the black man's president: the first to show any respect for their rights as men."

—Frederick Douglass on Abraham Lincoln

✦

"The purpose of leadership is to take others to the top."

—John Maxwell

✦

"My only goal was to be the best teammate anybody ever had."

—Jameer Nelson

✦

"The joy of leadership is helping others succeed."

—Roger Stilson

✦

"In a healthy organization, rewards come by empowering others, not by climbing over them."

—John Naisbitt

"Leadership is not a trumpet call to self-importance, it is an opportunity to serve."

—Mel Wallace

✦

"The greatest gift that one person can give another is friendship."

—Bill Russell

✦

"A pat on the back is only a few vertebrae removed from a kick in the pants, but it is miles ahead in results."

—Ella Wheeler Wilcox

✦

"To be an outstanding leader, one must be able to take a back seat without losing control of the steering wheel."

—O.A. Battista

✦

"There is nobody who would make me feel as good by saying, 'I like that,' as Walt."

—Marc Davis on Walt Disney

✦

"I've learned that people will forget what you said, people will forget what you did, but people will never forget how you made them feel."

—Maya Angelou

✦

"In 1998 and 1999, I was a 24-year-old entry level employee at the Reagan Foundation in Simi Valley, California. The best part of my job was I got to meet Ronald Reagan on several occasions. The onset of Alzheimer's had started, but Reagan still made public appearances. When I met him, he still had a presence about him. When Mr. Reagan shook my hand, he'd look me right in the eye, which made me feel like the only person in the world. He made me feel of value to him even though I was a nobody.

"I also met Reagan's daughter, Maureen, who was so personable—just like her father. The first time I met her, she came up and gave me a big hug, which made me feel very valuable to her. That hug shocked me at first; then I realized that touch is so important to people."

—Jefferson Ledgerwood

"The higher up the ladder you go, the more impact your words of encouragement have."

—Rich DeVos

✦

"He made a shy person feel at ease."

—Timothy Dwight on George Washington's people skills

✦

"Get to know the players. Nothing will serve you better."

—Buzzie Bavasi on success as a general manager in baseball

✦

"There is nothing more a coach should be than to see the full potential of a player unfolded, to see the future potential of another human being more than the player sees in himself."

—Steve Young

✦

"Let the senior among you become like the junior; let the leader act the part of the servant."

—Luke 22:26 (The Message)

✦

"Our chief want is someone who will inspire us to be what we know we could be."

—Ralph Waldo Emerson

✦

"They're all my sons—all 25 players—and I'll treat them all the same."

—Cal Ripken, Sr., when asked how he would handle managing his son

✦

"Choose to be a fountain, not a drain. A fountain is a giver. It bubbles up and gives us a drink. Being a fountain means looking for the positive first, rather than the negative. It means treating others with respect. A drain, on the other hand, is the opposite. It takes and sucks the good right out of us. A drain can suck the energy right out of a team. It even has its own sound. As a fountain, you bring an energy to your team."

—Mike Trapasso

"People are always talking about coaching basketball, but I always thought of myself as coaching people."

—Kay Yow

✦

"His greatest strength was the strength to love. He demonstrated that love is stronger than hate."

—John Perkins on Martin Luther King, Jr. as a leader

✦

"He's a person who is much more concerned with the group than he is about himself. He got over himself a long time ago. It's all about his team and what he can do, and he'll do whatever is best."

—Gregg Popovich on Manu Ginobili

✦

"Michael Jordan had the insight to incorporate teammates, those lesser angels, into his realm."

—Phil Jackson

✦

"The game of basketball teaches you how to take care of your teammates."

—Bill Russell

✦

"President George H.W. Bush always had a special sensitivity to the losing candidate in a race. He was famous for jotting off short letters of encouragement to the loser anywhere in the country—Democrat or Republican. 'I know how it feels,' he would always say, and 'You still matter to me.'"

—Doug Wead

✦

Life is mostly froth and bubble.
Two things stand like stone—
Kindness in another's trouble,
Courage in our own.

—Adam Lindsay Gordon

"What was the duty of the leader if not to inspire?"
—Carl Meredith

✦

"A coach I had in Italy told me once: 'Thirty seconds, every player, every day. You want to connect.'"
—Mike D'Antoni

✦

"Your players' lives are more important than your success."
—Norm Sonju

✦

"Teach, don't yell."
—Joe Callero

✦

"You must speak to his soul in order to electrify him."
—Napoleon on motivating the individual soldier

✦

"Leaders need to be leaders, not pointers."
—Johnny Hunt

✦

"Are you guys okay?"
—Thurmon Munson's last words to his two passengers after his plane crashed on August 2, 1979

✦

"When you come to practice, you cease to exist as an individual. You're part of a team."
—John Wooden to his players

✦

"If you make your people feel good about themselves, they will follow you."
—Joe Dumars on coaching

"Teamwork is more than one plus one equals two. In fact, it's much more than that."
—Buzz Aldrin

✦

"I tell them I love them. Why feel something about someone and not express it? What good does it do?"
—Dick Vermeil on his assistant coaches

✦

"When we select players, we are selecting people. In the final analysis, it's not the biggest and fastest that prevails. It's the best competitor. The best man [an old Marine] once told me, "I learned two things from the Marine Corps. Officers eat last, and the troops fight for each other.' They don't fight for their commanders. They don't fight for their division. They fight for their buddies. When I select a football player for the Giants, I can't help thinking of that. 'Will this guy be a good teammate? Will this be the kind of man that my players will fight for?' Because that's how you win."
—Ernie Accorsi

✦

"Coaching is really just teaching. A coach should ultimately be a teacher of the game."
—John Wooden

✦

"Avoid putting yourself before others and you can become a leader among men."
—Lao Tzu

✦

"It's not about me; it's about us."
—Slogan for the undefeated 1999 Florida State football team

✦

"Everybody he meets feels like they're real important, and that's a quality not many men have. He's everybody's dad. He calls to check with you."
—Mike Martz on Dick Vermeil

✦

"There was a genuine love on that football team, and I was glad to be a part of it."
—Paul Hornung on the Packers of the 1960s

"It is said that leadership is that unique quality which enables special people to stand up and pull the rest of us over the horizon."

—Bill Polian

✦

"What is good for us is good for one."

—Bill Walsh on loyalty to the team

✦

"What a great teacher does is make you want to please him or her. I'll never forget what he taught me. That was his greatest gift."

—Bill Curry on Vince Lombardi

✦

"I'm a relationship leader."

—Dick Vermeil

✦

"The common thing was that no one cared who got the credit. Everyone bought in."

—John Wooden on the common theme of his championship teams at UCLA

✦

"A career can be called a success if one can look back and say, 'I made a difference.'"

—Walter Cronkite

✦

"A manager is an assistant to his men."

—Thomas Watson, Sr.

✦

"The best leaders are those producing the most leaders."

—Allan Taylor

✦

"To check the passion level of any organization, stick a thermometer in the leader's mouth."

—Allan Taylor

"Shepherds ought to smell like sheep."

—Allan Taylor on leading up close

✦

"The leader is the rock that hits the pond and creates the first ripple. If there is no rock, there will be no ripples."

—Allan Taylor

✦

"I spoke to a waste management convention near Greensboro, Georgia, in August 2010. My topic was leadership and I mentioned how important it is to empower and encourage people. Afterwards a man came over to tell me a story related to my talk. His name was Kevin Woods: 'I used to live in Birmingham, Alabama, where I worked on the tall end of a garbage truck. One of the homes on our route belonged to Bart Starr. I'd see him in the morning and he'd always ask how I was doing and give me a word of encouragement and inspiration. He became like a second father to me. I never can thank that man enough. I've since been promoted into management and moved to Montgomery, but the impact of Bart Starr on my life will never leave me.' As Kevin told me this story, I could see tears welling up in his eyes."

—Pat Williams

✦

"You've got to care for one another. You have to love one another. Each player has to be thinking about the next guy. The difference between mediocrity and greatness is the feeling these players have for one another. Most people call it team spirit. When the players are imbued with that special feeling, you know you have yourself a winning team."

—Vince Lombardi

✦

After a mine collapse in Chili that trapped 33 miners who were still alive, this comment was made by Modesto Alonso, an Argentine psychologist and researcher: "In the face of such intense stress, some people literally die of fear and others find a resilience they didn't know they had. A key point will be the group dynamic and whether the miners have united and have developed a faith in their destiny as a unit" (*The Wall Street Journal*, August 24, 2010).

7

Occupying Your Mind

Hemera/Thinkstock

Your mind is a muscle that needs to be exercised every day. What you think about all day long ultimately becomes a reality in your life.

Read good books. Study the Bible. Feast on the wisdom of great motivators, and benefit from their teaching. Your mind must be kept as healthy as your body. Be mindful of the following truths. Read them and reap.

"The only two things in this world you can control are your effort and your attitude."
—Sue Enquist

✦

"Attitude is everything—pick a good one."
—Unknown

✦

"Next to love the most important word in the English language is *attitude*. You'll have down times and lofty times, but the right attitude will keep you on a level plane."
—Bart Starr

✦

"The three most important words in the English language are: 1. Attitude; 2. Attitude; 3. Attitude."
—Sherwood Strodel

✦

"The last of our human freedoms is to choose our attitude in any given circumstances."
—Viktor Frankl

✦

"What you hide in your heart, you'll find on your tongue. Once it goes into your mind, the journey is just begun. When you're glad, sad, or mad, it'll come out good or bad. What you hide in your heart, you'll find on your tongue."
—Sarah Moore, songwriter (from "What You Hide in Your Heart," recorded by Pat Williams' daughter Karyn)

✦

"You're not what you think you are; you are what you think."
—Brian Tracy

✦

"Attitude is the sum total of my outlook on life. Attitude creates my behavior. Behavior creates my habits. Habits create my performance. Improving my performance starts with attitude."
—Unknown

"The only disability in life is a bad attitude."

—Scott Hamilton

✦

"There is little difference in people, but the little difference makes a big difference. The little difference is attitude. The big difference is whether it is positive or negative."

—W. Clement Stone

✦

"Good thoughts bear good fruit. Bad thoughts bear bad fruit, and man is his own gardener."

—James Allen

✦

"An investment in knowledge always pays the best interest."

—Benjamin Franklin

✦

"Teaching skills are the foundation of all coaching."

—Bill Walsh

✦

"When someone questions me about retiring, I say, 'No. I have too much to learn yet.'"

—Tony Bennett at age 81

✦

"Being married to him is like being attached to one of those flying saucers they talk about. I never know when Walt's imagination is going to take off into the wild blue yonder and everything will explode."

—Lillian Disney on her husband Walt

✦

"Red was a visionary and was always ahead of other people. It was like he was sitting up above and looking down on the whole situation. He had a great grasp of the entire scene. Red had a feel for things that was a little above others."

—Dave Cowens on Red Auerbach

"If only closed minds came with closed mouths."

—A bumper sticker in Orlando

✦

"Some of your hurts have cured and the sharpest you still have survived, but what torments of grief you endured from evils which never arrived."

—Ralph Waldo Emerson

✦

"Other players would trash talk, but not him; they couldn't rattle him. Moses was so focused; he never heard a word they said."

—Calvin Murphy on Moses Malone

✦

"It's very important not to have the last pitch on my mind as I am throwing the next pitch."

—Greg Maddux

✦

"What Einstein was able to do was to think visually."

—Walter Isaacson

✦

"Visions are born in the soul of a man or a woman who is consumed with the tension between what is and what could be. Anyone who is emotionally involved, frustrated, brokenhearted, maybe even angry ... about the way things are in light of the way they believe things could be, is a candidate for a vision. Visions form in the hearts of those who are dissatisfied with the status quo."

—Andy Stanley

✦

"We are a 24-hour gym for your imagination."

—Sign at a Borders bookstore

✦

"Where there is no vision, the people perish."

—Proverbs 29:18 (KJV)

"If your body is willing, your mind can push it to do amazing things."
—Ed Viesturs, mountain climber

✦

"It is not enough in politics to be good. You have to have vision. You have to be able to see. If you can't they can tell and they'll retire you."
—Peggy Noonan

✦

"Leaders are people who focus attention on a vision."
—Warren Bennis

✦

"He had an ability to envision what the future would be."
—Pam Whitenack, Hershey, Pennsylvania archivist on Milton Hershey

✦

"Walt Disney didn't live in the real world. He was a big kid with child-like enthusiasm. Everybody else loses that stuff. He never lost it."
—Neal Gabler

✦

"When your memories are more exciting that your dreams, you've begun to die."
—Howard Hendricks

✦

"The most important side of an athlete's life is the mental side. I've seen a lot of talented athletes who don't succeed. You've got to have it between the ears. The mind is powerful and you have to discipline it. Many times I've hit the breaking point, but your mind can tell you what to do."
—Lisa Fernandez

✦

"1500 AD is considered the beginning of the modern era. From then to 1830, all known knowledge doubled. In 100 years, by 1930, it doubled again. Now knowledge doubles every 15 to 17 months."
—Jay Strack

"I don't design clothes, I design dreams."

—Ralph Lauren

✦

"I am a part of all that I have read."

—John Kieran

✦

"When I get a little money, I buy books, and if any is left I buy food and clothes."

—Erasmus

✦

"The average person has 50,000 thoughts a day. It's awfully boring to think the same thoughts all day, all year, or a whole lifetime. Reading is the most important thing you can do to keep acquiring new thoughts every day."

—James Davis

✦

"Because every day I go to the ballpark I learn something."

—Connie Mack at age 88, when asked why he was still managing the Philadelphia Athletics

✦

"The greatest regret I have is that I didn't study more and read more. I regret it because I feel, at times, I am empty of what I would like to have been."

—Billy Graham at age 87

✦

When Michelangelo was 13, he applied for an art apprenticeship in Florence, Italy. The man asked curtly, "Can you draw?" Michelangelo replied, "I have the capacity to learn."

✦

At age 84, Michelangelo was asked to summarize his life philosophy. He replied, in his native tongue, "Ancora Imparo" [...and I still learn].

"Book lovers never go to bed alone."

—Unknown

✦

"The man who graduates today and stops learning tomorrow is uneducated the day after."

—Newton D. Baker

✦

"Learning is not compulsory, but neither is survival."

—Edwards Deming

✦

"Learning leaders extract three to five times more information from opportunities and situations they encounter. As a leader, it's all about learning."

—J.P. Pawliw-Fry

✦

"In a time of drastic change, it is the learners who inherit the future. The learned find themselves equipped to live in a world that no longer exists."

—Eric Hoffer

✦

"Iron rusts from disuse, water loses its purity from stagnation ... even so does inaction sap the vigor of the mind."

—Leonardo da Vinci

✦

"Even Einstein died with something more to learn."

—Mickey Rooney

✦

"We never stop growing until we stop learning. People who are learning this simple truth will grow old but never get old."

—Charlie "Tremendous" Jones

"To me, leading is learning, and the moment you stop learning, you stop leading and your organization stops growing."

—Rick Warren

✦

"To teach is to learn twice."

—Plet Joubert, African soldier and statesman

✦

"Read. The book is still the greatest man-made machine of all—not the car, not the TV. I promise."

—Ken Burns

✦

"I have never spent a day in my adult life where I didn't learn something."

—Peter Jennings

✦

"If you read the Sunday *New York Times* from cover to cover, you will receive more information than a person living in colonial times received in his entire lifetime."

—Jay Strack

✦

Someone challenged Gandhi on his inconsistency: "How could you say one thing last week and now something different this week?"

Gandhi replied, "Ah, because I have learned something in the last week."

✦

"I will study and get ready and maybe someday my chance will come."

—Abraham Lincoln

✦

"The first rule of learning is the desire to learn."

—Phil Jackson

"Leadership and learning are indispensable to each other."
—John F. Kennedy

✦

"The average American spends 500 to 1,000 hours each year at the wheel. This equals three to six months of 40-hour weeks in your car and is the equivalent of one to two full-time university semesters. So turn off the music on your car radio and instead listen to books on tape or instructional tapes, and you will be one of the best informed professionals in your field."
—Brian Tracy

✦

During his retirement, Walter B. Wriston, former chairman of Citicorp Bank, wrote several books about business and technology and served on numerous boards. Small, innovative technology companies especially intrigued him. *Fortune* magazine asked him why. He responded, "Well, if I'm not awfully careful, I learn something."

✦

"A good book is like an unreachable itch: you just can't leave it alone."
—Laura Bush

✦

"Live as if you're going to die tomorrow, and learn as if you're going to live forever, because if you stop learning, you're through."
—John Wooden

✦

"Books."
—Malcolm X, when asked his alma mater

✦

On a typical day, former Defense Secretary Donald Rumsfeld would rise at 5 a.m., read for an hour to 90 minutes and then arrive at the Pentagon for a 12-hour day. At home, he would read for several more hours before turning in.

"The moment you stop learning, you stop leading."
—John Maxwell

✦

"In an abundant society where people have laptops, cell phones, iPods, and minds like empty rooms, I still plod along with books."
—Harper Lee, author (age 80)

✦

"Leaders are the ones who are constantly learning. You don't know a thing you don't learn from somebody else."
—John Wooden

✦

"Information is doubling every 63 days, and in the next three to five years, information will double every day."
—James Davis

✦

"I'm still learning and trying to improve. When you start taking things for granted, you're through. I think I'm finally figuring out how to do this job."
—Bob Shepherd, New York Yankees' public address announcer for 55 years

✦

"Learning a little every day soon puts you far behind whoever is learning a lot every day."
—Ashleigh Brilliant

✦

"I am quite unable to put down a book I have begun. I would rather read all night."
—Albert Schweitzer, missionary/physician, who slept four hours a night and blamed it on his insatiable appetite for reading

✦

"My pre-travel ritual is that it takes me 10 minutes to pack my clothes and somewhere between several hours and several days to choose the books I'll take along: a dozen for a four- to five-day trip."
—Tom Peters

"A room without books is like a body without a soul."
—Cicero

✦

"Old minds are like old horses: you must exercise them, if you wish to keep them in working order."
—John Adams

✦

"I consider my life primarily to be a continuing education course, and I am looking forward to learning more before the day is over."
—Ted Turner

✦

"What we become depends on what we read after all the professors have finished with us. The greatest university of all is a collection of books."
—Thomas Carlyle

✦

"Life was, to him, a school, and he was always studying and mastering every subject which came before him."
—Leonard Swett on Abraham Lincoln

✦

well-booked *adj*. Having access to a substantial number or a wide variety of books.

✦

"The cure for boredom is curiosity. There is no cure for curiosity."
—Ellen Parr

✦

"My mind is my best friend."
—Jerry West on his success in life

✦

"If you are an average reader (220 words a minute) and read just 20 minutes a day, you will have read 20 200-page books in a year."
—Zig Ziglar

"What could be more powerful than the intellectual capacity of an adult brain combined with a child's unawareness of limitation?"

—Unknown

✦

"I believer in overlearning. That way you are sure."

—Woody Hayes

✦

"The adult brain weighs about 1,350 grams; just three pounds, but it handles the information of 1,000 supercomputers. Note that the potential brain capacity is estimated as at least equivalent to that of 25 million volumes, a 500-mile-long bookshelf! Clearly, the brain is far more advanced than any computer ever produced."

—Pam Farrel

✦

"He had a lifelong quest to become an educated person."

—Doris Kearns Goodwin on Abraham Lincoln

✦

"I am not young enough to know everything."

—James A. Barrie

✦

"Take your mind out every now and then and dance on it. It is getting all caked up."

—Mark Twain

✦

"The ability to concentrate and to use your time well is everything."

—Lee Iacocca

✦

The centipede was happy quite until a toad, in fun, said,
"Pray, which leg goes after which?"
That worked her mind to such a pitch,
She lay distracted in the ditch,
Considering how to run.

—Unknown

"The strongest muscle in a superstar's body is in his head. His ability to push out harmful thoughts and focus on the now is uncanny."

—Todd Jones

✦

"Animal trainers carry a stool when they go into a cage of lions. They have their whips and their pistol at their side, but invariably they carry a stool ... it's the most important tool of the trainer. He holds the stool by the back and thrusts the legs toward the face of the lion. The lion tries to focus on all four legs at once. In the attempt to focus on all four, a kind of paralysis overwhelms the animal and it becomes tame, weak and disabled because its attention is fragmented."

—John Maxwell

✦

"Before every pitch for years and years he was on his toes, ready to move instantly alert. He always got ready as if he knew the ball was coming to him. Whenever a new guy would join the bullpen, he'd watch Brooks for a game or two and say, 'Holy cow, he's as good as they say.' We'd say 'Just watch him. He treats every pitch like there are two outs in the ninth.'"

—Pitcher Dick Hall on Brooks Robinson

✦

"Concentration is such an important aspect of baseball. When there are 30 seconds between pitches your mind has time to wander. You really have to fight that. One time in Kansas City, I looked down and noticed I was wearing a mismatched pair of cleats; then the ball was hit, and I didn't get it. I said, 'You should have had that,' but I wasn't concentrating."

—Brooks Robinson

✦

Ray Kroc served in the same military company during World War I as Walt Disney. Kroc remembered: "Walt was always drawing pictures while the rest of us were chasing girls. Therein lies a lesson because his drawings have gone on forever and most of those girls are now dead."

✦

In New York's Central Park, there's a little memorial to the late John Lennon. The section is called "Strawberry Fields." In the ground is a beautiful stone mosaic with one word on it: "Imagine."

"Harry Truman said he could never have functioned had he not read his eyes out about leaders who came before him. Before retiring at night, Truman donned a green eyeshade and put his hawk-like nose in a history book."

—Michael Beschloss

✦

"Not all readers become leaders, but all leaders must be readers."

—Harry S. Truman

✦

"Leaders must be readers."

—Donald Laird

✦

"You need to think about who you can influence, not who you can command."

—Tom Tierney, chairman and co-founder of Bridgespan Group

✦

"Listen to people with your heart and not just your head and ears."

—Michael Cooper

✦

"Every pore in his body was an ear."

—Dorothy Thompson on Franklin D. Roosevelt

✦

"Be a good listener. Your ears never get you in trouble."

—Frank Tyger

✦

"No man ever listened himself out of a job."

—Calvin Coolidge

✦

"Listening is also a sign of respect, and it is amazing how much people will allow you to say to them by way of criticism if you just bother to go listen to them first."

—Thomas Friedman

"The words 'listen and silent' are the same, save for the order of letters. We cannot listen clearly until we are silent."

—Lance Secretan

✦

"One of the best ways to persuade others is by listening to them."

—Dean Rusk

✦

"The opposite of talking isn't listening. The opposite of talking is waiting."

—Fran Lebowitz

✦

"Wise men and women are always learning, always listening for fresh insights."

—Proverbs 18:15 (The Message)

✦

"My greatest strength as a leader has always been the ability to listen to other people. I mean, really listen."

—Tom Ridge

✦

"He'll sit there and listen, I mean, really listen."

—Michael Irvin on former University of Miami coach, Jimmy Johnson

✦

"He was always asking, 'What do you think?' He wanted to know our opinions … and I think he wanted us to really think."

—Don Soderquist on Sam Walton

✦

"It's about listening and learning, instead of telling and directing."

—Blythe McGarvie on leadership

✦

"Listening, not imitation, may be the sincerest form of flattery."

—Dr. Joyce Brothers

"He possessed the gift of silence."
—John Adams on George Washington

✦

"Bud Selig's greatest strength as a leader is that he is talking 24/7 to his owners and listening to their problems. They all feel he cares about them, understands them, and wants to help them. The man's a great listener."
—Andrew Zimbalist

✦

A wise old owl sat in an oak.
The more he saw, the less he spoke.
The less he spoke, the more he heard.
Why aren't we like that wise old bird?
—E.H. Richards

✦

"The truth is Ronald Reagan believed everyone deserved an attentive ear."
—Dick Wirthlin

✦

"As courteous as he was tireless, General George Washington was a patient listener."
—Stanley Weintraub

✦

"John Schuerholz's greatest strength as a leader is that he hires very good people and then listens to them. He pays attention to what they have to say. That's a rare quality."
—Guy Hansen

✦

"You don't quit playing because you grow old. You grow old because you quit playing."
—Unknown

✦

"On my epitaph I want it written, 'He was curious to the end.'"
—Tom Peters

"The only factory asset we have is human imagination."

—Bill Gates

✦

"Nothing can stop the man with the right mental attitude and nothing on Earth can help the man with the wrong mental attitude."

—Thomas Jefferson

✦

"The man has no speed bumps between his brain and his mouth."

—David Brooks, *New York Times* columnist, on Joe Biden

✦

"People's brains Velcro to a story."

—Jack Canfield

✦

"In great teams conflict becomes productive. The free flow of conflicting ideas and feelings is critical for creative thinking and for discovering new solutions no one individual would have come to on his own."

—Peter Senge

✦

"Dr. Ross Edy, a well-known international neuroscientist and long-time friend of my husband, once told me that if you take two separate live heart cells from two separate mammals and put them pulsing in the same Petri dish, left alone, in a short time, they will find each other's rhythm and start to beat in time with each other. How profound is that!"

—Karen Connelly Armitage

✦

"His judgment was always clear because his mind was pure."

—Gouverneur Morris on George Washington

✦

"The human mind can bear plenty of reality, but not too much intermittent gloom."

—Margaret Drabble

"Thinking is when your mouth stays shut and your head keeps talking to itself."

—A nine-year-old boy

✦

"Ever wonder why you make a split-second decision and it comes out right? That's what it's about. You keep storing thoughts in the back of your brain kind of like cooking in a stew pot; then, boom! If you've done your homework, all the answers are there when you need them, in a blink."

—Joe Maddon

✦

"Watch your thoughts; they become your words. Watch your words; they become your actions. Watch your actions; they become your habits. Watch your habits; they become your character. Watch your character, for it will become your destiny."

—Hillel the Elder

✦

"I was still doing the same things: going home, playing video games, sitting around doing nothing when I wasn't in the pool. That's what I always do. I have no idea why I was in a rut."

—Michael Phelps, swimmer, on having an off year, after owning 2007

✦

"The secret of Bobby Jones' success was the strength of the man's mind."

—Ben Hogan

✦

"Men are not prisoners of fate, but only prisoners of their own minds."

—Franklin D. Roosevelt

✦

"We all have 60,000 thoughts a day. Further study disclosed that of those thoughts, 40 percent were about the future, and 99 percent of them never took place. 30 percent of the thoughts were about the past and nothing could be done to change that time period. Twelve percent of the thoughts were filled with doubt and 10 percent were worries about our health. In other words, 92 percent of our thoughts are not pictures of our reality."

—Brian Tracy

"Tell me a fact, and I'll learn. Tell me a truth, and I'll believe. Tell me a story, and it will live in my heart forever."

—Indian proverb

✦

"He still dreams."

—Ernie Accorsi on Joe Paterno at age 80

✦

"Your imagination is the most important tool you have."

—Robert Fulghum

✦

"When Walt got ideas, he visualized the whole thing 100 percent."

—Wilfred Jackson on Walt Disney

✦

"He took the ceiling off my brain."

—Oprah Winfrey on her lawyer

✦

"The genius of this man was his remarkable vision."

—Stephen E. Ambrose on Theodore Roosevelt

✦

"He was always seeing just beyond the horizon. You always felt that if you could just follow his gaze, you could stay ahead of everyone."

—Diane Sawyer on Roone Arledge

✦

"No one ever had a greater vision-thing than Roone."

—Barbara Walters on Roone Arledge

✦

"Imagination is the preview of life's coming attractions."

—Albert Einstein

"As president, George Washington had a vision and knew what he wanted to accomplish."

—Peter R. Henriques

✦

"I have seen the future and it is very much like the present, only longer."

—Woody Allen

✦

"I'm not afraid to think outside the box. There is a lot more space outside the box."

—Dennis Green

✦

"Lew Wasserman was the kind of visionary who always saw a few squares ahead on the board. That was Wasserman's great gift."

—George F. Custen

✦

"Success comes from having dreams that are bigger than your fears."

—Terry Litwiller

✦

"The manager has his or her eye always on the bottom line; the leader on the horizon."

—Warren Bennis

✦

"Kid, I got vision and the rest of the world has bifocals."

—Butch (Paul Newman) to Sundance (Robert Redford) in *Butch Cassidy and the Sundance Kid*

✦

"Leadership views the horizon, not merely the terrain."

—Unknown

✦

"If you can't see the invisible you can't do the impossible."

—Coach Gary Barnett

"President Reagan is a man of long vision."
—Donald Regan

✦

"You can't have a better tomorrow if you are thinking about yesterday all the time."
—Charles Kettering

✦

"Like Thomas Alva Edison, Walt Disney has eyes that see what no other man sees."
—Jerry Wald

✦

"My job is to live in the future, 20 years from today."
—Frank Moss, director of the Media Lab at MIT

✦

"Vision is the art of seeing things invisible."
—Jonathan Swift

✦

"When his father asked the school headmaster in Germany what profession young Albert Einstein should choose, he responded, 'It doesn't matter. He'll never make a success of anything.'"
—Steven M. Gillon

✦

"Why would I think about missing a shot I haven't taken yet?"
—Michael Jordan

✦

"Strength lies in the mind of a champion."
—A slogan on the back of a T-shirt

✦

"If you give a man enough time to work things out in his head, he can justify almost anything, even murder."
—A friend of Paul Byrd

"True wisdom is applying God's viewpoint to life. Wisdom—divine insight into how to make great choices—is available to all of us. We just need to ask."

—Tony Evans

✦

"The toughest thing about vision is you must see what is not yet obvious."

—Raymond McHenry

✦

"Strong leaders have to have intelligence because leadership has to do with ideas; to be able to see problems, and see solutions to problems."

—Father Theodore M. Hesburgh, former president of Notre Dame University

✦

"If you cannot see it before you see it, you'll never be able to see it."

—Orval Butcher

✦

"Teaching is not a bad way to learn your profession thoroughly."

—General Omar Bradley

✦

"The ability to learn is a defining characteristic of being human. The ability to continue learning is an essential skill of leadership. When leaders lose that ability they inevitably falter. When any of us lose that ability, we no longer grow."

—Warren Bennis and Robert Thomas

✦

"Sam's greatest asset was his unstoppable drive to learn from everybody."

—Todd G. Buchholz on Sam Walton

✦

"For lifetime leaders, learning is as natural as breathing. They squeeze all they can out of every acquaintance and encounter. They regard life's sterner, less pleasant side as a particularly instructive classroom."

—Warren Bennis and Robert Thomas

"He gave man speech and speech created thought, which is the measure of the Universe."

—Percy B. Shelley on God

✦

"Nadia Comaneci has a fantastic mind. She can block out the whole world. It's just her and the apparatus."

—Rod Hill, head manager of the United States Olympic Women's Team (1976)

✦

"General George Marshall possessed a breadth of vision which no nation can expect to find in its great men more than a handful of times in a century."

—Max Hastings

✦

"Hire people who make you squirm; that's how you get new ideas."

—Peter Skillman

✦

"Who dares to teach must never cease to learn."

—John Cotton Dana

✦

"Not really trying for long periods of time leads to a life called ordinary."

—Arron Chambers

✦

"The future belongs to those who see possibilities before they become obvious."

—John Sculley

✦

"A leader is one who sees more than others see, who sees farther than others see, and who sees before others do."

—Leroy Eims

✦

"Thomas Jefferson had a remarkable ability to focus on a single objective."

—Charles A. Cerami

"I don't look back and say, 'Oh, gee.' There's no use living that way. Do the best you can and look forward."

—Sandra Day O'Connor

✦

"You get instincts that come with reading so much history. Harry Truman seemed to see around corners, but that's because he read history. We just think he made the right decisions. At the time they were horrendously difficult."

—Ike Skelton

✦

"He wrote that a riverboat captain has to learn more than anybody should ever have to learn. That's pretty much what coaching is."

—Joe Paterno on Mark Twain

✦

"Both Lincoln and Washington had the ability to focus on their goals and not get distracted. In the case of Washington, it was to win freedom for the Colonies, and for Lincoln it was to keep together what Washington had built."

—David Clary, historian

✦

"The wonderful thing is when you practice effective listening other people will begin to find you fascinating. They will want to be around you. They will feel relaxed and happy in your presence.

"The reason why listening is such a wonderful tool in developing the art and skill of conversation is because listening builds trust. The more you listen to another person, the more he or she will trust you and believe in you. Listening also builds self-esteem. When you listen attentively to another person, his or her self-esteem will naturally increase, and finally listening builds self-discipline in the listener.

"Because your mind can process words at 500 to 600 words per minute, and we can only talk at about 150 words per minute, it takes real effort to keep your attention focused on another person's words. If you do not practice some self-discipline in conversation, your mind will wander in a hundred different directions. The more you work at paying close attention to what the other person is saying, the more self-disciplined you will become. In other words, by learning to listen well, you actually develop your own character and your own personality."

—Brian Tracy

"A word is dead when it is said some say. I say it just begins to live that day."

—Emily Dickinson

✦

"His secret was complete concentration on what he was doing."

—George Sidney, film director, on Frank Sinatra

✦

His genius lay in his capacity to look at the same thing as others were looking at but to see far more."

—Nelson Rockefeller, New York governor, at the funeral of David Sarnoff, December 1971

✦

"School is never out for the learner."

—Eugene Griessman

✦

"I'm not afraid of being a bad teacher. I'm afraid of being a bad learner."

—Celina Fraga

✦

"I tried to increase my knowledge all my life by reading and reading and reading, especially biography and history. There's nothing new in human nature. The only thing new in the world is the history you don't know."

—Harry S. Truman

✦

"I cannot live without books."

—Thomas Jefferson

✦

"He's enormously good company, partly because he is so well-read. He's read just about everything and remembered almost all of it: a veritable human sponge. As a result, he can intelligently discourse on virtually any subject."

—Frank Gifford on Roone Arledge

"He wants to come out of every meeting smarter than when he went in."

—Eric Dishman, Intel co-founder, on Andy Grove

✦

"Successful leaders have large libraries and small television sets."

—Unknown

✦

"I like nothing so well as writing and talking."

—Woodrow Wilson as a college student

✦

"Reading with me is a disease."

—Theodore Roosevelt

✦

"If you don't have good stories to tell on your deathbed, what good was living?"

—Sandra Bullock

✦

"The wonderful thing about visionaries is the clarity with which the future appears to them. They imagine it and pursue it, and all the rest is in service of realizing the dream."

—Michael Shapiro

✦

"You don't have a happy life if you can't read."

—Barbara Bush

✦

"The brighter you are, the more you have to learn."

—Don Herold

✦

"Nothing is more dangerous than to live in the temperamental atmosphere of a Gallup Poll, always feeling one's pulse and taking one's temperature."

—Winston Churchill in a speech to the House of Commons, September 30, 1941

"The wise are always listening. That's how they became wise. That's how they remain wise."

—Andy Stanley

✦

"To acquire knowledge, one must study, but to acquire wisdom, one must observe."

—Marilyn vos Savant

✦

"Mickey Mouse popped out of my mind onto a drawing pad when the business fortunes of my brother Roy and myself were at their lowest ebb and disaster seemed right around the corner."

—Walt Disney

✦

"I'm not an educator; I'm a learner."

—Bill Gates

✦

"Information is like eggs: the fresher, the better."

—George S. Patton

✦

"I seldom pass five minutes of my life in which I do not acquire some knowledge."

—Thomas Paine

✦

"Every time you speak, your mind is on parade."

—Unknown

✦

"The more you know, the higher you go. Only expertise makes you an expert."

—Bill Walsh

✦

"There is no quicker way for executives to get out of touch than to retire to the seclusion of their offices and write each other notes."

—Alec MacKenzie

You may call me old-fashioned, but from supper till bed,
It is reading a book that will get you ahead.
When I raised my three children, when supper was done,
We grabbed a good book and we all sat and read.
Oh, they begged and they pleaded and got down on their knees,
And they tried to convince me with logic and pleas,
And enriched with the culture in those DVDs.
But I challenged their logic with some that I had,
"When I was a child, long before I was Dad,
When supper was finished, we drank from our books,
And I really don't think that I turned out that bad."
Did I do the right thing? Was I strict and too hard,
To protect them from joysticks and rich DVDs?
Should I not have policed them; should I not have stood guard?
Last June, all three signed my Father's Day card,
"Love Amanda and Aaron and Abbey, PhDs."

—Swen Nater

✦

"You can't fake listening. It shows."

—Raquel Welch

✦

"It's still a coach's game. Make no mistake. You start at the top. If you don't have a good one at the top, you don't have a cut dog's chance. If you do, the rest falls into place. You have to have good assistants and a lot of things, but you first have to have the chairman of the board."

—Bear Bryant

✦

"In adding players to our roster I'm looking for guys with something to prove…to themselves, their former teams, their families, the media, etc."

—Joe Dumars, general manager, Detroit Pistons

✦

"Every big idea that works is marked by simplicity, by clarity. You can understand it when you hear it, and you can explain it to people."

—Peggy Noonan

"He is a great listener in a body of poor listeners. This makes it easy to deal with him."
—John McCain, senator, on Senator Ted Kennedy

✦

"It was fun. We all wanted to be here. His enthusiasm captured us all."
—Bob Schieffer, journalist, on working with Walter Cronkite at CBS News

✦

"I don't look much further past 7:05 and tonight's game."
—Nick Swisher

✦

"No lover ever studied every whim of his mistress as I did those of President Roosevelt."
—Winston Churchill

✦

"Words are the only things that last forever."
—Winston Churchill

✦

"The journey has been enjoyable and well worth making—once!"
—Winston Churchill's last words

✦

"Dreams are extremely important. You can't do it unless you first imagine it."
—George Lucas

✦

"Judgment gets impaired by arrogance."
—Tom Coburn

✦

"We can lick them all with quality."
—Walt Disney

"Everyone needs a spark because people think they're doing their best when in reality they aren't. So motivation is necessary."

—Tommy Lasorda

✦

"His greatest intellectual gift was for picking on essentials and concentrating on them."

—"Jock" Collins, Winston Churchill's personal secretary

✦

"He used an artillery of words."

—A writer on Winston Churchill's verbal skills during World War II

✦

In an interview, Roy Disney recalled how his Uncle Walt came to see him when he had chicken pox as a boy, enthralling him with a story he wanted to make into a film about a wooden puppet named Pinocchio. "He scared me to death with the stuff about the whale and everything else," Roy Disney said. "I remember it very, very sharply and very clearly, but when the movie came out, it was a big letdown for me. It was nowhere near as good as Uncle Walt's version."

✦

"One must keep one's compasses in the eyes."

—Michelangelo

✦

"He was always looking ahead during the course of a game. He was anticipating the seventh, eighth, and ninth innings from the start of the game. He owned those last three innings."

—Bill Lee, pitcher, on Dick Williams as a manager

✦

"Working with Walt you're going to leave the room more inspired than when you came in. To me that's leadership."

—Bob Gurr on Walt Disney

✦

"I just love walking to home plate every night. I just love that competition."

—Bruce Froemming

"I love to be thought of that I was a gamer which means that you're willing to meet whatever challenges have faced your team today. When you're called a gamer, that's the highest compliment."

—Cal Ripken, Jr.

✦

"Life is not a final. It's a daily pop quiz."

—Ann Crittenden

✦

"My greatest strength as a consultant is to be ignorant and ask a few questions."

—Peter Drucker

✦

"Go and get it, 'cuz it's not coming to you."

—Gregg Popovich

✦

"Great hopes make everything possible."

—Benjamin Franklin

✦

"I'm calm on the inside, too. When you are prepared, there is no reason to sweat."

—Jim Caldwell on why he appears so calm on the sidelines during an NFL game

✦

"Formal education will make you a living; self-education will make you a fortune."

—Jim Rohn

✦

"No man really becomes a fool until he stops asking questions."

—Barry Goldwater

8

Noting What Is Important

Ryan McVay

It is important to develop your greatest talents to their highest levels. It is, however, equally important to be a well-rounded person, and to fish in many of life's different ponds.

Push yourself to become knowledgeable about music, theater, sports, and history. Be a lifelong learner so that you can feast on a buffet of the best life has to offer. Digest the accomplishments and character of those who achieve greatness and reveal loving kindness.

"Fathers and mothers, if you have children, they must come first. You must read to your children and must hug your children and you must love your children. Your success as a family, our success as a society, depends not on what happens in the White House, but on what happens inside your home."

—Barbara Bush, during a 1990 commencement address at Wellesley College

✦

"The five most dangerous words in business may be: everybody else is doing it. So at Berkshire Hathaway, let's start with what is legal, but always go on to what we would feel comfortable about being printed on the front page of our local papers and never proceed forward simply on the basis of the fact that other people are doing it."

—Warren Buffett

✦

"Show me your friends, and I'll show you your future."

—Danny Holland

✦

"There are only two ways to come out of the trauma of struggle, and that's either bitter or better. You have a choice."

—Natalie Cole

✦

Smiling is infectious.
You catch it, like the flu.
When someone smiled at me, today,
I started smiling too.
I passed around the corner
And someone saw my grin.
When he smiled, I realized
I'd passed it on to him.
I thought about that smile
And realized its worth.
A single smile, just like mine
Could travel 'round the Earth.
So, if you feel a smile beginning,
Don't leave it undetected.
Let's start an epidemic quick,
And get the world infected.

—Unknown

Viktor Frankl was a Jewish psychiatrist who lived in Austria. He and his family were assigned to concentration camps during the Holocaust and Frankl lost his entire family in the process. Frankl watched the thousands of people struggling for survival. Some just gave up and died; others fought on valiantly. In his study of human behavior, Frankl concluded, "We who lived in the concentration camps remember the men who walked throughout the huts comforting others, giving away their last piece of bread. They have been few in number, but they offer sufficient proof that everything can be taken away from a man but one thing: the last of the human freedoms—to choose one's attitude in any given set of circumstances, to choose one's own way."

✦

"My friends, no one not in my situation can appreciate my feelings of sadness at this parting to this place and the kindness of these people. I owe everything to his care, commending you as I hope in your prayers you will commend me. I bid you an affectionate farewell."

—Abraham Lincoln at the Springfield, Illinois, train station as he left for Washington as the new President (1861)

✦

"You've got to have strong people around you. You've got to give them credit. You can't be out there hogging credit for yourself all the time."

—George H.W. Bush

✦

"A leader must run the risk of incurring people's displeasure sometimes, or he will never do them any good in the long run."

—John Adams

✦

"A president has to know where he is going and why."

—Harry S. Truman

✦

"Leadership is nothing more than simply knowing what to do and then doing it."

—James Baker

✦

"He noticed little things that would make a big difference."

—One of Walt Disney's associates

"The really impressive thing was that he listened just as well as he talked. If you made a good suggestion, Lombardi embraced it and put it in the playbook. If you told him something wasn't working, he wasn't afraid to acknowledge that, too."

—Pat Summerall on Vince Lombardi

✦

"I made it my business as president to listen to people in all walks of life and in all fields of endeavor and experience. I always tried to be a good listener."

—Harry S. Truman

✦

"He'd listen so hard that it was deafening. He didn't miss anything. He was, by far, the greatest listener I have ever experienced in a musical group."

—Bassist Gary Peacock on Miles Davis

✦

"Ever the diplomat, Dwight D. Eisenhower was practiced in the art of listening politely without agreeing."

—Michael Korda

✦

"He would sit and listen and listen, without saying a word, having a good time all along, but letting his companion do the talking."

—An unknown observer on Ulysses S. Grant

✦

After the 272-word Gettysburg Address, former Massachusetts governor Edward Everett, who was considered the greatest orator in the country at that time, wrote to Abraham Lincoln: "I should be glad if I could flatter myself that I came as near to the central idea of the occasion in two hours as you did in two minutes." Lincoln replied: "I am pleased to know that in your judgment the little I did say was not entirely a failure," and told his attorney general, James Speed, that he "never received a compliment he prized more highly."

✦

"My fellow Americans, our long national nightmare is over. Our Constitution works. Our great republic is a government of laws and not of men. Here, the people rule."

—Gerald R. Ford at his inauguration as president on September 9, 1974

"Bad news is not like wine. It does not get better with age."
—Colin Powell

✦

Years after *Snow White* was completed, Walt Disney was still fretting over the wobbles in her construction. He said, "The bridge of her nose floats all over her face."

✦

"Look, the thing that's going to make Disneyland unique and different is the detail. If we lose the detail, we lose it all."
—Walt Disney

✦

"This is the biggest thing I can think of in Walt's career: Quality came first in his opinion; the box office will follow quality."
—Ben Sharpstein on Walt Disney

✦

"I can't stand the sight of dwarfs. I predict that nobody'll ever pay a dime to see a dwarf picture."
—Walt Disney's wife, Lillian, on *Snow White*, which became the highest-grossing film of its time

✦

"You can afford to have one donkey, but you can't have two because they'll breed."
—Al McGuire on team chemistry

✦

"Peacock today, feather duster tomorrow."
—Joe Lapchick on coaching

✦

"Every boy has two questions about his father:
1. Do you delight in me and love me?
2. Do I have what it takes?
All sons want delight and validation from their dads."
—John Eldredge

"From Stettin in the Baltic to Trieste in the Adriatic, an Iron Curtain has descended across the continent. Behind that line lie all the capitals of the ancient states of Central and Eastern Europe. Warsaw, Berlin, Prague, Vienna, Budapest, Sofia, Belgrade, and Bucharest. All these famous cities and the population around them lie in what I must call the Soviet Sphere and all are subject, in one form or another, not only to Soviet influence but to a very high and in some cases increasing measure of control from Moscow."

—Winston Churchill at Westminster College in Fulton, Missouri on March 5, 1946

✦

"Of all the things I've ever done. I'd like to be remembered as a storyteller."

—Walt Disney

✦

"Thank you very much, ladies and gentlemen. You know how bad my voice sounds. Well, it feels just as bad ... There's been so many lovely things said about me. I'm glad I had the opportunity to thank everybody. Thank you."

—Babe Ruth, April 27, 1947

✦

Diane Sawyer's 82-year-old mom, Jean, is no different than any mother. At age 56 Diane said, "To this day I get messages about clothes that didn't look good or how I didn't sit in a ladylike position. She thinks if she just says the right thing, one day I'll get it right."

✦

"People smoke about 5.7 trillion cigarettes worldwide every year, enough to make a continuous chain from the Earth to the sun and back, with enough left over for a few side trips to Mars. The World Health Organization estimates that 10 million people will be dying annually from cigarettes by the year 2020—a third of those in China. Cigarettes, which claimed about 100 million lives from the 20th Century, could claim close to a billion in the present century."

—Robert Proctor

✦

"I wonder how far Moses would have gone if he'd taken a poll in Egypt? What would Jesus Christ have preached if He'd taken a poll in Israel? It isn't polls or public opinion of the moment that counts. It's right and wrong."

—Harry S. Truman

"When two people in business always agree, one of them is unnecessary."

—William Wrigley

✦

"Wisdom is the ability to make retrospective judgments prospectively."

—Jonas Salk

✦

"One year, I got a call from an agent of one of our pitchers. The call came in July at the All-Star break. The agent said, 'Why does your manager dislike my client so much?'

"I replied, 'What are you talking about?'

"The agent told me, 'Your manager hasn't spoken one word to this pitcher since opening day. How do you expect him to feel?'

"That was a real eye-opener to me about the importance of communicating with players."

—Kevin Malone, former Major League Baseball general manager

✦

"The only thing new in the world is the history you don't know."

—Harry S. Truman

✦

"Old men are always advising young men to save money. That is bad advice. Invest in yourself. I never saved a dollar until I was 40 years old."

—Henry Ford

✦

"One of the things he has, which I think is very important in any profession, is he knows how to learn. Wherever he went, he studied. Who's good and why are they good? Who knows more than I do, and how can I learn from that? Bill clearly did just that."

—David Halberstam on Bill Belichick

✦

"There are two words you need to ask yourself repeatedly: What else? What else can I do to help improve myself?"

—Brandon Steiner

"Learning how to learn is the most precious thing we have in life."
—John Naisbitt

✦

"I'm only smart in spots, but I stay around those spots."
—Thomas Watson, Sr.

✦

"The education of a man is never completed until he dies."
—Robert E. Lee

✦

Carlos Tosca tells the story of the time he released a player at Triple-A Richmond in 2001. For the first time in his career, a player threw it back in Tosca's face that he'd never played the game for pay. "His direct quote to me was, 'You're nothing but a teacher.' I guess that was supposed to be derogatory, but I took it as a compliment."

✦

"School is never out for the pro."
—Cavett Robert

✦

"Knowledge is king; experience is essential."
—Harry Hutt

✦

"A brash young musician asked Mozart for advice on how to go about writing a symphony. The legendary composer noted his youthful age and tactfully replied, 'You are quite young. Why not begin with a simpler form, such as ballads?'

"The cocky man resisted that counsel and remarked, 'But you composed symphonies when you were 10 years old.'

"Mozart then tartly responded, 'Yes, but I didn't have to ask how.'"
—W. E. Thorn

✦

"Words with me are instruments."
—Theodore Roosevelt

"If I went back to college again, I'd concentrate on two areas: learning to write and to speak before an audience. Nothing in life is more important than the ability to communicate effectively."

—Gerald R. Ford

✦

"Learning is not compulsory, but neither is survival."

—W. Edwards Deming

✦

"The seven smartest words in the English language are: I don't know, but I'll find out."

—Larry Lucchino

✦

"Bill certainly has a great deal of self-confidence, but he's got the humility to know that he can always learn from somebody that's successful. To me, the smarter you are, the more you want to learn."

—Ernie Accorsi on Bill Belichick

✦

"If you took all the information on the Internet in one month, and put it in books averaging 250 pages, and stack those books on the Earth, the stack would go 200 million miles beyond the sun, and it's 93 million miles from the Earth to the sun."

—James Davis

✦

"I teach in order to learn."

—Robert Frost

✦

"Give attention to reading, to exhortation, to doctrine."

—1 Timothy 4:13 (NKJV)

✦

"An organization's ability to learn and to translate learning into action rapidly is the ultimate competitive business advantage."

—Jack Welch

"When hard times come, be a student, not a victim."

—Jim Warren

✦

"Your education begins when what is called your education ends."

—Oliver Wendell Holmes

✦

"A child who enters the ninth grade and graduates four years later will be exposed to more new information than their grandparents absorbed in their entire lifetime."

—Jay Strack

✦

"A man only learns in two ways: one, by reading and the other by association with smarter people."

—Will Rogers

✦

"I'm an owl. I hope to watch, to learn, and be wise."

—Norman Schwarzkopf

✦

"Experience is overrated. I've had some crummy, experienced players."

—Dennis Franchione

✦

"Experience is a good teacher, especially if it is other people's experience. There's no point in learning something the hard way if someone else has already paid the price."

—Andy Stanley

✦

"The best substitute for experience is being 16."

—Raymond Duncan

✦

When friends said they feared his assassination, Abraham Lincoln said: "God's will be done. I am in His hands."

"What is it like to be a Christian? It is like being a pumpkin. God picks you from the patch, brings you in, and washes all the dirt off you; then he cuts off the top and scoops out all the yucky stuff. He removes the seeds of doubt, hate, greed, etc.; then He carves you a new, smiling face and puts His light inside of you to shine for all the world to see."

—Unknown

✦

"I have a very small definition of faith: Faith is living as if God is telling the truth. The essence of faith is taking God at His word. If we want to please God, we had better know how to exercise faith. It's not hard to please God without faith—it's impossible. Not only that, but it's impossible to expect anything from Him without faith."

—Tony Evans

✦

I had walked life's way with an easy tread,
I had traveled where pleasures and comfort led.
Until, one day, in a quiet place,
I met the Master, face-to-face.
With station and rank and wealth my goal,
Much thought for my body, but none for my soul.
I had entered to win this life's mad race,
When I met the Master, face-to-face.
I built my castles and reared them high,
'Til their towers had pierced the blue of the sky;
I had sworn to rule with an iron mace,
When I met the Master, face-to-face.
I met Him, and know Him and blushed to see,
That His eyes, full of sorrow, were fixed upon me,
I faltered and fell at his feet that day.
While my castles melted and vanished away.
Melted and vanished and, in their place,
Nothing else could I see, but the Master's face.
My thoughts are now for the souls of men,
I've lost my life, to find it again;
Ever since that day, in a quiet place,
Where I met the Master, face to face.

—Unknown

"What's a gold medal when the streets are made with the stuff in Heaven?"

—Madeline Manning-Mims, Olympic gold medal winner in the 800-meter race

✦

"God's sovereign even in things we don't understand."

—Billy Graham

✦

"Take all of this book upon reason that you can and the balance on faith, and you will live and die a happier and better man."

—Abraham Lincoln, in 1864, to his friend Joshua Speed on the Bible

✦

"If you don't have a personal knowledge of God's Word, you have only two influences in your life: 1. Your emotions, and 2. What someone else tells you."

—Charles Swindoll

✦

"Can two walk together, except they be agreed?"

—Amos 3:3 (KJV)

✦

"Sanctify yourselves, for tomorrow the Lord will do wonders among you."

—Joshua 3:5 (NKJV)

✦

"Circumstances won't allow you to always be happy, but Jesus will help you look like you are."

—Charlie "Tremendous" Jones

✦

"It looked as if the answer was no, and I started to leave. As I was ready to walk out of the house, I said to Mrs. Davis: 'There's one thing I haven't told you. If Willie comes to Grambling, he's going to be in church every Sunday.'

"'Willie,' she said, 'you've got to go to that school.'"

—Eddie Robinson on recruiting Willie Davis

"God sees tomorrow like we see yesterday."
—Jay Strack

✦

In his book, *I Shall Not Want*, Robert Ketchum tells of a Sunday school teacher who asked her group of children if anyone could quote the entire 23rd Psalm. A golden-haired, four-and-a-half-year-old girl was among those who raised their hands. A bit skeptical, the teacher asked if she could really quote the entire Psalm. The little girl came to the front of the room, faced the class, made a perky little bow, and said, "The Lord is my shepherd. That's all I want." That may well be the greatest interpretation of the 23rd Psalm ever heard.

✦

"God is always up to something. It may not be pleasant, but it will be good."
—Bill Pannell

✦

"My job is to take care of the possible and trust God with the impossible."
—Ruth Graham Bell

✦

"We find out that God is all we need when God is all we've got."
—Rick Warren

✦

"Faith means believing in advance what will only make sense in reverse."
—Philip Yancey

✦

"He's good friends with God."
—David Wells on Andy Pettitte

✦

"If you work for a company, it's slavery (that's why people long for 5 o'clock and Fridays; they want to be free). If you work for money, it's a job (I will do no more than I'm paid for). If you work for the Lord, it's worship, and I hate to stop worshipping because it's so much fun."
—Charlie "Tremendous" Jones

"Prayer is thinking things through before God."
—Earl Palmer

✦

"I believe in Christianity as I believe in the sunrise, not because I can see it, but because by it I can see everything else."
—C.S. Lewis

✦

"Hope is faith in the future tense."
—A sign outside the Killarney Baptist Church, in Winter Park, Florida

✦

"Live today as you will wish you had lived when you stand before God."
—Unknown

✦

"And God spoke all these words, saying, 'I am the Lord your God, who brought you out of the land of Egypt, out of the house of bondage. You shall have no other gods before Me.'"
—Exodus 20:1-3 (NKJV)

✦

Hope is the thing with feathers
That perches in the soul
And sings the tune without the words
And never stops at all
And sweetest in the gale is heard.
—Emily Dickinson

✦

George H.W. Bush, a veteran of World War II, has a plaque hanging on his office wall that reads: CAVU. "When I was a pilot, 18 years old or 19, that was what we all prayed for. We didn't have GPS, we didn't have all this navigation stuff and radar and everything; therefore, what we prayed for at night, for the next day, was that we'd have Ceiling Absolute Visibility Unlimited. That's where my life is today."

"One day, I interviewed Billy Graham and asked him, 'If you could go back and change anything in your life, what would it be?'

"Dr. Graham replied, 'I'd do less ribbon-cutting and store openings and spend more time with the Lord in His Word.'

"I thought to myself, 'If Billy Graham feels that way, what about me?'"

—Terry Meeuwsen

✦

God's Hall-of-Fame

Your name may not appear down here
In this world's hall-of-fame,
In fact, you may be so unknown that no one knows your name.
The All-Stars here may pass you by, On neon lights of blue,
But, if you love and serve the Lord, Then, I have good news for you.
This hall of fame is only good as long as time shall be,
But, keep in mind God's hall-of-fame is for eternity.
To have your name inscribed up there, Is greater, yet, by far
Than all the halls of fame down here, And every man-made star.
This crowd on Earth may soon forget the heroes of the past,
They cheer like mad, until you fall and that's how long you last.
But, God, He never does forget, and, in His hall-of-fame,
By just believing in His Son, Inscribed, you'll find your name.
I tell you, friend, I wouldn't trade my name, however small,
That's written there, beyond the stars in that celestial hall.
For any famous name on Earth, or glory that they share,
I'd rather be an unknown here and have my name up there.

—Unknown

✦

Family: Twenty-eight percent of all children in the United States live in single-parent families. Thirty-four percent of American children live apart from their biological father. One million U.S. children under the age of 18 are newly affected by divorce each year. Thirty percent of all babies in the United States are born to unwed mothers. Forty percent of all children in America are expected to spend some of their formative years in a co-habiting household. In the United States there are 10 million single-mother families and two million single-father families.

—*Outreach*, July/August 2006

The Rose

It is only a tiny rosebud... A flower of God's design;
But I cannot unfold the petals with these clumsy hands of mine.
The secret of unfolding flowers
Is not known to such as I...
The flower God opens so sweetly
In my hands would fade and die.
If I cannot unfold a rosebud, this flower of God's design
Then how can I think I have wisdom to unfold this life of mine?
So, I'll trust in Him for his leading each moment of every day,
And I'll look to him for his guidance each step of the pilgrim way.
For the pathway that lies before me my heavenly Father knows...
I'll trust him to unfold the moments just as he unfolds the rose.

—Unknown

✦

According to the National Fatherhood Initiative, nearly 24 million American children live in homes without their biological father, and, perhaps more sobering, in about 40 percent of homes without dads, children haven't seen their fathers even once in the past 12 months.

✦

Harry S. Truman and his mother lost the family farm after his father's death. In later years, when asked if he considered his father a failure, Truman replied, "My father was not a failure. After all, he was the father of a President of the United States."

✦

"All the time I missed not having my father around. A woman can't teach a man how to be a man. You need a man to do that."

—Mike Tyson on growing up in Brooklyn without his father

✦

"If your wife doesn't treat you as she should, be grateful."

—Fred Smith

✦

"To focus on what's around you diminishes your ability to focus on what's before you."

—Andy Stanley

"My dad said, 'You take care of all the little things, you'll never have a big thing to worry about.'"

—Cal Ripken, Jr. at his Hall of Fame induction

✦

"Have you ever seen the second and third floors of a building in a place before the foundation is built? The foundation has to be in place first."

—Cazzie Russell

✦

"There are only two ways. One is right and the other is wrong. *About* is always wrong. Don't tell me it's about right. If it's only about right then it's wrong. If you come to a stream five feet wide and jump four-and-a-half feet, you fall in and drown."

—George Washington Carver

✦

"The secret of concentration is elimination."

—Howard Hendricks

✦

"I scrutinize every word and grade every line."

—Neil Diamond at age 64, on his songwriting

✦

"Make everyone aware that teams lose because of missed details."

—Marvin Lewis

✦

"If you do the small things right, big things can happen."

—Quote on a T-shirt in Rome, Georgia

✦

"There are no little things. Little things add up to one big thing."

—Randy Shannon

✦

"Retail is detail."

—James Sinegal, Costco CEO

"Coach Bryant was a stickler about paying attention to all the details. He'd tell us in meetings, 'Little things win. Little things make you a champion.'"

—Ray Perkins on Bear Bryant

✦

"At practice, the Orlando Magic staff wears T-shirts that have printed on the back, 'It's all the little things.'"

—Glenn Anton "Doc" Rivers

✦

"Sixty percent of the American population is sedentary, and 61 percent is overweight. If you will walk two miles in 30 minutes three times a week, or two miles in 40 minutes five times a week, there will be a 58 percent reduction in death by heart attack, stroke, and cancer. Your lifespan will increase by six years overall. Each hour spent exercising (up to 30 hours a week) adds about two hours to a person's life expectancy, according to the Harvard Alumni Study which has tracked deaths among 17,000 men for more than two decades. Even those who did not start exercising until mid-life had 23 percent lower risk of death over the next 20 years."

—John Cooper

✦

"Do you live as if you rent your body or as if you own it?"

—Mackie Shilstone

✦

"If you don't have hope, what do you have?"

—Danny Wuerfeel

✦

"You can't find meaning in achievement. If you live long enough, life will trash your trophies."

—James Dobson

✦

"Fifty years from now, I'll just be three inches of type in a record book."

—Brooks Robinson

"In September 1969, I was working at the Weather Station at the little airport in Waco, Texas. The door opened and in walked Neil Armstrong, who two months earlier had set foot on the moon. He was the most famous man in the world at that point, but was flying a plane from Waco to Houston. He checked in with me to get an update on the weather conditions, proving that no matter how high you get in life you still have to pay attention to the little things."

—Mike Looney

✦

"The more weak links I hire, the less likely it is that I'll be the weakest."

—An advertising panel in the Atlanta airport

✦

When Johnny Weissmuller was playing Tarzan in the movies, he spoke to a group of young actors, all hoping for their big break. One of them asked, "What's the best advice you can give us?" He simply answered, "Don't let go of your vine."

✦

"When you borrow, try to borrow from a pessimist. He won't expect to get it back."

—Abraham Lincoln

✦

On one occasion, President John F. Kennedy went to Florida and toured the Space Center. During his tour, the president stopped to chat with one of the janitors. The president asked, "What is your job here?"

The janitor replied, "Mr. President, my job is to put a man on the moon by the end of this decade and return him safely to Earth."

✦

"You have to let your husband be himself, and you have to pretend he's someone else."

—Rita Rudner

✦

At his 103rd birthday party, a man was asked if he thought he'd be around for his 104th. He stated: "I certainly do. Statistics show that very few people die between the ages of 103 and 104."

"The redhead is so careful of the truth, he uses it very sparingly."
—A sportscaster on Larry MacPhail

✦

"I conquered anorexia."
—On the T-shirt of an overweight man

✦

"A person with a haunting fear that someone, somewhere is happy."
—H.L. Mencken's caricature of a Puritan

✦

"Ken-ya catch me?"
—Phrase on the back of a T-shirt at the start of the 2003 Chicago Marathon

✦

"To me, old age is always 15 years older than I am."
—Bernard Baruch

✦

"Clearly the trick is to die young as late as possible."
—Slogan on the back of a T-shirt at the 2004 Book Expo in Chicago

✦

"Did it occur to you that nothing ever occurs to God?"
—Johnny Hunt

✦

Winston Churchill, British Prime Minister, will always be remembered for his quick wit and lively comebacks. Someone once remarked to him, "Who would want to live to be 90?" Churchill is rumored to have replied, "Everyone who is 89."

✦

"Don't look forward to the day you stop suffering, because when it comes, you're dead."
—Tennessee Williams

"My second favorite household chore is ironing—my first being hitting my head on the top bunk until I faint."

—Erma Bombeck

✦

"My theory of housework is if the item doesn't multiply, smell, catch on fire, or block the refrigerator door, let it be. No one cares. Why should I?"

—Erma Bombeck

✦

"When you look like your passport photo, it's time to go home."

—Erma Bombeck

✦

"You know what really hurts? When you go into a store and the clerk asks, 'Is it for Father's Day, or would you like to see something more expensive?'"

—Unknown

✦

"I was one of the few he called by my first name. He called me Joe."

—John Drebinger on Babe Ruth, who was notoriously poor at remembering names

✦

"I can only please one person per day. Today is not your day. Tomorrow doesn't look good either."

—Unknown

✦

Once, famous baseball manager, Casey Stengel, took struggling Mets player Marv Throneberry aside and told him, "You know, Marv, when they make the announcement before the ballgame that anyone touching a thrown or batted ball will be ejected from the park? Well now, Marv, they don't mean you!"

✦

"Everywhere is within walking distance if you have the time."

—Steven Wright

"New wife to her friend: 'Housekeeping is like threading beads on a cord with no knot at the end.'"

—Lewis Stultz

✦

"All men make mistakes, but those who are married find out about them sooner."

—Richard Bernard "Red" Skelton

✦

"I'm as frustrated as a stray dog at a whistler's convention."

—Unknown

✦

During a flight on a small airplane, the flight attendant asked a passenger if he would like to have dinner. "What are my choices?" asked the passenger. "Yes or no," the flight attendant replied.

✦

"L.A. Dodgers announcer, Vin Scully, told the *Chicago Sun Times* about former big league infielder, Gene Freese. 'He once got back to the hotel after a night on the town, dialed the front desk and asked for a 7 a.m. wake-up call. The operator said, 'You just missed it.'"

—Tom Fitzgerald

✦

"My first major interview? The phone rang, and my wife told me it was *Sports Illustrated*. I cut myself shaving and fell down the steps in my rush to get to the phone. I said, 'Hello,' and the voice on the other end said, 'For just 75 cents an issue...'"

—William "Speedy" Morris

✦

"I just let my mind wander, and it didn't come back."

—Unknown

✦

"I think men who have a pierced ear are better prepared for marriage. They've experienced pain and bought jewelry."

—Rita Rudner

"With all the sadness and trauma going on in the world at the moment, it is worth reflecting on the death of a very important person, which almost went unnoticed last week. Larry LaPrise, the man who wrote *The Hokey Pokey,* died peacefully at the age of 93. The most traumatic part for his family was getting him into the coffin. First, they put his left leg in, and then the trouble started."

—Unknown

✦

"People tell me, 'Gee, you look good.' There are three ages of man: youth, middle age, and 'Gee, you look good.'"

—Red Skelton

✦

"The main purpose of children's parties is to remind you that there are children worse than your own."

—Katharine Whitehorn

✦

"When my kids become wild and unruly, I use a nice safe playpen. When they're finished, I climb out."

—Erma Bombeck

✦

"My favorite cartoon character, Charlie Brown, displayed an attitude with which many of us can identify. He and Linus were talking about their problems. Linus said, 'I guess it's wrong always to be worrying about tomorrow. Maybe we should think about today.'

"Charlie Brown replied, 'No, that's giving up. I'm still hoping that yesterday will get better.'"

—John Maxwell

✦

"George W. has always been surrounded by strong, smart women, sometimes by choice, sometimes by birth."

—Barbara Bush

✦

"The best advice for teenagers is leave home now while you still know everything."

—Unknown

"I majored in aeronautical engineering. That meant if I couldn't make it in the NBA, I could always be a skycap."

—Charles Barkley, NBA TV analyst and former all-star, speaking about his college experience

✦

"And now, as we come to the end of the convention, let me leave you with this thought, something to take home with you—as if the soap, the shampoo, the conditioner, and the towels aren't enough."

—Bob Orben

✦

"I have dieted continuously for the last two decades and lost a total of 758 pounds. By all calculations, I should be hanging from a charm bracelet."

—Erma Bombeck

✦

"We are not in an easy profession. A recent survey showed that in our business, one of the three basic food groups is Maalox."

—Unknown

✦

"I told my wife I'd be home by 11. Fortunately, I didn't say what day."

—Unknown

✦

"Given a choice between the man of your dreams and a plumber, choose the latter. Men who can fix your toilet on Sundays are hard to come by."

—Erma Bombeck

✦

"Leadership is influence, and influence can be taught."

—John Maxwell

✦

"The true measure of leadership is influence...nothing more, nothing less."

—John C. Maxwell

"The Titanic was larger than many modern cruise ships. At the time it was built, it was the largest moving object ever constructed by man. It was 882 feet long and stood 11 stories high. It's hard to wrap our minds around the size of that kind of sailing ship, but what may be harder still to reconcile is the fact that a rudder only 78 feet steered the enormous vessel."

—Robert Morris

✦

"Whether we want to admit it or not, we're all hero worshipers. We don't have cowboys anymore. We don't have war heroes to admire. So most of the heroes today are athletes."

—Bobby Bowden

✦

"You can manage without being a leader, but if you do you'll lose."

—General Tommy Franks on his advice to baseball managers

✦

"Maturity in leadership is the ability to see things not just from your standpoint, but also see them from the other person's viewpoint. Followers can't do this because they see things only from their own viewpoint."

—John C Maxwell

✦

"The leader must know, must know that he knows, and must be able to make it abundantly clear to those about him that he knows."

—Clarence A. Randall

✦

"A leader who does not inspire is like a river without water. Every follower yearns to be inspired by his or her leader."

—Lance Secretan

✦

"Leadership is solving problems and the day people stop bringing you their problems is the day you stop leading."

—Colin Powell

"There are natural-born leaders, but there are so few of them that they do not make any difference in the great scheme of things."

—Peter Drucker

✦

"There's a line I like from Socrates. When he was unjustly imprisoned and facing imminent death, the jailers asked, 'Why aren't you preparing for death?' Socrates said, 'I've been preparing for death all my life, the life I've led."

—John Wooden

✦

"The day before my inauguration, President Eisenhower told me, 'You'll find that no easy problems ever come to the President of the United States. If they are easy to solve, somebody else has solved them.' I found that hard to believe, but now I know it is true."

—John F. Kennedy

✦

"Developing leadership capabilities is like a three-legged stool. The first leg is seeing yourself as a leader. The second is having the right skills. The third leg is paying attention to opportunities to lead."

—John Eldred

✦

"In a recent study, it was discovered that 71 percent of people who left companies would have stayed if they could have worked with another manager."

—Brian Tracy

✦

"You can build a throne with bayonets, but you can't sit on it for long."

—Boris Yeltsin

✦

"Coaching is overrated. Leadership is not."

—Pat Riley

✦

"Leadership can't be taught, but can be learned."

—Jim Collins

"If I had to name a single all-purpose instrument of leadership, it would be communication."

—John Gardener

✦

"Martin Luther once observed that he would prefer to be governed by a smart Turk than a stupid Christian."

—Doug Bandow

✦

"To understand the importance of a leader, try working without one."

—An advertisement in the Phoenix airport

✦

"The gift of oratory is synonymous with leadership."

—Adam Witty

✦

"All progress known to mankind is dependent upon leaders shaping the world to themselves, not people shaping themselves to the world."

—Adam Witty

✦

"Here is a timeless principle of leadership:

- Get the right people on the bus.
- Get the wrong people off.
- Get people in the right seats, then figure out where to drive the bus."

—Jim Collins

✦

"Given a choice of hearing a brilliant story badly told, or a trivial story well told, an audience will always take the trivial."

—Robert McKee

✦

"He was always asking, 'What do you think?' He wanted to know our opinions, and I think he wanted us to really think."

—Don Soderquist on Sam Walton

"You are not in the baseball business, but the people-discernment business. It's getting the right people on your team in the right places at the right time. Without this ability, you will fail and never make it. After integrity, this is the most important component of leadership."

—Ed Young, Sr. to a young baseball manager

✦

In 1977, George Steinbrenner outlined those things by which a manager should be judged. They were known as George's Seven Commandments:

- Does he win?
- Does he work hard enough?
- Is he emotionally equipped to lead men?
- Is he organized?
- Does he understand human nature?
- Is he prepared for each game?
- Is he honorable?

✦

"When you are introduced to Bill Clinton, it's as if you are the only person in the room."

—Carol Bartz

✦

"Show me a coach or a boss who doesn't listen—really listen—and I'll show you a loser."

—Brad Gilbert

✦

There is an old adage often attributed to George Herbert, a seventeenth-century poet, which goes like this:

For want of a nail, the shoe is lost.
For want of a shoe, the horse is lost.
For want of the horse, the rider is lost.
For want of the rider, the battle is lost.
For want of the battle, the war is lost.
For want of the war, the nation is lost.
All for the want of a horseshoe nail.

"It's important to stress the little things, because—in tight competition—they will be the difference between winning and losing. Inevitably, the outcome of the game will come down to some detail."

—Raymond Berry

✦

"Competition breeds excellence. Without competition, mediocrity sets in."

—Mike Huckabee

✦

"We must not confuse dissent with disloyalty."

—Edward R. Murrow

✦

"If anything goes wrong, I have my money. I will buy an island, be king on my island. My money will save me."

—Uday Hussein

✦

"You can hit me and I won't think much of it, but you can say something and hurt me very much."

—Floyd Patterson

✦

When the pleasure you are viewing,
Any work that one is doing,
And you like him or you love him, tell him now.
Don't withhold your approbations,
'Til the parson makes orations,
And he lies with snowy lilies on his brow.
Now's the time to show it to him.
'Cause a man can't read his tombstone when he's dead.

—Unknown

✦

"Anyone can get old. All you have to do is live long enough."

—Groucho Marx

"I personally stay away from natural foods. At my age, I need all the preservatives I can get."

—George Burns

✦

"The memories of a man in his old age are the deeds of the man in his prime."

—Pink Floyd, "Free Four"

✦

"Remember, your life is all connected."

—Zig Ziglar

✦

"Patience is the ability to be slow to anger rather than being quick-tempered."

—James Merritt

✦

"If I was running a university, I would insist that these three things be taught:

- Memory training
- Speed reading
- How to recognize opportunities and take advantage of them."

—Rich Wolfe

✦

"Wisdom comes from knowing your days are short."

—James Dobson

✦

"All men die, but not all men really live."

—Mel Gibson, *Braveheart*

✦

"There's nothing wrong with teenagers that reasoning with them won't aggravate."

—Bob Plant

✦

"Everyone likes a compliment."

—Abraham Lincoln

"I don't stay in touch with people. That's clearly my biggest regret. Voters are the source of all wisdom. You have to conduct an ongoing dialogue with them."

—Gray Davis

✦

"The greatest compliment that was ever paid to me was when someone asked me what I thought, and attended to my answer."

—Henry David Thoreau

✦

"He can't last. I tell you flatly, he can't last."

—Jackie Gleason on Elvis Presley

✦

"Love is what's left of a relationship after all the selfishness has been removed."

—Cullen Hightower

✦

"That speech went on so long my foot went to sleep, and the rest of me wanted to join it."

—Bob Orben

✦

"Some guys can't coach a lot of talent. No one can coach no talent."

—John Wooden

✦

"The higher a monkey climbs the more you see of his behind."

—General Joe Stillwell

✦

"My one regret in life is that I am not someone else."

—Woody Allen

✦

"Selling ideas is the most crucial of all jobs. I've been selling all my life."

—Joyce Hall, founder of Hallmark Cards

David Douglas Duncan is generally acknowledged to have taken the best pictures ever of Americans in combat. He and his camera joined the Marines during their freezing Iliad during the Korean War. Slogging south one December day, Duncan came upon some exhausted troopers prodding at the frozen contents of a can of beans. The incessant wind dropped for a moment and Duncan broke the silence to ask a question: "If I were God, what would you want for Christmas?" The Marine lifted his eyes and said: "Give me tomorrow."

✦

"This is a game of personalities, and it's a game of selling. You make the call, and you have to sell it."

—Bruce Froemming on umpiring in the Major Leagues

✦

"Here lies a man who knew how to enlist into his service people better than himself."

—Andrew Carnegie's epitaph

✦

"Winning's a very precious thing."

—Bill Parcells

✦

"Never in the field of human conflict was so much owed by so many to so few."

—Winston Churchill, August 16, 1940 to British Airmen

✦

"There are five steps to being an effective storyteller:

1. Establish a mood and a specific time for the story; "Once upon a time..."
2. Establish a setting.
3. Introduce the central characters of the story.
4. Pose the dilemma or the situation that seems insurmountable.
5. Reveal the resolution that is identified with the central character."

—John Eldred

✦

"*Store* and *stories* sound alike for a reason. People will remember stories long after they have forgotten your bullet points."

—Laurie Beth Jones

"There are essentially three types of people in the world:

1. Those who think before they speak
2. Those who think while they speak
3. Those who think after they speak (Having written that, I now realize there may actually be a fourth type: Those who just speak and never think. I've met a few of those types of people over the years.)"

—Robert Morris

✦

"They were a colony of storytellers."

—Historian Theodore White on his Harvard history professors

✦

"As governor of Texas he was awful. He has improved mightily and is a master now."

—Jack Valenti, former LBJ aide, on George W. Bush's speaking style

✦

"Stories are the created conversion of life itself into a more powerful, cleaner and more meaningful experience."

—Robert McKee

✦

"Watching Ronald Reagan rehearse a speech was like watching Babe Ruth taking batting practice."

—Dick Wirthlin

✦

"He was a man for whom oratory was somewhere between an art form, a sport and a drug."

—Thomas Keneally on Abraham Lincoln's approach to public speaking

✦

"He mobilized the English language and sent it into battle."

—John F. Kennedy on granting U.S. citizenship to Winston Churchill in 1963

✦

"The only reason to give a speech is to change the world."

—Nick Morgan

"Martin, if you continue to use such lofty and flamboyant language, you will never be very effective in your public speaking."

—One of Martin Luther King, Jr.'s college professors frowned on his use of mighty expressions and defended a poor grade given

✦

"My saving grace has been my words. Words are the only things that endure."

—Nipsey Russell

✦

"A lot of managers aren't bad at public speaking, but not bad ain't good enough."

—Tom Peters

✦

"Not since Lincoln or Winston Churchill in Britain has there been a President who has so understood the power of words to uplift and to inspire."

—Margaret Thatcher on Ronald Reagan's 83rd birthday gala, 1994

✦

"I've always been guided by the three Cs: be clear, be concise, and be correct."

—Bob Shepherd

✦

"Can he talk! Anyone who has heard him speak knows that Powell can talk for an hour straight with fluency and polish without ever glancing at a note."

—Kathleen Parker on Colin Powell

✦

"We stood transfixed upon his appearance and one square inch of flesh was not covered with goose pimples. It was one of the greatest thrills I shall ever know ... that towering figure, impeccably attired, froze you in place and electrified the air."

—A young soldier wrote to his family after attending an address by General George S. Patton

✦

"Winston Churchill, through the power of his words on the radio, got people to go fight in the streets, and he did it without PowerPoints."

—Patricia Fripp, speech coach

"Communism is neither an economic nor a political system—it is a form of insanity, a temporary aberration which will one day disappear from the Earth because it is contrary to human nature."

—Ronald Reagan, May 1975, in his radio address

✦

"In your hands, my dissatisfied fellow countrymen, and not mine, is the momentous issue of Civil War. The government will not assail you. You can have no conflicts without being yourselves the aggressors."

—Abraham Lincoln's inauguration address, 1861

✦

"I ask you to stop and think for a moment what it would mean to have nuclear weapons in so many hands: in the hands of countries large and small, stable and unstable, responsible and irresponsible, scattered throughout the world. There would be no rest for anyone then, no stability, no real security, and no chance of effective disarmament."

—John F. Kennedy in a televised address to the nation in July 1963

✦

"It is no coincidence that our present troubles parallel and are proportionate to the intervention and intrusion in our lives that result from unnecessary and excessive growth of government."

—Ronald Reagan's inauguration speech, January 1981

✦

"Men talk of the Negro problem, but there is no Negro problem. The problem is whether the American people have loyalty enough, patriotism enough, honor enough to live up to their own Constitution."

—Frederick Douglass in 1892

✦

"I speak today not as a Massachusetts man nor as a northern man, but as an American ... I speak today for the preservation of the Union."

—Daniel Webster (January 1850) speaking to Congress

✦

"When I'm asked what teams gave us the most trouble, my answer is always the same: the teams with the best players."

—John Wooden

"Two thousand years ago the proudest boast was *Civis Romanus Sum*. Today, in the world of freedom, the proudest boast is, *Ich bin ein Berliner*. Freedom has many difficulties, and democracy is not perfect, but we have never had to put a wall up to keep our people in, to prevent them from leaving us."

—John F. Kennedy at the Berlin Wall, June 26, 1963

✦

"With malice toward none; with charity for all; with firmness in the right, as God gives us to see the right, let us strive on to finish the work we are in; to bind up the nation's wounds; to care for him who shall have borne the battle and for his widow, and his orphan ... to do all which may achieve and cherish a just and a lasting peace among ourselves and with all nations."

—Abraham Lincoln issued his historic plea to his fellow countrymen

✦

"People have forgotten how to tell a story."

—Steven Spielberg

✦

"The universe is made up of stories, not atoms."

—Muriel Rukeyser

✦

"You can never have too much talent. Even the 1927 Yankees didn't win every year."

—Buzzie Bavasi

✦

"The better horse I have, the better I can ride."

—Phillies' manager Charlie Manuel on talent

✦

"It's a talent business, and you must be able to manage talent. It takes a strong hand to handle talent and put them in a position to win."

—Randy Pfund

✦

A fan asked Yankee coach Don Zimmer: "What makes Joe Torre such a good manager?" Zimmer replied, "Good players."

"The success of the Celtics was that the first thing they looked at was ability. The second thing was ability. The third thing was ability."

—Bill Russell

✦

"I've always thought you'd rather have talent as the main thing and experience would be second, but the best would be 'experienced talent.'"

—Roy Williams

✦

When Sparky Anderson's team acquired a good player in a trade, he'd say, "I just got smarter."

✦

"If you don't want to get beat by Oklahoma, get better players."

—Billy Tubbs, when coaching at the University of Oklahoma

✦

"Never underestimate the value of talent."

—Jerry Steele

✦

"I give the same halftime speech over and over. It works best when my players are better than the other coach's players."

—Chuck Mills

✦

"Maddux, Glavine, Smoltz, and a few Cy Young awards had a lot to do with it."

—Leo Mazzone, former Atlanta Braves' pitching coach, on his success there

✦

"The proof that you know something is that you are able to teach it."

—Aristotle

✦

"Snow is a beautiful example of what God can do with a bunch of flakes."

—Rick Warren on teamwork

"Everyone and everything begins with people. If the people part is not right, we know where the rest of it is going."

—Dan J. Sanders and Galen Walters

✦

"A house divided against itself cannot stand."

—Abraham Lincoln, accepting his party's nomination for the U.S. Senate in 1858

✦

"When you don't take care of the team first, the baseball gods won't let you get away with it."

—Todd Hundley

✦

"You aren't the center of the universe. That job is already taken."

—Unknown

✦

"Two are better than one, because they have a good return for their work: if one falls down, his friend can help him up. But pity the man who falls and has no one to help him up! Also, if two lie down together, they will keep warm. But how can one keep warm alone?"

—Ecclesiastes 4:9-11 (NIV)

✦

"The most important single ingredient in the formula of success is knowing how to get along with people."

—Theodore Roosevelt

✦

"Talent alone is not enough. They used to tell me you have to use your five best players, but I've found that you win with the five who fit together best."

—Red Auerbach

✦

"No man will make a great leader who wants to do it all himself, or get all the credit for doing it."

—Andrew Carnegie

"It's about what we can do together. You could have a great game, you could have a maximum performance, and you could break all of your own personal records, but if we don't win the game, all those things are empty; they're shallow. Consider the tiger versus the lion. One-on-one, the tiger will win every time. The tiger family is very selfish, but if there are 10 lions and 10 tigers, the lions will win every time because the lions care about each other, and really, that's what it takes."

—Bill McCartney

✦

Mike Krzyzewski's Five-Point Play (Fist): Communication, Trust, Collective Responsibility, Caring, and Pride

✦

"The United States was founded ... not by isolated acts of individual heroism, but by the concerted revolutionary activities of people who had learned the power of working together."

—Ray Raphael

✦

"Without everybody embracing what we want to do, we haven't got a prayer."

—Jack Welch

✦

1. Be on time.
2. Play hard.
3. Know your job.
4. Know when to shoot and when to pass.

That's when I know you've arrived, because that's how you get team chemistry.

—Hubie Brown's four basic rules for each player

✦

In 1980, Herb Brooks coached the U.S. Olympic hockey team that beat the Soviets. The team was built on personal chemistry and many of the greatest college players were omitted. In the movie version *Miracle*, Brooks tells his assistant, "I'm not looking for the best players, Craig. I'm looking for the right players."

✦

"You're only as good as the people you hire."

—Ray Kroc

"The challenge for every organization is to build a feeling of oneness, of depending on one another, because the question is usually not how well each person works, but how well they work together."

—Vince Lombardi

✦

"I tried to explain to my players that every person has a role and every role is important, so fill your role. What good is an engine if you lose a wheel?"

—John Wooden

✦

"We can make a nice sound together. It all gets down to love. If we have love, we'll be good. If we don't, we'll be bad."

—Al McGuire to his players

✦

"There are three ingredients to team chemistry:
Trust in one another.
Have a common cause.
Build respect for each others' role on the team."

—Marty Schottenheimer

✦

"You can't make the team if you don't understand teamwork."

—John Heisman

✦

"One who attempts mighty feats had better be capable of recruiting a mighty team."

—*Zondervan Study Bible*

✦

"Talent can't beat chemistry. I'm sorry. Chemistry will win all the time."

—Darvin Ham

✦

"If it is about one person, I think you should run track."

—Larry Brown on his basketball philosophy

How tight were the 1960 Eagles? Tom Brookshier recalled a pre-season game played in Roanoke, Virginia. A group of the players, including Clarence Peaks, boarded the hotel elevator. Peaks, a black running back, was told he needed to step out and use the freight elevator. "Where's the freight elevator?" asked Billy Ray Barnes, a North Carolinian. "We'll all take the freight elevator."

✦

On September 1, 1971, the Pittsburgh Pirates played the Philadelphia Phillies. Manager Danny Murtaugh started the game with nine black players for the first time in Major League history. When a reporter asked Murtaugh if he realized his lineup had nine blacks, Murtaugh replied, "I thought I had nine Pirates out there on the field."

✦

Peter Drucker's religion teacher asked him a haunting question: "What will you be remembered for?" Drucker wrote when in his 80s: "I'm always asking that question."

✦

"We exaggerate yesterday. We overestimate tomorrow. We underestimate today."
—John Maxwell

✦

"He's day-to-day, but aren't we all."
—Charley Steiner on an injured baseball player's condition

✦

"Live Now."
—Tattoo on the right bicep of Carmelo Anthony

✦

"This is the greatest day in the history of the world; even better than yesterday, though that seemed an impossibility yesterday."
—Jack Kent Cooke

✦

"In an interview with Barbara Walters, Jimmy Carter was surprised by one question. She asked him to reflect on his colorful life—engineer, naval officer, peanut farmer, governor, president—and name what phase he most enjoyed. He thought for a minute, then he smiled that famous smile and said, 'Now.'"
—Philip Yancey

"There's no such thing as 'the good ol' days.' Who cares? Today's a good day! Tomorrow might even be better. That's the way you have to look at it."

—Johnny Pesky

✦

"A man can stand anything except a succession of ordinary days."

—Goethe

✦

"Would that I could stand on a busy corner, hat in hand, and beg people to throw me all their wasted hours."

—Bernard Berenson

✦

"My best day is today, and my next best day is tomorrow."

—Larry Hagman

✦

"Don't let yesterday use up too much of today."

—Will Rogers

✦

"Forever is composed of nows."

—Emily Dickinson

✦

There is a tide in the affairs of men,
Which, taken at the flood, leads on to fortune;
Omitted, all the voyages of their life
Is bound in the shallows and in miseries...
And we must take the current when it serves,
Or lose our ventures.

—William Shakespeare

✦

"The thing I lose patience with the most is the clock. Its hands move too fast. Time is really the only capital that any human being has and the one thing they can't afford to lose."

—Thomas Edison

"Its brevity."

—Billy Graham when asked what he was most surprised by in life

✦

"The sports writer, Red Smith, once said to me, 'I'm going to give the best advice you will ever get: make a memory every day.' And that's what I try to do."

—Lesley Visser

✦

"We have only this moment, sparkling like a star in our hand and melting like a snowflake."

—Sir Francis Bacon

✦

"Today is yesterday's pupil."

—Ben Franklin

✦

"To some people, instant gratification isn't fast enough."

—Greg Ehrbar

✦

"Don't let yourself become paralyzed by yesterday or hypnotized by tomorrow. It's important to stay riveted on today."

—Johnny Hunt

✦

"All of them!"

—Comedian Arte Johnson on his best day

✦

"Nearly every world problem makes it right to the desk of the Oval Office, and you've got to have a clear vision about what the world ought to look like."

—George W. Bush

✦

"He had the ability to see around the corners, to see the future before it's here."

—Bill Bradley on Woodrow Wilson

"Tomorrow is the most important thing in your life. It comes into us at midnight very calm. It's perfect when it appears and it puts itself in our hands. It hopes we've learned something from yesterday."

—John Wayne's epitaph

✦

"Leadership is the ability to enlarge men's vision about the future and give them expectations of a less uncertain and more gratifying future."

—Dick Wirthlin

✦

"Martin Luther King, Jr. was endowed with the gift to see beyond his years. You might call it a dream, but I think it was a vision of what America could become. Dr. King was the greatest communicator in the history of America, and could get others to see his vision as he shared with them what he visualized. As a result, he had the ability to get people to follow him."

—John Lewis, U.S. Congressman from Georgia

✦

"The balloon soon cleared the obstruction and floated up and out of the River Seine. Fifty-thousand spectators had witnessed that stunning achievement of the Montgolfier Brothers, Joseph and Etienne ... and the beginning of manned flight on November 21, 1783. Benjamin Franklin had to watch from his carriage so crippled was he with gout. One of the witnesses turned to Franklin to ask him what practical use it was. The most practical man on Earth answered simply: 'What is the use of a newborn baby?"

—William Bennett

✦

"Sports serves one master: winning. That is all that matters."

—Mitch Albom

✦

"Success. Success. It's fun if you know it's temporary and don't inhale. Neither of us ever did."

—David Brinkley after he and Chet Huntley won their first Emmy

✦

"There's no such thing as a success story."

—Ken Davis

"Whenever I am at a book signing, I sign the books in one of five ways. These are the five keys to success in life:

1. Dream Big
2. Enjoy Life
3. Work Hard
4. Be true to yourself.
5. Learn every day."

—Newt Gingrich

✦

"All of us live for one of three reasons: survival, success, or significance."

—David Uth

✦

"My belief has always been in executive leadership, not executive rulership."

—John Nance Garner

✦

"Dreams have only one owner at a time. That is why dreamers are lonely."

—Erma Bombeck

✦

"Speaking from the heart to the heart, directly ... Not too complicated, relatively brief sentences and words that are clear to everyone."

—Theodore C. Sorensen on effective public speaking

✦

"The nation yearns for leadership."

—Lead editorial in *The New York Times* (January 29, 2008)

✦

"I never concern myself about any game but the next one and the game we're playing tonight."

—Bill Russell

✦

"Leadership is of utmost importance. Indeed, there is no substitute for it."

—Peter Drucker

"The only thing worse than not reading a book in the last 90 days is not reading a book in the last 90 days and thinking that it doesn't matter."

—Jim Rohn

✦

"It's Recognition, Appreciation, and Encouragement, and that combination is more powerful than the fuel they use to send rockets to the moon."

—Lee Cockerell on the RAE Theory

✦

"The vacuum now is leadership."

—*Wall Street Journal* editorial (October 10, 2008)

✦

"The alternative to discipline is disaster."

—Vance Havner

✦

"Keep it clean and keep it friendly after I'm gone, and everything will be all right."

—Walt Disney on Disneyland

✦

"There's an old racetrack saying: No jockey ever runs faster than his horse."

—Bill Lyon

✦

"A quarterback's main job is to win games."

—Bill Belichick

✦

"Football's not about X's and O's. It's about people. Everything in life is based on people."

—Mike Ditka

✦

"The whole point of failure is to learn from it."

—Sidney Harman

"Experience is not what happens to a man. It is what a man does with what happens to him."

—Aldous Huxley

✦

"Good players—very, very good players."

—Terry Francona on being 8-0 in the World Series with the Red Sox

✦

"All politics is about is being a little better than the other guy."

—John Sears

✦

"I suppose leadership at one time meant muscles, but today it means getting along with people."

—Gandhi

✦

"You simply cannot lead if you cannot tell the other guy what it is you want and expect. If you can't rouse the crowd, you cannot lead effectively."

—Bob Crandall

✦

"When I first started coaching at LSU, I went to visit John Wooden, to pick his brain. We spent an entire day together and, at the end of that day, Coach said to me: 'Let me give you three key points to remember:

- Make certain you have better players than your opponents.
- Those players must put the team above themselves.
- Always practice simplicity with constant repetition. Don't give your players too much information.'"

—Dale Brown

✦

"Leadership is one of the performing arts, and the leader always has to sell himself or herself to the audience."

—Warren Bennis and Robert Thomas

"A leader can never listen too much."

—Warren Bennis

✦

"There's a sign in my office that says one word: Communication. I don't always do the best job of that, but I know it's the most important thing you can do."

—Mike Ditka

✦

"FDR never did talk to me confidentially about the war or about foreign affairs or what he had in mind for peace after the war."

—Harry S. Truman to his daughter, Margaret

✦

"I sit here all day trying to persuade people to do the things they ought to have sense enough to do without my persuading them ... That's all the powers of the president amount to."

—Harry S. Truman

✦

"In your hands, my dissatisfied fellow countryman, and not in mine, is the momentous issue of Civil War. The government will not assail you."

—Abraham Lincoln (March 4, 1861) at his first inauguration

✦

"A strong leader doesn't say, 'We're going to treat everyone the same.' A strong leader says, 'We treat everyone fairly.' It's a cop-out to say that you're going to treat everyone the same way."

—Roy Williams

✦

"Albert Einstein was asked to be the second president of Israel, but he declined, saying that he lacked the people skills."

—Noah D. Oppenheim

✦

"If you want to get elected, learn to speak; if you want to stay elected, learn to listen."

—Tom Daschle

"You can't motivate someone else. Motivation is an inside job. We can't motivate others, but we can inspire them."

—Kevin Eikenberry

✦

"When Dr. Martin Luther King's sermons started to gain altitude, his father, Daddy King, was known to lean forward and whisper, 'Keep it simple, son, keep it simple.'"

—Tom Brokaw

✦

"Lord, grant me the wisdom to know what is right and the courage to do it. Amen."

—Clarence Thomas, Supreme Court Justice, at his swearing-in ceremony, offered this silent prayer

✦

"I think there are only two kinds of prayers: 'Thank you, God,' and 'Help me, God.'"

—Gloria Gaither

✦

"Finding the right person for the job is far more important than finding a person to fill the job."

—Monica Wofford

✦

"Tommy Lasorda made a career out of remembering everyone's name and their birthdays."

—Bill Plaschke

✦

"Management consultant Nancy Austin says that when she looked under the bed in her room of one of her favorite hotels, she was surprised to find a card. It said, 'Yes, we clean under here, too!' Austin said, 'I don't remember the lobby or the number of chandeliers or how many square feet of marble cobbled together to make our underfoot experience pleasant.' What she remembered was that card. The housekeeping staff had anticipated what was important to her and had served her well."

—John Maxwell

"Who you know is not more important than what you know."

—Bobby Jindal

✦

"If it were not for hope, the heart would break."

—Unknown

✦

"You won't know what kind of teacher you are until 28 years after the fact."

—John Wooden

✦

"The real problem with our society is that we've taken the word responsibility and turned it into entitlement, and we sit around thinking that's an option."

—Roger Ailes

✦

"The greatest leaders in world history have had great teachers in their lives, and generally have been great teachers themselves."

—Mark Swick

✦

"The words of the president have an enormous weight and ought not to be used indiscriminately."

—Calvin Coolidge

✦

"Discipline yourself, and others won't need to."

—John Wooden

✦

"In the business world, everyone is paid in two coins: cash and experience. Take the experience first. The cash will come later."

—Harold Geneen

✦

"Patience is the companion of wisdom."

—Saint Augustine

"In any contest between power and patience, bet on patience."

—W.B. Prescott

✦

"He that can have patience can have what he will."

—Benjamin Franklin

✦

"Our growth depends not on how many experiences we devour, but on how many we digest."

—Ralph W. Sockman

✦

"My limo driver in Omaha, Walter, told me he has driven Warren Buffett and Bill Gates together at times. Both men do a lot of kidding. On one occasion, Bill Gates said, 'Walter, you better not have a wreck with us in this limo. It will have a bad effect on the nation's economy.'"

—Pat Williams

✦

"Hope deferred makes the heart sick."

—Proverbs 13:12 (NIV)

✦

"At the end of the day its managing people."

—Sam Mitchell on coaching in the NBA

✦

"Believe me, you start raising your voice to me right now, and I'm getting ready to turn you off. You start talking to me like a man and I'm going to listen to what you have to say."

—Lovie Smith

✦

"I learned a long time ago that when you win as a team the individual honors follow."

—John Paxson

"I love to see little things done correctly. In my experience that may be as close to anything that I can identify as being the secret of success: little things done right." In fact, there are no big things, only an accumulation of little things done well."

—John Wooden

✦

"Always remember that there are only two kinds of people in the world: the realists and the dreamers. The realists know where they're going. The dreamers have already been there."

—Bob Orben

✦

"If you've got one foot in yesterday and one foot in tomorrow, you're missing today."

—Liza Minnelli

✦

"The only job where you start at the top is digging a hole."

—Unknown

✦

"Every idea you present must be something you could get across easily at a cocktail party with strangers."

—Jack Welch

✦

Value people (I want to know you as a person)

Interested in people (Not bored with them)

Needs of people concern you (What can I do to help meet your need? Don't neglect others.)

Encourage people (A pat on the back goes a long way)

—Dwight Bain's V.I.N.E. Formula for connecting with people on a personal level

✦

"It doesn't make much difference how much knowledge and experience an executive possesses. If he is unable to achieve results through people, he is worthless as an executive."

—J. Paul Getty

"Being Barack Obama's speech coach is like being Ted Williams' batting coach."
—Young speechwriter for Barack Obama

✦

"He was an aerobic listener."
—Anna Quindlen on David Halberstam

✦

"Words are the most powerful drug used by mankind."
—Rudyard Kipling

✦

"Leadership gravitates to the man who can talk."
—Lowell Thomas

✦

"The ability to deal with people is as purchasable a commodity as sugar or coffee, and I will pay more for that ability than for any other under the sun."
—John D. Rockefeller

✦

"Not everyone—not everybody, but you! Remember, you are talking to one person."
—A taped sign by the microphone at the studios of WGN Radio in Chicago

✦

"There ain't no fun telling a boring story."
—Jim "Mudcat" Grant

✦

"Don't tell them more than you know."
—Al Neuharth gave this advice to his executives upon launching *USA Today* as the Nation's newspaper

✦

"The chemistry on a team comes with the talent. Believe me, if you don't have the talent, you can have the greatest chemistry in the world and it's not going to work."
—Carl Yastrzemski

"I only hope that we don't lose sight of one thing—that it was all started by a mouse."
—Walt Disney

✦

"Why is that wall there?"
—Ronald Reagan in West Berlin, 1982

✦

"What has become clear to you since we last met?"
—Ralph Waldo Emerson greeting old friends after a time of absence

✦

"The illiterates of the 21st Century will not be those who cannot read or write, but those who cannot learn, unlearn, and relearn."
—Alvin Toffler

✦

"You can crash and burn or you can crash and learn. Choose to learn from those situations."
—Johnny Davis on his experiences as a head basketball coach

✦

"We are all living to hear seven words at the end of our lives: 'Well done, thou good and faithful servant.'"
—Jentezen Franklin

✦

"These are the most capable men in the country. I'm going to need them by my side."
—Abraham Lincoln on picking his team of rivals as Cabinet members

✦

"So much of what we call 'management' consists in making it difficult for people to work."
—Peter Drucker

✦

"Ultimately, leadership is responsibility."
—Colin Powell

"The key is to get into the stores and listen."
—Sam Walton

✦

"Effective teamwork is the universal bedrock for organizational success."
—Patrick Lencioni

✦

"Is he a good teammate?"
—Jerry West's barometer on a prospect for his teams

✦

"The reality is basketball is based on chemistry—guys who want to play together, want to share the work together, want to sacrifice for each other and learn how to do that."
—Phil Jackson

✦

"Good players."
—Yogi Berra when asked what makes a good manager

✦

"We are all Republicans. We are all Federalists."
—Thomas Jefferson at his inauguration

✦

"Taxation without representation is tyranny."
—James Otis, Boston attorney (February 24, 1761)

✦

"I learned recently that the healthiest thing a person can do is to keep having birthdays. The more you have, the longer you live."
—Bill Ellis

✦

"Everybody is motivated, but everybody is motivated differently. Each individual has a unique and distinct motivational type. What motivates one person can demotivate another. No one motivational type is better than any other."
—Tamara Lowe

"As Gertrude Stein lay dying in the July heat in Paris in 1946, she mumbled to someone, 'What is the answer?' When there was no answer, she said, 'Then, what is the question?'"

—William Shirer

✦

"Everyone, sooner or later, sits down to a basket of consequences."

—Robert Louis Stevenson

✦

"Speak properly, and in as few words as you can, but always plainly, for the end of the speech is not ostentation, but to be understood."

—William Penn

✦

"There are no passengers on spaceship Earth. We are all crew."

—Marshall McLuhan

✦

"I've said a thousand times, there are two kinds of coaches—the ones who coach great players and ex-coaches."

—Geno Auriemma

✦

"Do not say a little in many words, but a great deal in a few."

—Pythagoras

✦

"Nobody would remember me if we hadn't won."

—Norman Schwarzkopf

✦

"Give them quality. That's the best kind of advertising."

—Milton Hershey

✦

"Life is the sum of all your choices."

—Albert Camus

"As a leader, work towards being the best electrician possible. Study how each person is wired and what it takes to motivate them to reach their full potential. You need to know how those wires can best be configured."

—Greg DiCenzo

✦

"Lead from your strengths and build a team around you to cover your weaknesses."

—Peter Drucker

✦

"Outstanding leaders give off the aura that 'I am listening.' They stay focused and engaged with you and close the circle around you. They are not looking over your shoulder, trying to spot someone else more important than you."

—Sheila Murray Bethel

✦

"I can calculate the motions of heavenly bodies, but not the madness of people."

—Sir Isaac Newton

✦

"We have a saying: 'Trust the pass.'"

—Doc Rivers

✦

Mitt Romney once asked his wife, "When we were young, did you ever, in your wildest dreams, think I might be president?" She replied, "Honey, you weren't in my wildest dreams."

✦

"The most important thing in communication is hearing what isn't said."

—Peter Drucker

✦

"The best asset a coach can have is selective hearing."

—Chuck Daly

"Listening is squinting with one's ears."
—Thomas Cronin

✦

"He knew how to listen. It was the secret of his success: great ears."
—Bill Russell on Red Auerbach

✦

"Laughter is America's most important export."
—Walt Disney

✦

"He is truly wise who gains his wisdom from the experience of others."
—R.E. Littlejohn

✦

"As soon as you are complicated, you are ineffectual."
—Konrad Adenauer

✦

"In light of my past experience, and my future hopes and dreams, what's the wise thing to do?"
—Andy Stanley

✦

"I knew what my job was; it was to go out and meet the people and love them."
—Diana, Princess of Wales

✦

"There aren't any time-outs in life. The clock is always running."
—Andy Stanley

✦

"Few things offer greater return on less investment than praise—offering credit to someone in your organization who has stepped up and done the job."
—Bill Walsh

If I Were a Leader

If I were a leader I'd like to say;
"You did an excellent job today."
I'd look for a man, or woman or boy
Whose heart would leap with a thrill of joy
At a word of praise, and I'd pass it out
Where others could hear what I talked about.

If I were a leader I'd like to find
The person whose work is the proper kind;
And whenever to me a good thing came
I'd like to be told the toiler's name,
And I'd go to the person who had toiled to win,
And I'd say, "That was perfectly splendid, Lynn!"

Now a bit of praise isn't much to give,
But it's dear to the hearts of all who live;
For there's never a person on this old earth
But is glad to know that one's been of worth;
And a kindly word, when the work is fair,
Is welcomed and wanted everywhere.

If I were a leader I'm sure I would
Say a kindly word wherever I could;
For those who have given their best by day
Want a little more than their weekly pay.
They like to know, with the setting sun,
That the leader's pleased with the work they've done.

—Unknown

✦

"Living a life is like constructing a building—if you start wrong, you'll end wrong."
—Maya Angelou

✦

"The players have to know their jobs."
—Vince Lombardi on what makes a winning team

"Jack made everyone he met feel significant. He didn't believe his own press reports."
—Mike Calhoun on Jack Wyrtzen as a leader

✦

"His love for people."
—Suzy Welch on Jack Welch's greatest strength as a leader

✦

"You are who you are and your record is what it is."
—Denny Green

✦

"In the end, all leadership eventually stems from production."
—Brian Billick

✦

"NBA titles are won by teams with elite talent and good role players."
—Daryl Money

✦

"Mentor, model, motivator, monitor."
—Jay Strack on the four Ms that every child needs while growing up

✦

"People are the heart of your organization."
—Bill Walsh

✦

Steve Jamison on the three common traits of John Wooden and Bill Walsh:

"1. They knew their stuff.
2. They placed a great priority on the environment they taught in and wanted it to be the best. They were very demanding and got what they wanted, but treated people fairly.
3. They were creative in what they did and were always looking for new ideas (example: Walsh's West Coast offense and Wooden's pressing defense)."

"Every big idea that works is marked by simplicity, by clarity. You can understand it when you hear it, and you can explain it to people."

—Peggy Noonan

✦

"A coach's job is to solve problems."

—Bobby Bowden

✦

"In adding players to our roster, I'm looking for guys with something to prove—to themselves, their former teams, their families, the media, etc."

—Joe Dumars

✦

"Hire, fire, pay, promote. If you hire well, everything else becomes very easy; you won't have to fire, and paying and promoting will be a pleasure."

—David Moore on the four keys to building a business

✦

"It was his manifest self-regard, his complete lack of humility, that lay a deep fissure at his very core. In the end it split wide open and destroyed him."

—William Manchester on Douglas MacArthur

✦

"What a great teacher does is make you want to please him or her."

—Bill Curry

✦

"A manager is an assistant to his men."

—Thomas Watson, Sr.

✦

"I know only one method of operation: to be as honest with others as I am with myself."

—Dwight D. Eisenhower

"Those who talk too much dominate communication. Those who listen and ask questions control communication."

—Walter Winston

✦

"Every great team needs at least one guy who enjoys picking up the trash."

—Sparky Anderson

✦

"They better like you."

—Bo Schembechler on coaching players

✦

"Guys ask me, 'Don't you get burned out?' How can you get burned out doing something you love?"

—Tommy Lasorda

✦

"A smart person knows that you learn first and decide next."

—Bob Iger

✦

"Your players have to believe in you. They have to understand that you are doing everything you can to make them better. With players you always put a positive act in their heads—never a negative thought."

—Tommy Lasorda

✦

"They were trying to get inside each other. The air was electric in there. They just stared and stared at each other. Oh, what a pair, those two!"

—Clyde Sukeforth later gave his impression of the meeting's opening stare-down (the Jackie Robinson/Branch Rickey meeting on August 28, 1945)

✦

"Read my lips: no new taxes."

—George H.W. Bush

"A person without self-control is like a house with its doors and windows knocked out."

—Proverbs 25:28 (The Message)

✦

"In my study of great military leaders, the common trait that they all have possessed is boldness when it comes to decision-making."

—Brian DeToy

✦

"There isn't any pressure when you have confidence."

—Rick Barry

✦

"In an age that has stamped itself as the era of the go-getter, he was a go-giver."

—Father O'Donnell on Knute Rockne

✦

"Whether you were a starter or a 12th man, he made us all feel like we were the most important player who ever played for him."

—Larry Brown on Dean Smith

✦

"You can't ignore reality. You can't just wish it away. It doesn't work that way. You have got to pay attention to the facts."

—Peter Vegso

✦

"People often say that motivation doesn't last. Well, neither does bathing; that's why we recommend it daily."

—Zig Ziglar

✦

"I only wish I could have done more for you all."

—John Wooden at age 98 to his players when named by *The Sporting News* as the greatest coach in sports history

"Simplicity is the ultimate sophistication."
—Steve Jobs quoting Leonardo da Vinci

✦

"Education is an investment, never an expense."
—Nick Goble

✦

"The key to successful leadership today is influence, not authority."
—Kenneth Blanchard

✦

"I visited Disney's Hollywood Studios on December 20, 2009, and all over the park were banners with these words: Celebrate Today."
—Pat Williams

✦

"He doesn't say much. He doesn't have to."
—Jack Burns, longtime Major League Baseball player and coach, on Joe DiMaggio

✦

"Don't just be yourself, but, more importantly, be comfortable with yourself."
—Ernie Harwell, giving advice to Drew Sharp

✦

"Audacity, audacity, always audacity!"
—George Danton

✦

"The best thing is experienced talent. The second best is talent."
—Roy Williams, coach

✦

"If each of us hires people who are smaller than we are, we shall become a company of dwarfs, but if each of us hires people who are bigger than we are, we shall become a company of giants."
—David Ogilvy

"It's real simple. When I ride, I ride to win."
—Eddie Arcaro, jockey

✦

"I like to teach because that's the way I learn."
—Peter Drucker

✦

"Communicate everything you possibly can to your partners. The more they understand, the more they'll care. Once they care, there's no stopping them."
—Sam Walton

✦

"I very strongly possess a Ph.D. in people."
—John McDonough

✦

"The game is simple but the people are complicated."
—Chuck Daly

✦

"This moment is yours."
—Herb Brooks to his Olympic hockey team in 1980 before the Russian game

✦

"If you think education is expensive, try ignorance."
—Harvey MacKay

✦

"I'm in a hurry and God isn't."
—Philip Brooks

✦

"If you are not teaching, you are not leading."
—Earl Suttle

"I'm here to make decisions."

—Harry S. Truman, April 5, 1945

✦

"Make sure that the best thing to happen to your customer today is you."

—Christopher Chanski

✦

"The three most important words a leader can use are: 'I need help.'"

—Rob Waldman

✦

"If I had won some more ballgames, I would have signed another five-year contract. That's how good I feel, but I didn't win enough dad-gum games."

—Bobby Bowden on January 1, 2010, at age 80, after coaching his last game

✦

"Listen to the customers. If you ask, they will tell you exactly what to do."

—John Chambers

✦

"Go see for yourself."

—A Toyota leadership maxim known as *genchi genbutsu* in Japanese

✦

"You do not raise morale in an organization. It always filters down from the top. There are no bad soldiers under a good general."

—Brian Tracy

✦

"Leaders conduct themselves as though everyone is watching even when no one is watching."

—Brian Tracy

✦

"There ain't no right way to do the wrong thing."

—Waylon Jennings

"The glue of the military ethos is what the Greeks call *Philia*—friendship, comradeship, or brotherly love."

—Mackubin Thomas Owens

✦

"This is no time to go wobbly, George."

—Margaret Thatcher to George H.W. Bush at Camp David at the launch of Desert Storm

✦

"One thing I've observed about the great football coaches—they are patient and they are very good teachers and they could teach under pressure. After watching for 50 years, I'm convinced you couldn't be a great coach without being a great teacher."

—Keith Jackson

✦

"Bear Bryant treated all the players the same in different ways. He knew the particular needs of each of his players and what it took to motivate them. What other way is there? You can't just yell at them."

—Allen Barra

✦

"The true depth of his character became clear when things didn't work out the way he had planned. That's what makes him a hero for any age."

—Jonathan Eig on Lou Gehrig

✦

"The best question a leader can ask is: 'What do you think?'"

—Liz Wiseman

✦

"In three words, I can sum up everything I've learned about life. It goes on."

—Robert Frost

✦

"My wife Turi Ann and I have been married for 58 years—the shortest 58 years of my life."

—Keith Jackson

"Leadership is a matter of having people look at you and gain confidence in seeing how you react."

—Tom Landry

✦

"When I became president, believe it or not, there were only 50 sites on the entire worldwide web. There have been more than that added since I started talking."

—Bill Clinton on May 16, 2010 at a commencement address at West Virginia University

✦

"This problem like most problems will seem simple when solved."

—Chinese proverb

✦

"I was 25 and had just concluded my playing days in the NFL. I was starting my coaching career with the legendary Steelers' coach, Chuck Noll. I had no idea what I was meant to be doing and no one had told me anything. I went up to Chuck one day and asked, 'What do you want me to do?' He said to me: 'Your job is to help our players play better.' That one statement has stayed with me my whole life and formed the foundation of my philosophy as a head coach in the NFL."

—Tony Dungy

✦

"I heard Bear Bryant address his team before an Alabama/Georgia Tech game. The whole room went into an oral shutdown. Afterwards, the head of the English department, who was a guest that day, said to me: 'If I could reach my students like that, I'd teach for nothing.'"

—John Underwood

✦

"I like Chuck Tanner for being so positive and upbeat. He was the only manager I had who came out of the dugout to pat me on the back if I moved a runner from second to third with nobody out."

—Ken Berry

✦

"Martin Luther King was not really an organizer. He was an inspirer."

—Bayard Rustin, organizer of the March on Washington

"Bear Bryant was a people person. He loved his players. On Sunday afternoon after our film session and team meeting, he'd tell us, 'I love every one of you … now go call your mamas.'"

—Butch Hobson

✦

"You better play together as a team or you sit."

—John Wooden

✦

"Is what I am doing, or about to do, getting us closer to our objective—winning."

—Sign on football coach George Allen's desk

✦

"The single biggest problem in communication is the illusion that it has taken place."

—George Bernard Shaw

✦

"Look at what's happened to you in the past. Look at where you want to go in the future. That tells you what's important now. That's the W.I.N. theory—What's Important Now."

—Lou Holtz

Conclusion

This final section provides some thought-provoking quotes for you to ponder as you cool down from your workout.

"If you're a leader, lives should be better because of the influence you've had."
—Tony Dungy

✦

"I am happy being remembered as a man of integrity. I like that."
—John Wooden, two weeks prior to his death

✦

"From a child, I was fond of reading, and all the little money that came into my hands was ever laid out in books."
—Benjamin Franklin

✦

"We have to say memorable things in memorable ways in order to communicate well."
—Ed Young, Jr.

✦

"An army of a thousand is easy to find, but how difficult to find a general."
—Chinese proverb

✦

"As we look ahead into the next century, leaders will be those who empower others."
—Bill Gates

✦

"I don't know how to describe a leader, but I can recognize one."
—Bear Bryant

"Coach could get more out of you than you wanted to give. He just made players play better."

—Danny Ford on Bear Bryant

✦

"The only thing that kills you in coaching is losing. Just don't lose."

—Stan Van Gundy

✦

"He made an indelible impression on you if he knew you for 50 years, 5 minutes, or 5 seconds. As a friend, if you reached out to him, he'd always reach out to you."

—Jamaal Wilkes at John Wooden's memorial service

✦

"He possessed a complete understanding of the art of communication and had the ability to say more in one sentence than most of us could in one hour."

—Al Michaels in his opening remarks at John Wooden's memorial service

✦

"It takes a very steady hand to hold a full cup."

—James Dobson

✦

"I never learned a thing while I was talking. That would be my motto."

—Larry King

✦

"I never met a good, strong leader who wasn't mentally tough and could take the ups and downs and not let things bother him."

—Darwin Holt

✦

"I didn't like you all the same, but I tried to love you all the same."

—John Wooden to his players

✦

"Boy, do I love to win; everything is right in the world when I do."

—Venus Williams

"A commander, no matter how weary, should never be seen burying his head on his desk, lest someone interpret it as a loss of hope. He must always give the impression of optimism."

—General John Pershing to General George C. Marshall

✦

"I learned that it's important to cede part of your own individual potential to the group and in the process have the group be able to achieve more."

—Bill Bradley on his basketball career

✦

"I've always believed that it takes a lot of unspectacular preparation to get spectacular results."

—Roger Staubach

✦

"All great leaders are willing to stand in the gap for those underneath them."

—Walter Harris

✦

"In my career I have learned that people don't want to follow overly cautious leaders."

—Stanley McChrystal

✦

"He had a better vision of the country's potential than any other founder."

—John Murray on Alexander Hamilton

✦

"Did they know how to win on the battlefield?"

—Stephen W. Sears on the test Abraham Lincoln applied to all his generals

✦

"These leaders can look at an acorn and see a giant oak tree with its great limbs spreading upward and outward in the years to come. Some people in Washington, D.C. take a look at an acorn and all they can see is just an acorn. Even give them a magnifying glass, or even a pair of spyglasses, or even a telescope, they just shake their heads and all they can say is, 'I'm sorry. I can't see anything but an acorn there.' I call this acorn thinking."

—Harry S. Truman

"He was thoroughly prepared every day. He was so organized, I think he counted his chews at breakfast."

—Jim Dent on Ara Parseghian

✦

"To this day dad cannot picture himself as a great man, or a great President."

—Margaret Truman on Harry S. Truman

✦

"He was an avid reader. That was one of the reasons he was able to take on so rapidly the immense problems he had to deal with."

—W. Averell Harriman on Harry S. Truman

✦

"Bear Bryant was not a gusher when it came to praise. He didn't run around praising everybody and everything. When our unit came off the field and we'd done well he'd say, 'Good job.' That's all we needed to hear. As a leader it's important to know how to praise and when to praise. If you are always praising it doesn't mean much. I like sugar, but not a whole truckload of it. John Wooden was like Coach Bryant ... make your praise mean something."

—John Croyle

✦

"Big things are accomplished only through the perfection of minor details."

—John Wooden

✦

"Coach Bryant would say to his assistants, 'You teach them what to do. I'll get them ready to do it.'"

—John Mitchell on Bear Bryant

✦

"Father had the ability to peer into the future and begin planning for it."

—Margaret Truman on Harry S. Truman

✦

"I'll never say no to anything. You don't know which is the one that will work."

—Joan Rivers

"I never made a bad move; some just didn't work out as well."
—Chuck Tanner

✦

"You don't lose your way all at once; just a little at a time."
—Bill Simmons

✦

"When I was 15 I decided it was time for me to start shaving. That would be the mark of manhood for me, even though I had only one hair on my face. I kept bugging my dad to teach me how to shave. So one day he relented and took me into the bathroom. I'm old enough to remember his straight-edged razor and the leather strop to sharpen it. He got me ready and then said, 'Dick, it's a lot easier to shave in the morning if you don't mind looking at your face in the mirror.' At that point he walked out of the room, leaving me in a state of confusion. I didn't understand what he meant, but I do now. My dad lived until age eighty-one. That shaving story was the most important lesson he ever taught me."
—Dick Bunce

✦

"I found that most of the really great ones (famous people) never thought they were great."
—Harry S. Truman

✦

"Bear Bryant didn't coach football. He coached people."
—Bum Phillips

✦

"The most underrated virtue in America is discipline."
—Colin Cowherd

✦

"Positive thinking won't let you do anything, but it will help you to do everything better than negative thinking will."
—Zig Ziglar

"I had an idea and dream about a ranch for neglected children here in Alabama. I went to Coach Bryant to get his views on it. In the middle of the meeting his secretary, Rebecca, came in and said, 'I've got Bob Hope, Roone Arledge, and Spiro Agnew all on hold. What should I do?'

"Coach said, 'Tell them to wait.' Then he turned back to me and said, 'Now, tell me more about your ranch idea.'

"He always told us that his players took precedence over anybody else. That day he proved to me that he backed up what he said. His message to me was, 'Go build the ranch. Follow your dreams.' He knew that I was built to do this."

—John Croyle on Bear Bryant

✦

"The best players don't always win, but those that play the best always do."

—Lou Holtz

✦

"Coaching is teaching. Teaching is the ability to inspire learning."

—Nick Saban

✦

"Franklin Roosevelt had a very clear vision of what the United States should look like when he was done and what the horizon should look like for our citizens."

—Jeff Shesol

✦

"President Truman said that he liked problems."

—Harold D. Smith

✦

"The second-team defense would be on the field. Our first team would be standing behind Coach Bryant. One day they couldn't stop the other team and Coach turned to our unit and said simply, 'Go stop 'em!' That was it. Call that clarity of mission."

—John Croyle on Bear Bryant

✦

"He knew how to win and he knew how to lose and he knew that coaching was about a lot more than winning and losing."

—Rick Barnes on Dean Smith

"Great leaders like Coach Bryant possess two key qualities:

1. They know exactly where they are going, and
2. They persuade others to go with them.

They find motivated people and steer them in the way to go. They don't force them against their will."

—John Croyle on Bear Bryant

✦

"The key to leadership is this: How will you be remembered? There are three possibilities:

1. Did you impress people?
2. Did you impact people?
3. Did you inspire people for greatness?

Category three will be Coach Bear Bryant's legacy."

—John Croyle

✦

"We were playing at Louisiana State University one year when Bert Jones was their quarterback. I kept hitting him and thought I was doing well. After one series I came to the sidelines and Coach Bryant said to me, 'When are you going to get him?' Oh, he hit my button with that one. That really lit me up. Coach knew exactly how to motivate you."

—John Croyle on Bear Bryant

✦

"Hey, left-hander. Don't forget just how good you are."

—Robin Roberts to Cole Hamels after a disappointing 2009 postseason

✦

"He was the best listener I've ever seen in my life. He was a great listener."

—Bill "Brother" Oliver on Bear Bryant

✦

"One leader of vision impacts millions who toil in his shadow."

—E. Gaylon McCollough

"When purpose and passion line up, you have unbelievable power."
Dwight Bain

✦

"In his old age, the Duke of Wellington was asked what he'd do differently if he could. He replied: 'I'd give more praise.'"
—Unknown

✦

"What we have here is a failure to communicate."
—The warden in *Cool Hand Luke*

✦

"I played for Bear Bryant and Tom Landry. The common traits they possessed were their organizational skills and thorough preparation. They were always focused on how to improve their teams and get players to think better. As a result, we wanted to do what they were teaching and not because they demanded it."
—Lee Roy Jordan

✦

"Bear Bryant was a really good football coach, but he really coached people."
—Jim Bob Harris

✦

"When a role is right for him, he's peerless."
—Pauline Kael on Paul Newman

✦

"A player who makes the team great is better than a great player."
—John Wooden

✦

"Leadership is an attitude before it is an ability."
—Jim Peterson

✦

"The best way to improve the team is to improve yourself."
—John Wooden

Epilogue

Congratulations! You have completed the running trail and should be filled with inspiration and motivation.

Now, I must break some news to you: inspiration and motivation does not last. Just like a daily shower only lasts one day, so it goes with inspiration and motivation.

Therefore, turn back to page one and start all over again. Daily doses of these powerful and insightful quotes will keep you running for a lifetime.

And if you come across some good quotes, pass them along to me at pwilliams@orlandomagic.com. Who knows? They might end up in another volume of mine.

Lace up those running shoes, and keep pounding away.

About the Authors

Pat Williams is the senior vice president of the NBA's Orlando Magic. As one of America's top motivational, inspirational, and humorous speakers, he has addressed thousands of executives in organizations ranging from Fortune 500 companies and national associations to universities and nonprofits. Clients include AllState, American Express, Cisco, Coca-Cola, Disney, Honeywell, IBM, ING, Lockheed Martin, Nike, PricewaterhouseCoopers, and Tyson Foods to name a few. He is also the author of over 55 books.

Williams served for seven years in the United States Army, spent seven years in the Philadelphia Phillies organization—two as a minor league catcher and five in the front office—and has also spent three years in the Minnesota Twins organization. Since 1968, he has been in the NBA as general manager for teams in Chicago, Atlanta, Philadelphia—including the 1983 World Champion 76ers—and now the Orlando Magic, which he co-founded in 1987 and helped lead to the NBA finals in 1995. Twenty-three of his teams have gone to the NBA playoffs, and five have made the NBA finals. In 1996, Williams was named as one of the 50 most influential people in NBA history by a national publication.

Williams has been an integral part of NBA history, including bringing the NBA to Orlando. He has traded Pete Maravich as well as traded for Julius Erving, Moses Malone, and Penny Hardaway, and he has won four NBA draft lotteries, including back-to-back winners in 1992 and 1993. He also drafted Charles Barkley, Shaquille O'Neal, Maurice Cheeks, Andrew Toney, and Darryl Dawkins. He signed Billy Cunningham, Chuck Daly, and Matt Guokas to their first professional coaching contracts. Nineteen of his former players have become NBA head coaches, nine have become college head coaches, while seven have become assistant NBA coaches.

Pat Williams and his wife, Ruth, are the parents of 19 children, including 14 adopted from four nations, ranging in age from 24 to 38. For one year, 16 of his children were all teenagers at the same time. Pat and his family have been featured in *Sports Illustrated, Reader's Digest, Good Housekeeping, Family Circle, The Wall Street Journal, Focus on the Family, New Man* magazine, plus all of the major television networks, *The Maury Povich Show*, and *Dr. Robert Schuller's Hour of Power*.

Williams co-teaches an adult Sunday school class at First Baptist Church of Orlando and hosts three weekly radio shows. In the last 14 years, he has completed 55 marathons—including the Boston Marathon 13 times—and also climbed Mt. Rainier. He is a weightlifter, Civil War buff, and serious baseball fan. Every winter he plays in Major League Fantasy Camps and has caught for Hall of Famers Bob Feller, Bob Gibson, Fergie Jenkins, Rollie Fingers, Gaylord Perry, Phil Niekro, Tom Seaver, and Goose Gossage.

Williams was raised in Wilmington, Delaware, earned his bachelor's degree at Wake Forest University, and his masters degree at Indiana University. He is a member of the Wake Forest Sports Hall of Fame after catching for the Deacon baseball team, including the 1962 Atlantic Coast Conference Championship team. He is also a member of the Delaware Sports Hall of Fame.

Ken Hussar is a comedian who has presented over 4,000 programs in the past 40 years.

He retired from the Penn Manor School District, Millersville, Pennsylvania, in 1997 after 31 years as an elementary school teacher. During his teaching career, he received five awards for teaching excellence, and in 1994 he was named the district's Outstanding Elementary Educator.

Hussar is a graduate of Delaware County (PA) Christian School, Millersville University, and Temple University. He worked as a brakeman on the Strasburg Rail Road for 22 summers and continues to entertain on the railroad's Lee Brenner Dining Car.

Hussar has written 442 *Short and Snappy* humor columns for the *Lancaster New Era*. Additionally, Hussar has worked with Pat Williams on over 50 book projects.

Hussar and his wife, Carolyn, have three grown children, Caryn, James, and Stephanie, daughter-in-law, Beatriz, son-in-law, David Baxter, and three grandsons, Gabriel, Camilo, and Carter. Ken and Carolyn live in Lancaster County, Pennsylvania.

To contact Ken Hussar regarding entertainment, send inquiries to:

Ken Hussar
174 Ridings Way,
Lancaster, PA 17601
Phone: (717) 898-0024
ridingsway@netzero.net

You can contact Pat Williams at:

Pat Williams
c/o Orlando Magic
8701 Maitland Summit Boulevard
Orlando, FL 32810
Phone: (407) 916-2404
pwilliams@orlandomagic.com

Visit Pat Williams' website at:

www.PatWilliamsMotivate.com

If you would like to set up a speaking engagement for Pat Williams, please write or call his assistant, Andrew Herdliska, at the above address, or call him at (407) 916-2401. Requests can also be faxed to (407) 916-2986 or e-mailed to aherdliska@orlandomagic.com.

We would love to hear from you. Please send your comments about this book to Pat Williams at the address provided. Thank you.